D1592350

The ABC's of
GW-BASIC

SYSTEM	Ends GW-BASIC and returns to DOS.
USR()	Calls a machine language subroutine.
WHILE/WEND	Creates a logically terminated loop.

Event Trapping

COM() ON|OFF|STOP	Enables/disables trapping the com port.
KEY() ON|OFF|STOP	Enables/disables trapping of keystrokes.
ON COM() GOSUB	Defines an event trap for communications.
ON ERROR GOTO	Enables error trapping.
ON KEY() GOSUB	Defines an event trap for keystrokes.
ON PEN GOSUB	Defines an event trap for a light pen.
ON PLAY() GOSUB	Defines an event trap for playing music.
ON STRIG() GOSUB	Defines an event trap for the joystick triggers.
ON TIMER() GOSUB	Defines an event trap for timer events.
PEN ON|OFF|STOP	Enables/disables trapping of light pen events.
STRIG() ON|OFF|STOP	Enables/disables trapping of joystick trigger state.
TIMER ON|OFF|STOP	Enables/disables trapping of timer events.

Mathematical Functions

ABS()	Calculates the absolute value.
ATN()	Calculates the arctangent in radians.
CDBL()	Converts a value to double precision.
CINT()	Rounds to the nearest integer.
COS()	Calculates the cosine of an angle in radians.
CSNG()	Converts a value to single-precision.
EXP()	Calculates the power of **e** of a number; returns **e** to the x power.
FIX()	Truncates a number to an integer.
INT()	Rounds down to the next integer.
LOG()	Calculates the logarithm of a number.
SGN()	Returns the sign of a number.
SIN()	Calculates the sine of a number.

SQR()	Calculates the square root of a number.
TAN()	Calculates the tangent of a number in radians.

String Functions

ASC()	Converts a character into an ASCII code.
CHR$()	Converts an ASCII code into a character.
HEX$()	Converts a number into a hexadecimal string.
INSTR()	Locates a substring within a string.
LEFT$()	Extracts the left side of a string.
LEN()	Gets the length of a string.
MID$	Replaces a substring.
MID$()	Extracts a substring.
OCT$()	Converts a number into an octal string.
RIGHT$()	Extracts the right side of a string.
SPACE$()	Returns a string of spaces.
STRING$()	Returns a string of characters.
STR$()	Converts a number to a string.
VAL()	Converts a string into a number.

Other Functions

DATE$	Sets the current date.
DATE$	Gets the current date.
ERL	Gets the line number that caused the last GW-BASIC error.
ERR	Gets the error code for the last GW-BASIC error.
ERROR	Simulates a program error.
RANDOMIZE	Resets the random number generator.
REM	Remark statement; does nothing.
RND()	Gets a random number.
SHELL	Executes DOS commands without exiting GW-BASIC.
TIME$	Sets the current time.
TIME$	Gets the current time.
TIMER	Gets the number of seconds since midnight.
VARPTR()	Gets the memory address of a variable or file control block.
VARPTR$()	Gets the memory address of a variable as a string.

The ABC's of GW-BASIC®

William J. Orvis

SYBEX®

San Francisco • Paris • Düsseldorf • Soest

Acquisitions Editor: Dianne King
Developmental Editor: Vince Leone
Copy Editor: Muriel Solar
Technical Editor: Michael Gross
Word Processors: Scott Campbell, Deborah Maizels, Chris Mockel
Book Designer: Jeffrey James Giese
Chapter Art: Suzanne Albertson
Technical Art: Jeffrey James Giese
Screen Graphics: Delia Brown, Jeffrey James Giese
Typesetter: Bob Myren
Proofreader: Rhonda Holmes
Indexer: Nancy Guenther
Cover Designer: Thomas Ingalls + Associates
Cover Photographer: David Bishop
Screen reproductions produced by XenoFont

To B.J. and Skye, because they can read now—
and they love to see their names in print

Preface

BASIC was the first computer language I ever learned, and I still find myself coming back to it again and again to solve those tasks that don't rate a major program development effort, but that are well beyond the capabilities of a hand calculator. The reason? Nearly everything is already done for you in BASIC. You may not have the fanciest screens when you're finished, but then you didn't have to spend a year developing them either. On the other hand, if you want the fancy screens, you can have them too with a little more effort.

When the chance to write this book came along, I originally thought "Doesn't everyone already know how to program in BASIC?" I mean, learning BASIC is like learning to use a fork. It's just one of those things that you pick up while you're getting to know computers. I spoke to some friends and acquaintances, and I found out the answer is no, that there are a lot of people who know how to use computers but somehow have never learned BASIC. For those of you who fit this description, who are just getting your feet wet in programming, get ready for an adventure. Programming is addictive, far more than any video game or puzzle. When you are programming, you are the one who is making the computer work and react—and not the other way around. Your creations don't just sit there and look pretty; they move and react according to your directions and no one else's.

I had a lot of help at Sybex with this project, including Rudy Langer and Dianne King who convinced me to do it, developmental editor Vince Leone who tried to keep me on track, and copy editor Muriel Solar.

I also had a lot of help at home. My one-year old, Shane, loves to type on the keyboard. I didn't dare leave the machine on when he was around or whole pages of strange type appeared. More than once, while I was engrossed in thought (that's a polite way of saying that I was staring at the wall, trying to figure out what to write next), a small arm would snake its way up over the edge of the table and madly hit as many keys as it could reach before I grabbed it.

My three-year old, Sierra, has finally learned to leave the computer alone. She used to sleep on my lap while I typed; now she wants me to move over so she can have her turn. My four-year old, Skye, is getting more interested in the wires and connections in back than in the keyboard. Luckily, however, she only tested the on/off switch once while Daddy was typing. Very luckily, Mommy rescued her while Daddy was getting his heart started again (although he knows better, he hadn't saved anything for the last hour).

Next, there is my seven-year old, B.J., who wants to know when I am going to get him his own computer, or could I please get out of the way so that he can play a few rounds of the latest computer game. Finally, there is Julie, who held my hand, poured the coffee, and fought off the kids so that I could get some work done. Many times, she gathered them up to go to the park so that I could be alone for a while. She does tell me that my turn is coming as soon as I finish this thing (I wonder what she means by that).

I hope this book fills a void in your knowledge and sparks a lifelong interest in these marvelous little machines. I hope I have given you a tool to help build your dreams.

William J. Orvis
Livermore, California

Contents at a Glance

Table of Contents

6 Program Flow and Control Functions   97

7 Understanding Functions and Subroutines   121

Introduction

When considering computer languages for the IBM-PC and compatible computers, you might wonder why you should consider GW-BASIC. Why not get a modern language like Pascal or C? The first reason is that you probably already own GW-BASIC. The second is that it is a good, easy-to-use programming language that is appropriate for many useful tasks. Its utility is demonstrated by the fact that you can create a fully functional one-line program in GW-BASIC that does something useful. Most modern languages require far more than that just to print Hello on the screen. GW-BASIC takes care of all of the nuances of communicating with the microprocessor and the different devices (screen, keyboard, and so forth) for you. For example, to print on the screen, all you have to do is type PRINT followed by what you want printed. You don't have to open a device driver, execute initialization routines, or set environmental variables. All that is taken care of by GW-BASIC, so you can spend your time worrying about what it is you want the computer to do rather than about how to do it.

The computer language BASIC was developed at Dartmouth College by Professors Thomas Kurtz and John Kemeny. They wanted students at the college to learn about computers without having to spend an inordinate amount of time learning a computer language. In May of 1964, they had the first version of BASIC available for use.

Since that time, BASIC has grown as a computer language. In the '70s, some form of BASIC was generally available on most of the new microcomputers that were showing up. BASIC was often fixed in ROM (read-only memory) in those machines and was available whenever you turned the machines on. In many cases, BASIC was the only system available to control them, since disk operating systems like MS-DOS were not available yet. In the late '70s, disk operating systems appeared, and several people worked on developing versions of BASIC to use with them. One of those developers was Bill Gates and his people at Microsoft, Inc. They developed a version of BASIC known as GW-BASIC (for Gee Whiz BASIC) that eventually was available in some form on many machines.

In the early '80s, when IBM designers were looking for an operating system for their new IBM-PC, they chose Microsoft's newly developed MS-DOS for the operating system—and included GW-BASIC with it. The IBM version of the operating system was renamed PC-DOS, and the IBM version of GW-BASIC was broken into three parts: a simple BASIC interpreter built into its hardware plus two disk-based versions (the advanced disk version called BASICA is IBM's version of GW-BASIC). With the advent of PC-compatible computers, Microsoft marketed its own version of the operating system (MS-DOS) to run on the compatibles—and also included GW-BASIC. Thus, either GW-BASIC or the IBM version BASICA are available on most IBM-PC, XT, AT, and compatible computers.

GW-BASIC and BASICA

Functionally, these equivalent versions (GW-BASIC and BASICA) are nearly identical. The major difference is that BASICA runs only on the IBM-PC series of computers (XT, AT, PS2), and GW-BASIC runs on the IBM-PC and most compatibles. This is because of the low-level BASIC interpreter in ROM (known as casette BASIC or ROM BASIC). Both BASIC and BASICA expect it to be there, and they make extensive use of it when it is. Since most PC-compatible computers don't have ROM BASIC, however, BASICA won't run on them. GW-BASIC, on the other hand, is complete in itself, and doesn't need ROM BASIC. Thus, it ignores the ROM BASIC and runs on IBM-PCs or any of the compatible computers.

Manufacturers of PC-compatible computers often sell their own modified versions of MS-DOS and may or may not include GW-BASIC. The examples in this book were written using MS-DOS (Version 3.3) and GW-BASIC (Version 3.22) on a Today 286 AT-compatible computer. If some of the statements or functions do not seem to work as I describe them, check your owners' manual to see whether the operation or syntax of that statement or function is different. If you have older versions of GW-BASIC or BASICA, most of the examples should work, but that is not guaranteed. Earlier versions (2.xx) do not recognize directory paths in file names, and they don't have networking capabilities. There are other differences that vary from manufacturer to manufacturer.

Hardware Requirements

To run GW-BASIC, you need an IBM-PC or PC-compatible computer with 256K of memory. Though you can use it on systems with a single floppy-disk drive, two drives are suggested as the minimum system (two floppy disks or one floppy and one hard disk). If you have only a single-drive system, add another drive if possible; it doesn't cost much more than a very good dinner for two, and it will make your life much easier. Better yet, get a hard disk that holds at least 20 MBytes (1 megabyte equals 1 million bytes, and 1 byte stores 1 character). Larger hard disks hold more than 50 times as much data as floppy disk drives—but their cost is nowhere near 50 times as much.

MS-DOS Version 3.2 or later must be installed for GW-BASIC Version 3.22 to run. In general, if you have installed MS-DOS, you probably have already installed GW-BASIC. While all the examples in this book were run on a Today 286 AT-compatible computer with an EGA monitor and card, they will all run on a dual-floppy PC-compatible with a monochrome monitor.

Readability and Understandability

Throughout this book, I comment about how this or that convention makes a program more readable or more understandable. I do this for a reason. Many times, I have had to use or modify someone else's program or a program of my own that I wrote a year or more ago. The first thing I must do, before modifying a program is figure out how it works. If the program lacks comments or uses uncommon algorithms, understanding it can be almost impossible, and modifying it is even harder. Even my own programs are difficult to understand if I haven't inserted enough comments.

Unless you don't plan to save a program after you have run it once or twice, be sure to insert comments wherever the actions are not obvious. It may seem like adding a lot more work now, but it will save you much more work in the future.

For Those Who Don't Want to Type the Examples

For those of you who want to try all the examples but would rather not type them all yourself, they are available on disk. In addition to the examples from this book, the disk contains many other examples of GW-BASIC statements and functions. Please note that GW-BASIC Version 3.22 (included with MS-DOS 3.3) is *not* included on this disk, and remember that GW-BASIC Version 3.0 or later is required to be able to run the examples. Earlier versions of GW-BASIC may not be able to run all the examples.

To obtain this disk, send your name, address and $20.00 in U.S. funds (check or money order) to the address below, and I will send you a disk by first-class mail. Be sure to indicate that you want the BASIC Examples Disk when you place the order. For orders from countries other than the U.S. and Canada, please add an additional $1.00 to cover the increased cost of overseas shipping. California orderers, please add your local sales tax. There is a form at the back of this book to assist you with the order.

Send your order to: William J. Orvis

226 Joyce St.

Livermore, CA   94550

Conventions Used in this Book

Throughout this book, what you are expected to type is written in boldface and what the computer types back to you is not. BASIC keywords (that is, those words and names that form the GW-BASIC statements and functions) are printed in bold capital letters, but capital letters are not required when you type them because GW-BASIC makes no distinction between upper- and lowercase in its keywords and variable names. If you type a program in lowercase and then print it on the screen, all the keywords and variable names will be automatically converted to uppercase.

The GW-BASIC Reference

A complete reference to GW-BASIC is in Appendix A. All the operators, statements, and functions are alphabetically listed there, including their complete syntax and usage. Use this reference in conjunction with the chapters of this book to learn the GW-BASIC language. Inside the front and back covers is another list of these same GW-BASIC statements and functions, grouped by function this time instead of alphabetically. Appendix B contains a list of the GW-BASIC error messages.

Installing GW-BASIC

In many cases, MS-DOS and GW-BASIC are already installed on your machine when you receive it. In the event that they are not, you must install them. See your MS-DOS manual for instructions for installing MS-DOS. Whether you have a hard- or floppy-disk-based system, the program GWBASIC.EXE must be available on your working disk. On a hard-disk system, copy GWBASIC.EXE from the Supplemental Programs disk into the directory where you keep your DOS commands and programs. On a floppy-disk-based system, copy the system files, COMMAND.COM, GWBASIC.EXE, and any other commands that you use regularly (like FORMAT.COM) onto a working floppy, and use that floppy to run GW-BASIC.

L et the Tour Begin

Get ready for a fast and furious introduction to the GW-BASIC language. If you don't understand a statement or function, don't be afraid to experiment with it. Try different variations and see what happens. You cannot hurt the hardware, and the worst that you could do is to erase your disk—and the likelihood of that happening is quite small. Since you always keep backup copies of your disks (you *do*, don't you?) that could easily be corrected if it should happen.

The chapters of this book follow these general topics:

- Chapter 1 is a quick, get-your-feet-wet example, to demonstrate the ease with which a GW-BASIC program can be written.

- Chapter 2 introduces the programming environment. It describes how to invoke GW-BASIC, how to create and edit programs, and how to save and later reload them.

- Chapter 3 covers input and output operations with the screen, printer, keyboard, and disk.

- Chapter 4 describes numbers, variables, and assignment statements for doing the calculations your programs require.

- Chapter 5 describes manipulating strings, string variables, and string assignment statements.

- Chapter 6 discusses the flow control statements. These are the statements that make decisions and control what a program does next.

- Chapter 7 covers user-defined functions, subroutines, and block-structuring your codes to make them understandable and verifiable.

- Chapter 8 covers using random-access disk files.

- Chapter 9 discusses the art of debugging a code.

Within these chapters are numerous short examples, and towards the end of a chapter, a larger main example program. As you progress through the book, the main example program gets longer and more complex, using more and more of the capability of GW-BASIC. It also does

more and demonstrates more of the capabilities of GW-BASIC. Here is
a list of the example programs:

Chapter 1:   The Straight-Line Depreciation Calculator.

Chapter 2:   The Price Markup Calculator.

Chapter 3:   The Computer-Usage Journaling Programs.

Chapter 4:   The Loan-Payment Calculator.

Chapter 5:   The Mail Merge Program.

Chapter 6:   The Computer-Usage Report Generator.

Chapter 7:   The Amortization Table Program.

Chapter 8:   The Inventory Maintenance Program.

Chapter 9:   Various Debugging Aids.

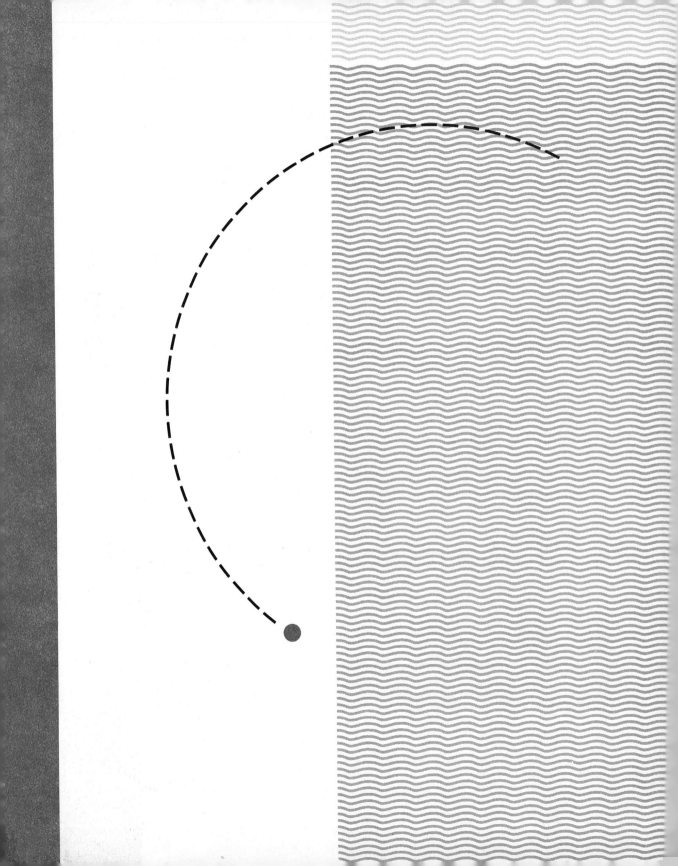

CHAPTER

1

Getting the
Feel of GW-BASIC

There are many reasons for exploring and learning—and using—GW-BASIC. Perhaps you have just bought an IBM PC-compatible computer and would like to know just how much you can do with it. Maybe you're already using a computer as a word processor and would like to try doing some programming yourself. Or maybe you simply want to find out more about this computer language that came with the MS-DOS operating system. GW-BASIC, a later version of the original BASIC, is a computer language that is easy for the beginner to learn and use but is sophisticated enough to do a significant amount of practical computing.

BASIC was probably the first computer language to bring the power of programming to the average computer user. Using English-like statements, you can control the inner workings of your computer and cause them to work for you. While the language is chiefly calculational in nature, it also has the ability to handle text. You can use it to create and maintain accounts and records, numerically integrate differential equations, or edit documents. It can do all these tasks over and over again, very quickly, without getting either tired or bored. All you need do is write the program—which tells the computer what you want it to do—and GW-BASIC will do the rest.

In this first chapter, I'll give you a feel for programming with GW-BASIC. You'll create and run a simple program that calculates the depreciation on an asset using the straight-line method. As you will see, programming is a relatively straightforward process that anyone can do, rather than than an arcane science known only to especially initiated persons.

Invoking GW-BASIC

In most cases, if your computer has a hard disk, both the MS-DOS operating system and GW-BASIC will already have been installed. Simply turn on the power and the computer will boot itself. If GW-BASIC is not present, you must copy the program GWBASIC.EXE from the MS-DOS distribution disk onto your hard disk (see your DOS manual for more information). If your system instead has only floppy disks, insert the working copy of the system disk into drive A, turn on the power, and the computer will boot from that disk. In either case, the MS-DOS operating system will be loaded into memory and will be running.

As the system is booting, you may be asked to input the date. If the date shown is correct, press Enter. Otherwise, type the correct date in the format shown on the screen, followed by Enter. You will next be asked to input the time. Respond in the same way, with Enter if the time is correct or the right time if it is not. You should now see the DOS prompt, usually a letter designating the current drive, followed by a greater than symbol (for example, A> for a floppy disk system or C> for a hard disk system). Figure 1.1 shows what you should see if your computer has booted correctly on a floppy-disk system. If you do not get a system prompt, review the installation of your system software to determine why the computer has not booted correctly. Check your DOS manual or a book such as Judd Robbins' *Mastering DOS*, also published by SYBEX, for more information.

Assuming that the screen now shows the system prompt, type **GWBASIC**, press Enter, and see whether it starts up. If GW-BASIC does start up correctly, your screen should look like Figure 1.2. If your screen doesn't look like the figure and yours is a floppy-disk system, you must insert the disk containing GW-BASIC in drive A. With a hard-disk system, change to the directory containing GW-BASIC using the **CD** (change directory) command.

```
Current date is Fri  1-Ø4-1991
Enter new date (mm-dd-yy):
Current time is 23:36:35.27
Enter new time:


Microsoft(R) MS-DOS  Version 3.3Ø
           (C)Copyright Microsoft Corp 1981-1987


A>
```

Figure 1.1: The DOS screen after booting a floppy-disk system

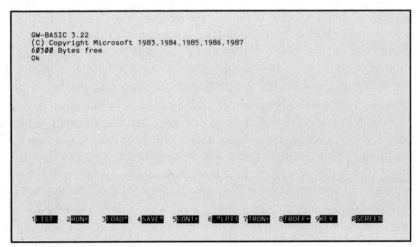

Figure 1.2: GW-BASIC start-up screen

Typing a Simple Program

Straight-line depreciation is the simplest of the depreciation methods. It is based on the assumption that an asset is used up evenly from the beginning to the end of its lifetime and is calculated using the formula

$$SL = \frac{(COST - SALVAGE)}{LIFE}$$

where COST is the asset's initial cost and SALVAGE is the remaining value at the end of its lifetime, LIFE.

In the following program, the numeric values for the variables COST#, SALVAGE#, and LIFE are input by the user in lines 50 through 90. Numeric variables can be set to any numeric value (hence the name). Here the variables represent the three numbers that will be input. In line 110, the program calculates the depreciation, printing it in line 120.

```
10 REM SLDEP.BAS Depreciation Calculator
20 CLS
30 PRINT "Straight-Line Depreciation Calculator"
40 PRINT "Initial cost of the asset ($)";
50 INPUT COST#
60 PRINT "Salvage value of the asset ($)";
70 INPUT SALVAGE#
80 PRINT "Lifetime ";
90 INPUT LIFE
100 PRINT
110 SL# = (COST#-SALVAGE#)/LIFE
120 PRINT USING "The depreciation is$$###,.##";SL#
130 END
```

To try this program, type it exactly as shown, including the line numbers and punctuation and pressing Enter at the end of each line. If you make a mistake before pressing Enter, correct it by backspacing over the error and retyping it. You can replace a line after pressing Enter by typing it again, starting with the line number. Simply typing a line number and pressing Enter will delete the line with that number. To check what you have typed, type **LIST** and press Enter, and the program will be listed on the screen. You can add more lines or make any corrections that are necessary. In the next chapter I will discuss additional ways to edit a program.

Running the Program

When you think everything has been entered correctly, type **RUN** and press Enter, and the program will begin running. If something is wrong, GW-BASIC will give you an error message and then stop. In this program, the worst you should get is Syntax error, which means you have typed something incorrectly. If this happens, the problem line will be displayed with the cursor in it. Correct the error and press Enter (the cursor can be anywhere in the line when you press Enter).

If the program runs, line 20 clears the screen, and line 30 prints the words Straight-Line Depreciation Calculator at the top. Line 40 prints Initial cost of the asset ($). Line 50 then appends the ? and waits for you to type a value for COST#. Type **10000** ($10,000.00) and press Enter.

Line 60 prints Salvage value of the asset ($), and line 70 adds the ? and waits for you to type a value for SALVAGE#. Type **2750** ($2,750.00) and press Enter. Line 80 prints Lifetime; line 90 appends the ? and waits for you to type a value for LIFE. Type **10** (10 years) and press Enter.

Line 100 prints a blank line. Next, line 110 calculates the value of the depreciation and stores it in SL#. Line 120 prints The depreciation is followed by the value of the depreciation stored in SL#. Finally, line 130 ends the program. Your screen should now look like Figure 1.3. If it does, congratulations! You have just written your first BASIC program. If your screen doesn't resemble the figure, list the program again with the LIST command, and find and correct the error.

Once the program is working correctly, you can run it again and again, using different values for the cost, salvage value, and lifetime. Each time, the program calculates the depreciation for the numbers you input.

Saving the Program and Quitting GW-BASIC

To save this program for loading later, type **SAVE "SLDEP.BAS"** and press Enter. The program will be saved in the current directory under the

```
Straight-Line Depreciation Calculator
Initial cost of the asset ($)? 10000
Salvage value of the asset ($)? 2750
Lifetime ? 10

The depreciation is  $725.00
Ok
```

```
1LIST  2RUN◂  3LOAD"  4SAVE"  5CONT◂  6."LPT1  7TRON◂  8TROFF◂ 9KEY   ØSCREEN
```

Figure 1.3: Calculating depreciation

name SLDEP.BAS. A file name can contain up to eight alphanumeric characters, a decimal point, and a three-character file-type extension. If the file-type extension is omitted, GW-BASIC assumes that it is a BASIC program and adds .BAS. To load the program again at some later time, type **LOAD "SLDEP.BAS"** and press Enter. When you finish working with the program, quit GW-BASIC and return to DOS by typing **SYSTEM** and pressing Enter.

*S**ummary: Getting the Feel of GW-BASIC***

The object of this first chapter was to give you a feel for GW-BASIC by letting you type and run a simple program. Later in this book, I will describe each of the statements and steps contained in that program in greater detail.

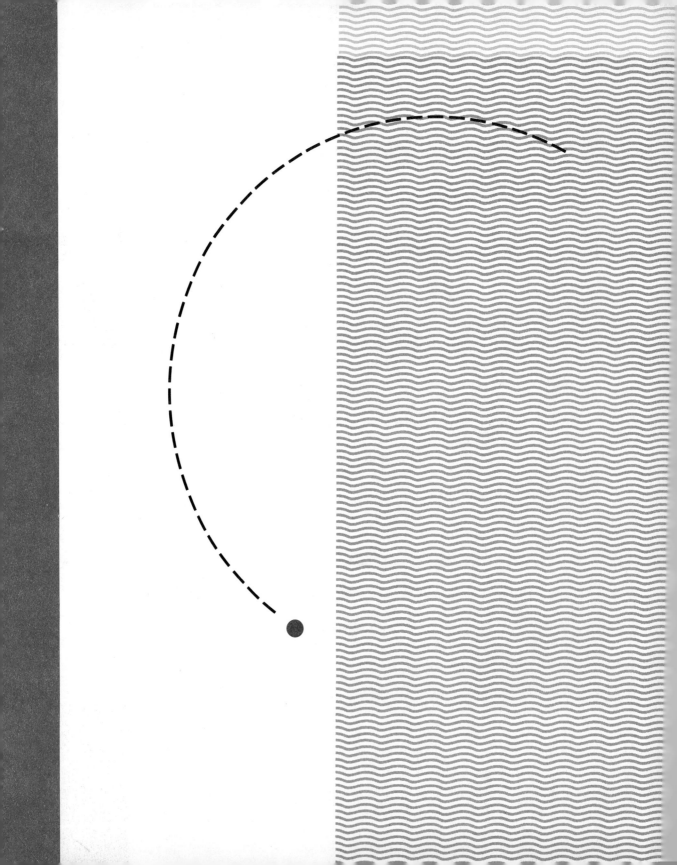

CHAPTER 2

Using the Programming Environment

GW-BASIC is one of the more popular PC programming languages. One of the major reasons for that popularity is availability: It is included with every copy of MS-DOS—and MS-DOS is included with nearly every IBM PC-compatible computer. Beyond availability, however, GW-BASIC is popular because it is also a reasonably good programming language and environment. Further, the language is interpreted, rather than compiled, so that programs are ready to run as soon as you finish typing them.

In a compiled language, a program must be compiled before it can be executed. That is, the compiler converts programs into machine language—the binary numbers that your computer's central processing unit (CPU) understands. The CPU is the integrated circuit chip (an 8088 or 8086 chip in a PC or PC/XT, an 80286 in an AT, or an 80386 in some of the newer machines) where all the instructions are executed. This conversion is done only once; whenever the program is run, the machine language codes are already available and can be directly executed by the CPU.

In an interpreted language, the program statements can be executed as soon as they are typed. The interpreter reads one line from your program and sends the appropriate instructions to the CPU for execution. When that line is complete, the interpreter moves on to the next line and interprets and executes it. Having a program immediately ready to run after any changes have been made makes program development much faster.

There is a cost for this development speed, however, and that cost is a decrease in the program's execution speed and usually an increase in the size of the program file on disk. The file size is rarely a problem for short programs, but the decrease in speed can range from a factor of 10 to 100 (depending on the program). Whenever the program is run, each line is separately interpreted and executed every time it is encountered. It is the reinterpretation of every line that makes an interpreted program run more slowly than a compiled program. On the other hand, the absence of a separate compilation step before a program can be run does make program development faster with an interpreted language. You will probably never notice the loss in execution speed for most small programs, especially compared with the significantly decreased time needed to create them.

In this chapter, I will describe invoking GW-BASIC, using direct mode to calculate and print values immediately, using the editor to create and edit a program, and listing, saving, loading, and executing programs.

Starting GW-BASIC

The simplest way to invoke GW-BASIC was shown in the previous chapter. With your computer running and the DOS prompt displayed, type **GWBASIC** and press Enter. The screen should look like that shown in Figure 1.2.

Notice that the DOS system prompt is replaced by the GW-BASIC Ok prompt, and a list of function key assignments is printed along the bottom. The function key assignments are shortcuts. Pressing the indicated key inserts, at the cursor location, the text displayed at the bottom of the screen.

Starting GW-BASIC in this way starts the interpreter and loads a blank program document. To load and execute an existing BASIC program, type **GWBASIC** followed by the name of the program. For example, the following line would start GW-BASIC and load and run the program we created in Chapter 1:

C> **GWBASIC SLDEP.BAS**

While there are other options and switches that can be used when invoking GW-BASIC, you will find that you rarely use them.

Understanding Direct Mode and Indirect (Program) Mode

At this point, you can either enter (and execute) a direct-mode statement or command, or enter a BASIC program in indirect mode. The difference here is that each statement in direct mode is immediately executed when you press the Enter key. In indirect mode, program lines are stored in memory, and are executed—as a program—when you type the RUN command. To use indirect mode, simply begin each line with a line number. To use direct mode, omit the line number.

A *statement*, in GW-BASIC, is any BASIC instruction. A statement generally consists of a *keyword* such as PRINT, followed by arguments and/or other keywords. Keywords are those words reserved exclusively for the use of GW-BASIC; they make up the GW-BASIC commands and functions. A function is a keyword that returns a value. A *command* is a keyword that causes an action to take place but does not return a value.

U*sing Direct Mode*

While direct mode is primarily used to execute the BASIC commands used for program development (NEW, SAVE, LOAD, RUN, and so forth), it is also used to execute other valid BASIC statements.

You can use direct mode to calculate a number quickly from a single-line equation when a calculator isn't handy. You can also use it to test mathematical functions and combinations of functions when you are unsure of their operation or what results to expect. Throughout this book, I use direct mode to demonstrate the use of different BASIC statements and functions. You should remember that in most cases, direct-mode statements can be changed into program statements by simply adding a line number before each statement.

While most BASIC statements can be executed in direct mode, only those that are prefaced with PRINT or ? will display any results. If you type

PRINT 1+1

and press Enter, GW-BASIC immediately prints the value 2, followed by the Ok prompt.

```
2
Ok
```

This is not too exciting, but let's say that you want to know the payment required on a four-year (48-month) automobile loan of $10,000 with an annual interest rate of 12 percent. The loan is compounded monthly at 1 percent (0.01 in decimal notation). The equation is

$$PAYMENT = \frac{PRINCIPLE \times INTERSEST}{1 - \left(\dfrac{1}{1+INTEREST}\right) NUMBER\ OF\ PAYMENTS}$$

and you can calculate it by typing

PRINT 10000*0.01/(1-(1/(1+0.01))^48)

and pressing Enter. The response is

```
263.3388
Ok
```

If you only wanted to know the value of one loan payment, then this direct-mode method would be a reasonable way to go. If you wanted to calculate the loan payments for several different loans, however, you should create a program to do it.

You can also type statements such as

    A=5+3

Here, A is given the value 8 when you press Enter. Nothing is printed because this statement only assigns a value to A. (Because it can be assigned a value, A is considered a *variable*). Next type

    PRINT A

which, when you press Enter, prints the value of A

    8
    Ok

Numbers stored in memory this way will remain there until you quit GW-BASIC, clear memory, or run a program.

Using Indirect (Program) Mode

A BASIC program is different from a direct-mode calculation in that the commands are stored and not interpreted until you execute the RUN command.

Another difference is that you can save a program for execution later; a direct-mode calculation is done and gone as soon as you press Enter. As you type the program statements, they are stored in memory. The statements remain there until you clear them with a command such as NEW or DELETE, load another program, or quit GW-BASIC.

Entering and Running a Program

Precede each statement in a GW-BASIC program with a line number as you type it. The line number not only marks the statement as a line from a program, it also determines the order of execution (from lowest to highest). For example, assume you want to calculate the markup on an item for sale. Type a line number followed by a statement assigning the fractional markup rate of 0.2 (20 percent) to RATE.

10 RATE = 0.2

When you press Enter, nothing appears to happen, but the statement has been stored in memory. Next, assign the cost ($15.75) of the item you want to mark up to VALUE by typing

20 VALUE = 15.75

Again nothing appears to happen when you press Enter. Calculate the markup by multiplying VALUE and RATE; then print it with a PRINT statement. Be sure to press Enter after each statement.

30 MARKUP = RATE*VALUE
40 PRINT MARKUP

Because these four statements have been entered as a four-line BASIC program, they will not be executed until you type RUN. Execute this program, by typing **RUN**, then pressing Enter. You can also execute this program by pressing the function key F2.

```
3.15
Ok
```

The 20 percent markup on $15.75 is $3.15. Each statement is calculated in order, and the result is printed on the screen. To see your program, type **LIST** (or press F1) and press Enter. Your program will be printed on the screen. In the following example (and subsequently throughout this book), boldface print will be used in program listings to indicate what you should type.

```
LIST
10 RATE = .2
20 VALUE = 15.75
30 MARKUP = RATE*VALUE
40 PRINT MARKUP
Ok
```

You could instead type LLIST, which sends your program to the printer.

Stopping a Program

Before we go any further, there is one command that you need to know—how to stop a running program. In the event that you start a program running that you really didn't want to run, or a program you're running has somehow gotten out of control, you need to be able to make it stop. The stop command in GW-BASIC is the same as for the DOS commands: press Ctrl-Break. If you can't remember this command, write it down and stick the note to the bottom of your monitor. Even if you can remember it, write the command down anyway so that when panic sets in, the command to stop the program is right in front of you.

As an example, add the following line 50 to the program currently in memory and then list it. Type **50 GOTO 10**, press Enter, and type **LIST** and press Enter. Your program will now read

```
10 RATE = .2
20 VALUE = 15.75
30 MARKUP = RATE*VALUE
40 PRINT MARKUP
50 GOTO 10
Ok
```

This line will make the program jump back to line 10 at the top and run the program over and over again forever. This is a not-uncommon coding error known as the *infinite loop*. Run this program by typing **RUN** and pressing Enter, and you will see a program out of control. Press Ctrl-Break and it will stop. It did stop, didn't it? When you have finished, delete line 50 by typing **50** and pressing Enter.

Using Line Numbers

Line numbers can range from 0 to 65529. It's common practice to start with line number 10 and to continue in incremental steps of 10. In this way, you leave yourself plenty of room to insert lines between the existing ones without having to renumber the whole program.

If you type another statement, it will be inserted in your program according to the line number that precedes it. For example, take the markup program. What we would really like to know is the final price of an item rather than the amount of the markup. To do this, we need to add the original cost to the markup. First, list the program by typing **LIST** (or pressing F1) and pressing Enter.

```
10 RATE = .2
20 VALUE = 15.75
30 MARKUP = RATE*VALUE
40 PRINT MARKUP
Ok
```

Insert a new line, 35, that adds VALUE and MARKUP to create the final PRICE, and change line 40 to print PRICE. (From now on, assume that you should press the Enter key at the end of each statement you type.) Type the new lines 35 and 40.

```
35 PRICE = MARKUP + VALUE
40 PRINT PRICE
```

Now list the program again to see the result of your change, and then run it to see whether it works.

```
LIST
10 RATE = .2
20 VALUE = 15.75
30 MARKUP = RATE*VALUE
35 PRICE = MARKUP + VALUE
40 PRINT PRICE
Ok
RUN
18.9
Ok
```

Note that while the new program line was typed out of order, it was inserted into the program in the correct location. Note also that the new line 40 replaced the existing line 40. As explained earlier, typing a statement with the same line number as an existing statement replaces the existing statement with the new one. If adding lines causes you to run out of available line numbers between two that have already been used, you can automatically renumber a program with the RENUM command. Renumber the markup program and list it to see the result.

```
RENUM
Ok
LIST
10 RATE = .2
20 VALUE = 15.75
```

```
30 MARKUP = RATE*VALUE
40 PRICE = MARKUP + VALUE
50 PRINT PRICE
Ok
```

*E*diting a Program

Suppose you want to change one of the statements in your program. You can simply retype the whole statement, complete with changes, replacing the previous one, or you can edit the existing statement. If the changes in the line are extensive or the line is short, retyping the statement is often the easiest way to make a change. Most changes are minor, however, in which case editing an existing line is the better alternative.

Any BASIC statement shown on the screen, including direct-mode statements, can be edited. Use the arrow keys to move to the statement to be changed, type the changes, and press Enter with the cursor anywhere in the statement (it does not have to be at the end). If you move the cursor out of the statement with the up arrow or down arrow keys before pressing Enter, the stored version of the line will not be changed, even though the version shown on the screen is. You must move the cursor back into the line and press Enter for the changes to be made to the program stored in memory. Table 2.1 contains a list of keys that are available to simplify editing programs.

You can recall statements to the screen for editing in either of two ways: LISTing the program or using the EDIT command. If the program is so large that it will scroll off the screen, list a range by using the LIST command followed by two line numbers separated by a hyphen. Only the statements between those two line numbers will be listed. To use the EDIT command to edit line 50, type EDIT 50:

EDIT 50
50 PRINT PRICE

The line is printed, with the cursor at the beginning of the line. Use the right arrow key until the cursor is at the P in PRICE. Because the editor defaults to overtype mode, press Insert (or Ctrl-R) to change to insert mode and type **"The marked-up price is $";**. Pressing Insert again or using the arrow keys will return the editor to overtype mode. Press Enter with the cursor still in the line, and then list the changes.

Table 2.1: Editing Keys

Key	Alternate Key	Function
Backspace	Ctrl-H	Deletes the character to the left of the cursor and shifts the balance of the line to the left.
Ctrl-Break	Ctrl-C	Aborts a running program (Ctrl-Break only), aborts the current line edit without saving changes, or stops automatic line numbering.
Ctrl-left arrow	Ctrl-B	Moves the cursor left one word.
Ctrl-right arrow	Ctrl-F	Moves the cursor right one word.
Down arrow	Ctrl--	Moves the cursor down one line.
Up arrow	Ctrl-6	Moves the cursor up one line.
Left arrow	Ctrl-]	Moves the cursor left one character.
Right arrow	Ctrl-\	Moves the cursor right one character.
Del (Delete)		Deletes the character under the cursor and shifts the balance of the line one space to the left.
Ctrl-End	Ctrl-E	Erases from the cursor position to the end of the line.
End	Ctrl-N	Moves the cursor to the end of the line.
Ctrl-Enter	Ctrl-J	Causes lines to wrap at the insertion point.

Table 2.1: Editing Keys (Continued)

Key	Alternate Key	Function
Enter	Ctrl-M	Enters a program line into memory or executes a direct-mode command.
Esc	Ctrl-[	Erases the entire line containing the cursor.
Ctrl-G		Rings the bell (beeps).
Home	Ctrl-K	Moves the cursor to the upper-left corner of the screen.
Ctrl-Home	Ctrl-L	Form feed; clears the screen and moves the cursor to the upper-left corner.
Ins (Insert)	Ctrl-R	Toggles between insert mode and overtype mode. The default mode is overtype.
Ctrl-NumLock		Program pause; press any key to resume.
Ctrl-PrtSc		Echoes characters to the screen and to the printer lpt1:.
Shift-Prtsc		Prints the current screen on the printer lpt1:.
Tab	Ctrl-I	Moves the cursor right to the next tab stop. Tab stops are every eight characters.

```
LIST
10 RATE = .2
20 VALUE = 15.75
30 MARKUP = RATE*VALUE
40 PRICE = MARKUP + VALUE
50 PRINT "The marked-up price is $";PRICE
Ok
```

At this point, you can use the arrow keys to move the cursor back into the line to make any other needed changes. Keep in mind that if you change the line number shown on the screen, you will end up with two copies of the statement in memory. One will have the old line number; the second will have the new one. This feature is useful for inserting a copy of a line elsewhere in a program.

*S*aving a Program

Be sure to save your program before you clear memory or turn off your machine, or everything will be lost. In fact, it's a good idea to save your program whenever you make a significant number of changes, to ensure that a system crash or power failure will not cost you hours of work. Use the SAVE command or function key F4, followed by the name of the file:

```
SAVE "RATE"
```

Because you've given no file extension, GW-BASIC automatically appends the .BAS extension. The program is saved in the current directory, in a file with the name RATE.BAS. As mentioned earlier, the file name can have up to eight characters plus a period and a three-character extension. (If you include an extension with the file name, GW-BASIC will not append .BAS).

Normally, the program is saved in binary format, which loads quickly and conserves disk space. Appending ,A to the command saves the file as text that can then be opened and edited with any text editor.

To save the program in a different directory, include a path with the file name. For example, typing

```
SAVE "C:\BASFILES\RATE.TXT",A
```

would save the program as a text file named RATE.TXT, on disk C, in directory BASFILES. Use the extension .TXT as a reminder that this is a text file.

Clearing a Program from Memory

Now that you have saved the program, you need to clear memory for a new one. Type **NEW** and press Enter to delete the current program from memory. Make sure you have saved your changes before executing NEW, or they will be gone forever.

To delete only certain statements, rather than the whole program, from memory, use the DELETE command. There are three ways to use this command:

- DELETE 30 deletes the single statement that has number 30 (or any other specified line).

- DELETE 30-50 deletes the statements with line numbers 30 through 50.

- DELETE 20- deletes statement number 20 and all statements after it.

To clear the screen without deleting a program from memory, use the CLS command. (We used CLS in the depreciation program in the last chapter to clear the screen before printing new material on it.)

Loading a Program into Memory

To load a program previously saved with the SAVE command or a BASIC program created as a text file, use the LOAD (F3) command. To load the program we just saved, type **LOAD "RATE"**.

GW-BASIC will delete any program currently in memory, search the current directory for a file with the name RATE.BAS, and load it into memory. If you include a file extension (such as .TXT), GW-BASIC will use that instead of .BAS in the search.

Copying and Deleting Files from within GW-BASIC

Most file maintenance (listing, creating, copying, and deleting disk files and directories) can be done from within GW-BASIC, without having to quit and return to DOS. Table 2.2 lists the GW-BASIC file maintenance commands. You can also use the SHELL command to run DOS without exiting GW-BASIC and losing the program currently in memory. Type **SHELL** and DOS is now running in the remaining memory. You can do any necessary file maintenance, using standard DOS commands, or run another program (assuming there is enough memory). To return to GW-BASIC, type **EXIT** at the DOS prompt.

If you type **SHELL** followed by a DOS command within quotation marks, the command will be executed and you will then return to the GW-BASIC OK prompt.

Table 2.2: GW-BASIC File Maintenance Commands

Command	Use
CHDIR	Change the default directory.
FILES	List the files in a directory.
KILL	Delete a file.
MKDIR	Create a new subdirectory.
NAME	Change a disk file name.
RESET	Close all disk files.
RMDIR	Delete a subdirectory.
SHELL	Execute an external program.

Quitting GW-BASIC

To quit GW-BASIC and return to DOS, type **SYSTEM**. Be sure you have saved your current program before typing **SYSTEM**, or any changes made since the last time you saved it will be lost.

Summary: The Programming Environment

In this chapter, you have learned how to invoke GW-BASIC and work in the GW-BASIC environment. I have discussed direct-mode commands and creating, editing, saving, and loading BASIC programs. You have also learned how to quit GW-BASIC and how to perform file maintenance without having to return to DOS.

- Load the BASIC interpreter by typing GWBASIC at the DOS prompt. To load and execute a BASIC program at the same time, type the program name after the GWBASIC command.

- The difference between direct-mode statements and indirect (program) statements is that the former are executed immediately, while the latter are saved in memory and executed as a whole with the RUN (F2) command. Program statements are preceded by line numbers, which both differentiate them from direct-mode statements and determine the order in which they will be executed.

- A running program can be stopped by pressing Ctrl-Break.

- Edit programs by changing the lines shown on the screen, and pressing Enter while still in the edited line. Lines can be listed on the screen with the LIST (F1) or the EDIT command. Edit the statements by moving to the location that needs changing with the arrow keys, and then typing in the changes. Table 2.1 contains a list of special editing keys to use while making changes to a program.

- Save BASIC programs with the SAVE (F4) command and load them with the LOAD (F3) command. In both cases, append the file name, within quotation marks, to the command. Files are normally saved in a compressed binary format but can be saved as text files by appending ,A to the SAVE command. The LOAD command will read either text or compressed binary files.

- You can perform most file maintenance operations from within GW-BASIC, using the commands in Table 2.2. You can also run DOS or any other program with the SHELL command. This command leaves intact GW-BASIC and any program you currently have in memory and runs DOS or some other program in the remaining memory. To return to GW-BASIC, quit the other program or use the EXIT command in DOS.

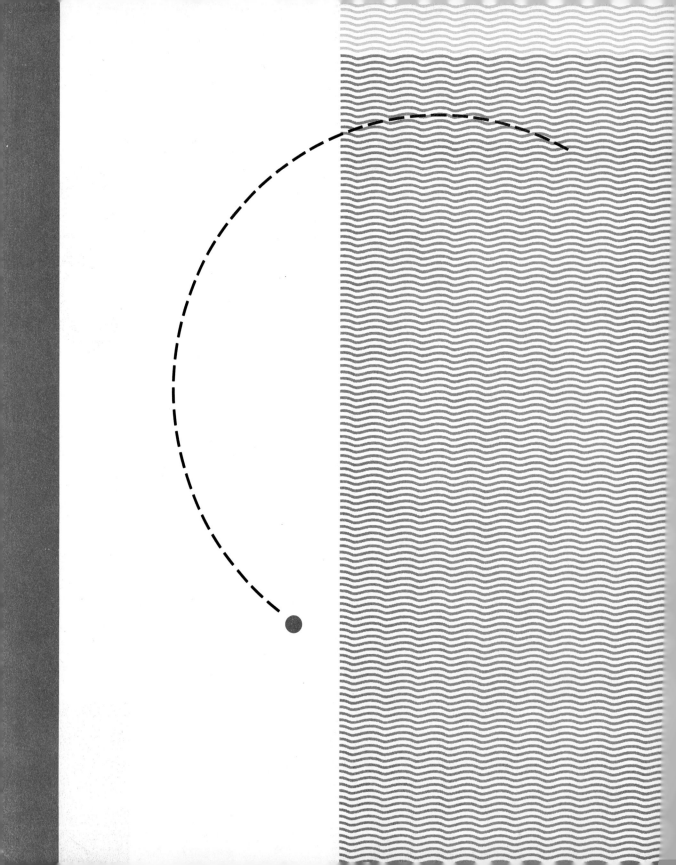

CHAPTER

3

Interfacing with
the Outside World

Input and output (I/O) deals with transferring information between memory and any device attached to your computer. Devices include keyboards, monitors, printers, floppy and hard disks, joysticks and mice, modems, and networks. GW-BASIC makes it easy for you to use these devices by handling all the requirements and protocols for you. To send data to and receive data from a device, you use the PRINT and INPUT statements. Whether the device is the screen or a floppy disk, you access each of them in essentially the same way. In this chapter, I will discuss I/O as it relates to screens, keyboards, printers, and simple sequential disk files.

Accessing Devices

Three steps are required to access a device with GW-BASIC.

1. Open a connection to the device with an OPEN statement.

2. Write to or read from the device using the PRINT or INPUT statement.

3. Close the connection when you have finished by using a CLOSE statement.

These three steps can be used to communicate with any standard device, including the keyboard, screen, printer, disk files, and serial ports, although access to the screen, printer, and keyboard automatically open whenever GW-BASIC is started. These devices therefore don't need the OPEN and CLOSE statements.

Printing on the Screen

The most used output medium on the computer is the screen, and one of the most basic operations of a program is printing on that screen.

Using PRINT

Printing text and numbers on the screen is accomplished with the PRINT statement. A PRINT statement consists of the word PRINT, followed by no, one, or several arguments. Arguments can be numbers, text, or the results of formulas. The arguments (or their results) are printed on the screen and followed by a carriage return. If there are no arguments, the PRINT statement merely provides a blank line (linefeed).

If the argument is a string of text enclosed in double quotation marks, it is printed exactly as it was typed between the marks. As an example, type the following direct-mode statement: **PRINT "What is the purpose of this session"**; press Enter and you will see

```
What is the purpose of this session
Ok
```

If the argument is a numeric value or a formula that returns a numeric value, the number will be printed with a leading space or minus sign plus a trailing space. Suppose you want to print the result of the division of 355 by 113. Type **PRINT 355/113** to get the following:

```
3.141593
Ok
```

The formula is calculated first, and then the result (which just happens to be a good approximation of the value of pi) is printed. Note the space before the 3 in the output. Had the numeric result been a negative number, a minus sign would have appeared there. The space following the number is not visible in this output.

Separating Arguments with Commas, Semicolons, or Spaces

A PRINT statement can have multiple arguments, separated by commas, semicolons, or blank spaces. (A printed line that exceeds the width of the screen will continue on the next line.)

- If you use a comma, GW-BASIC moves to the next tab stop (one every 14 character positions) before printing the next argument.

- If you use a semicolon, printing of the next argument starts immediately to the right of the last character printed.

- Although blank spaces usually give the same results as semicolons, in some cases blank spaces confuse GW-BASIC (I seldom use them for that reason).

If you end a PRINT statement with a semicolon, comma, or the SPC() or TAB() function, the carriage return is suppressed when the program is run. This is a useful feature for spreading the printing of a complicated line over more than one PRINT statement. While this is not usually required, it often does simplify program input and improve readability. Suppressing the carriage return is also used when you want the user to type the answer to a question on the same line as the printed question rather than on the next line down.

The following example demonstrates these different variations of the PRINT statement. Clear memory with **NEW**, and type the following program.

```
10 PRINT 10,20,30
20 PRINT 40;50;60
30 PRINT 70 80 90
40 A = 100
50 B = 200
60 C = 300
70 PRINT A B C
80 PRINT 400;
90 PRINT 500;
100 PRINT 600
110 PRINT "There are";A;"boxes on the shelf."
```

Now run the program with the RUN command.

```
RUN
10          20          30
40  50  60
708090
100  200  300
400  500  600
There are 100 boxes on the shelf.
Ok
```

The first line printed shows the tab-stop spacing produced by the commas in line 10. Note the double spaces between the numbers printed with line 20. Each number is printed directly after the preceding one with a preceding and a trailing space, providing two spaces between numbers.

Line 30 gives us an example of the problem with using blanks instead of semicolons. Because GW-BASIC can't tell that we are entering three separate numbers, it combines them into a single number. That problem could be corrected by assigning numbers to the variables A, B, and C as shown in lines 40, 50, and 60, and then using the letter variables instead of numbers, as shown in line 70. (Of course, the whole thing could have been avoided by using semicolons as in line 20.)

The last line of the example shows a combination of text and numeric output in the same PRINT statement. The contents of A are inserted between the two strings to create a sentence. Note that the spaces before and after the number are part of the printed number rather than the text.

Using PRINT USING

There are many occasions when it is helpful to *format* information that is displayed on the screen. *Formatting* is the act of putting the output into a particular arrangement. You can control the number of digits after the decimal point, the inclusion of commas and dollar signs within a printed number, and the number's location.

In the last chapter, I calculated the payment on a loan with the statement

```
PRINT 10000*0.01/(1-(1/(1+0.01))^48)
```

While we realized that the result (263.3388) was in dollars and cents, it would be helpful if this were more obvious. In this case, we would like the number to be preceded with a dollar sign and rounded to two decimal places. By adding a USING clause to the PRINT statement, we can get just that.

```
PRINT USING "$###.##";10000*0.01/(1-(1/(1+0.01))^48)
$263.34
Ok
```

Formatted output in GW-BASIC is produced by using the PRINT USING statement. You type a formatting string after PRINT USING to determine where and how the arguments of the statement are printed. The string is simply alphanumeric characters and symbols enclosed by double quotation marks. Such symbols as \, !, &, #, and $ are used to specify where and how the arguments of the PRINT USING statement are printed. Any alphabetic or numeric characters included in the formatting string are included in the output unchanged. The more commonly used symbols are shown here.

\ \   Two backslashes, separated by spaces, define a location for printing the contents of a string. The first character in the string is placed where the first \ is. Succeeding characters will fill in the spaces until the second \ is reached. Any text remaining in the string is skipped.

!   This symbol causes only the first character of the string to be printed at that location.

&   This causes the whole contents of the string to be printed no matter how long it is.

Pound signs mark the location for printing of a number. Put one pound sign where each digit of the number is to go. Place a decimal point between the signs where the decimal point should appear in the printed number. A comma placed anywhere to the left of the decimal point causes a comma to appear before every third digit to the left of the decimal in the printed number, correctly separating hundreds, thousands, millions, etc.

$ A dollar sign immediately to the left of a number inserts a dollar sign at the leftmost point of the defined area in the printed output. Because numbers are right-aligned within that area, there may be spaces between the sign and the number. On the other hand, two successive dollar signs to the left of a number puts the dollar sign up against the leftmost character in the number. The second dollar sign is counted as part of the field width for the number.

As an example, clear memory and type and run the following program:

```
NEW
Ok
10 PRINT USING "Some text, \          \, ######,.##";"A string
field",1234.5678
20 PRINT USING "Some text, \        \, $######,.##";"A string
field",1234.5678
30 PRINT USING "Some text, &, $$#####.##";"A string
field",1234.5678
40 PRINT USING "Some text, !, $$.##";"A string field",1234.5678
RUN
Some text, A string field,    1,234.57
Some text, A string , $    1,234.57
Some text, A string field,   $1234.57
Some text, A, %$1234.57
Ok
```

The first two words in the formatting string in line 10 (Some text) are printed because they are not formatting symbols. Next come two back-slashes separated by 12 spaces, defining a field 14 characters wide for printing the string A string field. Finally, the number 1234.5678 is printed in the numeric field defined with the pound signs. The comma within the numeric field places a comma between the hundreds and thousands. The decimal point in the numeric field indicates its location in the printed result. Since the number has more digits after the decimal than the field defined in the formatting statement, the number is rounded.

In line 20, the same string and number are printed. In this case, the string field has been shortened; because the whole string cannot fit the area, it is truncated after string. The numeric field has $ inserted to its left, which prints a dollar sign at the left side of the numeric field.

The & in line 30 specifies that the whole string is to be printed. Without the comma in the numeric field, hundreds and thousands are not delineated. This time the numeric field has $$ on the left, which prints a dollar sign immediately to the left of the number.

In line 40, the ! indicates that only the first character of the string is to be printed; in addition, the numeric field is too short for the number to fit. The percentage sign in the printed output indicates that the number would not fit in the field specified for it.

*P*rinting on the Printer

While the most common way to get printed output from a GW-BASIC program is to use LPRINT statements, an easier way to print simple results is to print a screen at a time. Let's start with this simple approach.

*P*rinting the Screen

The simplest method of printing your output is to print the screen with PrtSc or to turn on screen echoing with Ctrl-PrtSc. To use PrtSc (this key may be labeled somewhat differently on your keyboard), first print your results on the screen, then press PrtSc. Again depending on your keyboard and computer, it may be necessary to press Shift-PrtSc to send the output to the printer (in some cases, both methods work). In any event, everything on the screen will be printed on the printer.

To use screen echoing, press Ctrl-PrtSc first and then run your program. Everything that appears on the screen will also be printed on the printer. To turn off screen echoing, press Ctrl-PrtSc again.

*U*sing LPRINT and LPRINT USING

The more conventional method of getting printed results is to use LPRINT and LPRINT USING statements in place of the PRINT and PRINT USING statements. LPRINT and LPRINT USING work the same as PRINT and PRINT USING except that the output goes to the printer instead of to the screen. (Remember that you do not have to execute an OPEN statement before printing on the printer.)

*U*sing Control Characters

When printing on the printer, you will often need to advance the printer to the top of the next page. To accomplish this, you must send a form feed *control character* to the printer. The form feed character is produced in GW-BASIC by printing the function CHR$(12). If it is printed on the screen instead of the printer, it causes the screen to be cleared.

A control character is one of several characters that cause actions to take place on the printer or screen rather than causing symbols to be printed. Control characters are created in GW-BASIC by using the CHR$() function and placing the ASCII codes for the desired control character within the parentheses. The codes for several useful control characters are 7 (bell), 8 (backspace), 9 (tab), 10 (line feed), 12 (form feed), and 13 (carriage return).

*G*etting Input from the Keyboard

The most used input device on your computer is the keyboard. Like the screen, the keyboard is a special device whose communication path is automatically opened when GW-BASIC is started.

*U*sing INPUT

The INPUT statement is used to get data from the keyboard. When this statement is executed, the program stops, prints a ?, and waits for you to type some data. When you press Enter, the data is stored in the variables given as arguments of the INPUT statement, and the program continues running.

In the following example, the program prints a message on the screen, waits for you to type two numbers, and then prints a number back on the screen. Clear memory with NEW, type the program and then RUN it, answering the question when asked.

```
NEW
Ok
10 PRINT "Input the year and your age";
20 INPUT YR,AGE
30 PRINT "You were born in";YR-AGE
RUN
Input the year and your age? 1990,39
You were born in 1951
Ok
```

Line 10 prints a question on the screen. Note that it ends with a semicolon, which suppresses the carriage return. When the INPUT command is executed in line 20, it places a question mark on the screen at the current cursor position, just to the right of the word age. The question mark indicates that the INPUT statement is waiting for you to type something. At this point, since there are two numeric arguments (YR and AGE) in the INPUT statement, you must type two numbers separated by a comma. If you type anything else, GW-BASIC will print an error message and ask you to try again (Redo from start). Line 30 then prints the additional text and the difference between the numbers stored in YR and AGE.

The PRINT statement in line 10 and the INPUT statement in line 20 can be combined into a single INPUT statement. If the first argument of an INPUT statement is a string of text surrounded by quotation marks, that text will be printed on the screen (just as with PRINT) before INPUT stops and waits for your entry. For example, the program above could be edited to

```
10 INPUT "Input the year and your age";YR,AGE
30 PRINT "You were born in";YR-AGE
```

Using LINE INPUT

When you input a string with the INPUT command, it reads characters into the string variable until it encounters a comma or a quotation mark and then terminates. If you are trying to input a string that contains commas, you begin and end the string with quotation marks. INPUT will read it correctly, including everything but the quotation marks. If you want to include quotation marks in the string as well, you must use the LINE INPUT statement. The LINE INPUT statement only terminates reading data into a string variable when it encounters the carriage return at the end of a line.

Using a Sequential Disk File

In Chapters 1 and 2, we used the SAVE and LOAD commands to transfer programs between memory and disk files. The same process can be used with the data needed or produced by your program; that is, you can read data from a disk file and write data to one.

There are actually two different types of disk files, sequential access and random access. Sequential-access disk files are written to and read from in order from the beginning to the end. The first entry is placed at the beginning of the file, the second entry comes next, and so forth. Random-access files, on the other hand, can be read and written in any order, rather than from the beginning. (In this section I will discuss only sequential-access files. Random-access files will be discussed in Chapter 8.)

We use the PRINT# and INPUT# statements to read and write sequential-access files, much as we use PRINT and INPUT to print on the screen and read entries from the keyboard. The differences are the inclusion of the pound sign (#) and the use of a file number in the PRINT# and INPUT# statements.

Opening a Sequential Disk File

Before you can do anything with a disk file, you must open it with an OPEN statement. This statement specifies a file to be opened or created, a mode for opening the file, and assigns it a file number. The file number assigned with the OPEN statement is used to identify which file you are accessing when you use PRINT# and INPUT# statements.

```
OPEN "MYFILE.TXT" FOR INPUT AS #1
```

This statement opens the existing file MYFILE.TXT in the current directory, defines the mode of access as INPUT, and assigns the file number 1 to the file. If the file doesn't exist in the current directory, an error will result.

> OPEN "MYFILE.TXT" FOR OUTPUT AS #1

This statement opens, and allows you to write to, a sequential-access file. It will create a file if there is no file with this name in the default directory.

> OPEN "MYFILE.TXT" FOR APPEND AS #1

This case is similar to opening a file FOR OUTPUT, but any writing you do will be appended to the end of any data that already exists in the file. It will create a new file if there is no file with the name MYFILE.TXT in the current directory.

> OPEN "MYFILE.TXT" FOR RANDOM AS #1

Use this command to open a random-access file for reading or writing. Table 3.1 summarizes the mode commands and their effects.

The file number (i.e., the number you assign to the file when you open it) indicates which file to access. You can open a file more than once for input or random but not for output or appending:

> OPEN "MYFILE.TXT" FOR INPUT AS #1
> OPEN "MYFILE.TXT" FOR INPUT AS #2

Since only three files can be open at any one time, you are limited to file numbers 1, 2, and 3. File numbers can be reused by closing one file and then opening another with the same number.

Table 3.1: Effects of Modes in an OPEN Statement

Mode	Effect if no file exists	Opens file at	INPUT from	PRINT to
INPUT	Error	Beginning	Yes	No
OUTPUT	Creates it	Beginning	No	Yes
APPEND	Creates it	End	No	Yes
RANDOM	Creates it	Beginning	Yes	Yes

*W*riting Data with PRINT# and PRINT# USING

Once a file is open, writing to it is as simple as printing on the screen. Just insert a #, the file number, and a comma after the word PRINT, and the printing that would have appeared on the screen is directed into a file instead. The resulting file will be an ASCII text file that can then be printed with the DOS PRINT command, viewed with the DOS TYPE command, or opened with a word processor.

To write formatted text to a disk file, use the PRINT# USING statement, adding the file number after the pound sign. This statement provides the same result as the PRINT USING statement except that the text is directed into the specified disk file instead of the screen.

*W*riting Data With WRITE#

If you are storing data to later be reinput into GW-BASIC, you may want to use WRITE# instead of PRINT#. The WRITE# statement inserts quotes around printed strings and commas between different printed numbers. This makes it possible for the INPUT# statement to accurately separate the different data items. For example, if your program has a statement like

WRITE#1,"Jack and Jill", 1234, 567.8,"Hello there"

it would produce the following line in file number 1:

"Jack and Jill",1234,567.8,"Hello there"

*R*eading Data with INPUT#

To read data from a sequential-access disk file, insert a pound sign, the file number, and a comma after the word INPUT. Reading numeric data with the INPUT# statement starts with the first character and continues until a space, carriage return, line feed, or comma is encountered. With string data, any leading blanks are ignored and reading starts with the first actual character. If that character is a double quotation mark, reading continues until a second such mark is encountered. Otherwise, reading continues until 255 characters have been read or a comma, carriage return, or line feed is encountered.

Reading Data with LINE INPUT#

The LINE INPUT# statement is used to read an entire line of text from a disk file and store it in a string variable. In this case, the reading stops when a single carriage return is encountered or 255 characters have been read.

Closing a Sequential Disk File

When you have finished writing to or reading from a file or wish to reuse the file number, you must close it with the CLOSE statement. For example, to close file number 1, you use

    CLOSE#1

To close all open files, use

    CLOSE

Creating Computer Journaling Programs

The computer journaling programs developed here are designed to record and print statistics about computer use. The programs systematically record the amount of computer time you spend on different projects. You can use these records for billing purposes or to justify a business deduction for computer equipment. These programs are simple but effective: I have been using them for the last few years to separate the personal and business uses of my own computer.

The requirements of the journaling programs are that they record the date, time, and type of usage when you start your computer, when you change projects, and when you quit. The data must be stored in a way that will allow it to be retrieved later and analyzed with a BASIC program or some other program such as Lotus 1-2-3 or Microsoft Excel.

There are three nearly identical journaling programs to perform these functions as well as a program to print the results. The journaling programs, BUSUSE.BAS (used below to demonstrate I/O operations), CHANGE.BAS, and LO.BAS, record the usage at start-up, any change of usage within a session, and an ending entry at shutdown. The printing program, USERPT.BAS, reads the data file created by the journaling programs and sends it to the printer.

The BUSUSE.BAS Program

Clear memory and type the program as shown below. Note that when you run the program, it will ask you to type the purpose of this session and then print the date, time, and that purpose on the screen and in the disk file usage.txt.

```
NEW
Ok
1 REM BUSUSE.BAS
2 REM Computer-Usage Journaling Programs
3 REM Start-up Journal Entry
4 REM Call from AUTOEXEC.BAT
8 GOTO 20
9 REM Autosave segment
10 SAVE "c:\bususe.bas"
11 END
20 REM Start of Program
30 TAB$=CHR$(9)
40 PRINT "What is the purpose of this session";
50 INPUT PURP$
60 OPEN "c:\usage.txt" FOR APPEND AS #1
70 PRINT #1,DATE$;TAB$;TIME$;TAB$;PURP$
80 PRINT DATE$;TAB$;TIME$;TAB$;PURP$
90 CLOSE #1
100 SYSTEM
```

The first few lines of the program are my standard prologue, describing the program's name and function and automatically saving the current version. Lines 1 through 4 are remarks that describe the program's name and purpose. Since anything typed on the same line after the word REM or after a single quotation mark (') has no effect on the operation of the program, use remarks as much as possible. They take very little space, and they make a program much more understandable, especially several years from now when you—or someone else—must try to figure out just what it was that you did.

Next, the statements in lines 9 through 11 save the program with the correct file name. Line 10 is a SAVE statement that saves the current version of the program in the root directory of my hard disk (C). If you are

using a floppy-disk–based system, you will want to change the C to an
A. Line 11 causes the program to quit as soon as it has been saved.
(Whenever I make some changes to the program, all I have to do is type
RUN 10. The program will start running at line 10 and save itself.)

Line 8 is a GOTO statement that causes execution to skip to line 20
whenever the program is executed normally with a RUN command. This
prevents the program from saving itself whenever it is run.

At this point, you should save the program using the autosave
segment:

```
RUN 10
Ok
```

Line 20, another remark, is the actual beginning of the journaling program. Because the program will be using tabs, line 30 assigns the variable TAB$ the value of the tab control character using CHR$(9). Using
TAB$ is slightly faster than using CHR$(9) and makes the program more
readable.

Line 40 prints What is the purpose of this session. Line 50 causes the
computer to pause, print a question mark, and wait for you to enter some
text that describes the current use of the computer. The answer is then
stored in PURP$.

Line 60 opens the file usage.txt in the root directory of drive C. Again,
if you have a floppy-disk system, change the drive letter to A. The file is
opened using FOR APPEND so that any new text will be added to the end
of the file, and it is given the file number 1.

Lines 70 and 80 print the date, time, and usage to both the disk file and
the screen. The functions DATE$ and TIME$ return the current date and time
as stored in the system clock. The TAB$s separate the information on this
line in a manner acceptable to a spreadsheet program. Line 90 closes the
disk file, and line 100 quits GW-BASIC and returns you to DOS. While
you are working on this program, you may want to change line 100 to a
remark by inserting a REM after the line number. Otherwise, every time you
run the program it will end GW-BASIC and return to DOS.

The CHANGE.BAS Program

The CHANGE.BAS program, which is nearly identical to BUSUSE.BAS,
indicates changes in usage during a session. It first prints the end of one

type of usage before printing the start of another. You can, of course, type this program from scratch; a simpler way is to LIST BUSUSE.BAS and then edit it. Change the file name in line 10 first to be sure that you don't accidently write over BUSUSE.BAS. Don't forget to press Enter with the cursor in each statement that you have changed—otherwise the statement will not be changed in memory.

In line 40, use the variation of the INPUT statement that combines the capabilities of PRINT and INPUT in one statement. Type a blank line 50 to erase the original one because line 40 now fulfills its function. (Note that I have typed a line through line 50 to show that you should delete it.) Add the new lines 62 and 64 to write the date, time, and the word stop to the disk file and the screen. This indicates the end of the current session. The listing below shows all the new text in boldface.

```
LIST
1 REM CHANGE.BAS
2 REM Computer-Usage Journaling Programs
3 REM Change Journal Entry
4 REM Call from CHANGE.BAT
8 GOTO 20
9 REM Autosave segment
10 SAVE "c:\change.bas"
11 END
20 REM Start of program
30 TAB$=CHR$(9)
40 INPUT "What is the NEW purpose of this session";PURP$
50 INPUT PURP$
60 OPEN "c:\usage.txt" FOR APPEND AS #1
70 PRINT #1,DATE$;TAB$;TIME$;TAB$;PURP$
80 PRINT DATE$;TAB$;TIME$;TAB$;PURP$
90 CLOSE #1
100 SYSTEM
Ok
50
62 PRINT #1,DATE$;TAB$;TIME$;TAB$;"stop"
64 PRINT DATE$;TAB$;TIME$;TAB$;"stop"
```

Now LIST the new program.

```
LIST
1 REM CHANGE.BAS
2 REM Computer-Usage Journaling Programs
3 REM Change Journal Entry
4 REM Call from CHANGE.BAT
```

```
8 GOTO 20
9 REM Autosave segment
10 SAVE "c:\change.bas"
11 END
20 REM Start of program
30 TAB$=CHR$(9)
40 INPUT "What is the NEW purpose of this session";PURP$
60 OPEN "c:\usage.txt" FOR APPEND AS #1
62 PRINT #1,DATE$;TAB$;TIME$;TAB$;"stop"
64 PRINT DATE$;TAB$;TIME$;TAB$;"stop"
70 PRINT #1,DATE$;TAB$;TIME$;TAB$;PURP$
80 PRINT DATE$;TAB$;TIME$;TAB$;PURP$
90 CLOSE #1
100 SYSTEM
Ok
```

As soon as you have made all the changes, run the autosave segment
to save the program.

RUN 10
Ok

The LO.BAS Program

The third computer-usage journaling program, LO.BAS, is also nearly
identical to the other two. The difference is that this program doesn't ask
the user for a purpose. It just inserts the date, time, and stop to indicate the
end of a session. Create it in the same way as the last one, by editing the previous program. For the most part, all you have to do is to change the file
names and delete part of CHANGE.BAS. Save it by running the autosave
segment as soon as you have made all the changes.

```
LIST
1 REM ENDSES.BAS
2 REM Computer-Usage Journaling Programs
3 REM End of Session Journal Entry
4 REM Call from LO.BAT
8 GOTO 20
9 REM Autosave segment
10 SAVE "c:\endses.bas"
11 END
20 REM Start of program
30 TAB$=CHR$(9)
40 INPUT "What is the NEW purpose of this session";PURP$
```

```
60 OPEN "c:\usage.txt" FOR APPEND AS #1
62 PRINT #1,DATE$;TAB$;TIME$;TAB$;"stop"
64 PRINT DATE$;TAB$;TIME$;TAB$;"stop"
70 PRINT #1,DATE$;TAB$;TIME$;TAB$;PURP$
80 PRINT DATE$;TAB$;TIME$;TAB$;PURP$
90 CLOSE #1
100 SYSTEM
Ok
40
70
80
LIST
1 REM ENDSES.BAS
2 REM Computer-Usage Journaling Programs
3 REM End of Session Journal Entry
4 REM Call from LO.BAT
8 GOTO 20
9 REM Autosave segment
10 SAVE "c:\endses.bas"
11 END
20 REM Start of program
30 TAB$=CHR$(9)
60 OPEN "c:\usage.txt" FOR APPEND AS #1
62 PRINT #1,DATE$;TAB$;TIME$;TAB$;"stop"
64 PRINT DATE$;TAB$;TIME$;TAB$;"stop"
90 CLOSE #1
100 SYSTEM
Ok
RUN 10
Ok
```

*U*sing the Computer Journaling Programs

Because the program BUSUSE.BAS needs to be run whenever you start your computer, you can make its execution automatic by inserting the following line in your AUTOEXEC.BAT file.

GWBASIC BUSUSE.BAS

Execution of the CHANGE.BAS and LO.BAS programs can be simplified by creating two batch files called CHANGE.BAT and LO.BAT. Each of the two files would contain the single line shown here. For CHANGE.BAT, type

GWBASIC CHANGE.BAS

For LO.BAT, type

GWBASIC LO.BAS

Simply typing CHANGE or LO at the DOS prompt will then start GW-BASIC and run the desired program.

The USERPT.BAS Program

The report generator, USERPT.BAS, opens and prints the journal file. Since the standard prologue is nearly the same in each program, delete the rest of the previous program (load it if necessary), edit the prologue, type the rest of the new program, and run the autosave segment to save it.

```
DELETE 30-
Ok
LIST
1 REM USERPT.BAS
2 REM Computer-Usage Journaling Programs
3 REM Computer Usage Report
8 GOTO 20
9 REM Autosave segment
10 SAVE "c:\userpt.bas"
11 END
20 REM Start of program
Ok
30 OPEN "c:\usage.txt" FOR INPUT AS #1
40 IF EOF(1) THEN 80
50 LINE INPUT #1,USAGE$
60 LPRINT USAGE$
70 GOTO 40
80 LPRINT CHR$(12)
90 CLOSE #1
100 END
RUN 10
Ok
```

Here, line 30 opens the report file usage.txt FOR INPUT; change the disk drive letter if necessary.

Line 40 is an IF THEN statement. It tests to see if the next record in the file is the end-of-file record. If it is, the statement causes the program to jump down to line 80 and continue executing there. This is to prevent the program from attempting to read the end-of-file, which would cause an error. (I will discuss the IF THEN statement in more detail later.)

The *end-of-file (EOF)* is a special character that marks the end of a file. The EOF(1) function tests the next record in file number 1, to see if it is the end-of-file. If it is, the function returns true, otherwise it returns false.

Line 50 is a LINE INPUT# statement to input a line from the disk file and store it in USAGE$. I use the statement here because I want to be sure that I read a complete line from the file each time. If I had used an INPUT# statement instead, and the text that I typed to explain the purpose of a session included a comma, then the input to USERPT.BAS would have stopped at the comma instead of at the end of the line. Thus, line 50 reads a line of text from the file and line 60 prints it.

The process is repeated until the last line of data has been read and printed and EOF is reached. The IF THEN statement in line 40 then causes execution to jump to line 80 where we execute a form feed, close the disk file, and end the program. Figure 3.1 shows part of the printout generated with this program, using the data in my last year's file.

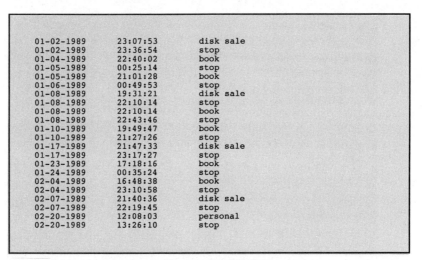

```
01-02-1989        23:07:53        disk sale
01-02-1989        23:36:54        stop
01-04-1989        22:40:02        book
01-05-1989        00:25:14        stop
01-05-1989        21:01:28        book
01-06-1989        00:49:53        stop
01-08-1989        19:31:21        disk sale
01-08-1989        22:10:14        stop
01-08-1989        22:10:14        book
01-08-1989        22:43:46        stop
01-10-1989        19:49:47        book
01-10-1989        21:27:26        stop
01-17-1989        21:47:33        disk sale
01-17-1989        23:17:27        stop
01-23-1989        17:18:16        book
01-24-1989        00:35:24        stop
02-04-1989        16:48:38        book
02-04-1989        23:10:58        stop
02-07-1989        21:40:36        disk sale
02-07-1989        22:19:45        stop
02-20-1989        12:08:03        personal
02-20-1989        13:26:10        stop
```

Figure 3.1: An example of output from the USERPT.BAS program

Summary: Input/Output Operations

As you continue to write programs, you will find that larger and larger amounts of your code will be devoted to I/O. The fancier a print-out or screen, the more code must be devoted to I/O. Therefore, most programmers are continuously enhancing the I/O of their code, especially if the code is going to be used by others.

In this chapter, I discussed the various methods used to transfer data between memory and the attached devices.

- Printing on the screen is accomplished with the PRINT statement. The word PRINT, followed by some arguments, will print the values of those arguments on the screen. To have more control over the printed values, use the PRINT USING statement, which includes a format string to control the location, the number of digits after the decimal, and the inclusion of commas and dollar signs in the printed number. The LPRINT and LPRINT USING statements perform the same functions for the printer.

- The INPUT statement is used to get data from the keyboard. Including a string of text after the word INPUT will cause that text to be printed on the screen before the INPUT statement waits for you to type in the desired data. LINE INPUT is a special form of the INPUT statement that reads a whole line of text into a string variable at one time. Punctuation within the file, such as a comma, will not stop the input as it does in a simple INPUT statement.

- The OPEN, PRINT#, INPUT#, and CLOSE# statements access disk files. Disk files are accessed by first opening a communication path to the files with the OPEN statement and assigning a file number to that path. Reading and writing data are also accomplished with the INPUT and PRINT statements, adding a pound sign and the file number to identify the file to which the data are being sent. When you are through with a disk file, you must close the communication path with a CLOSE statement.

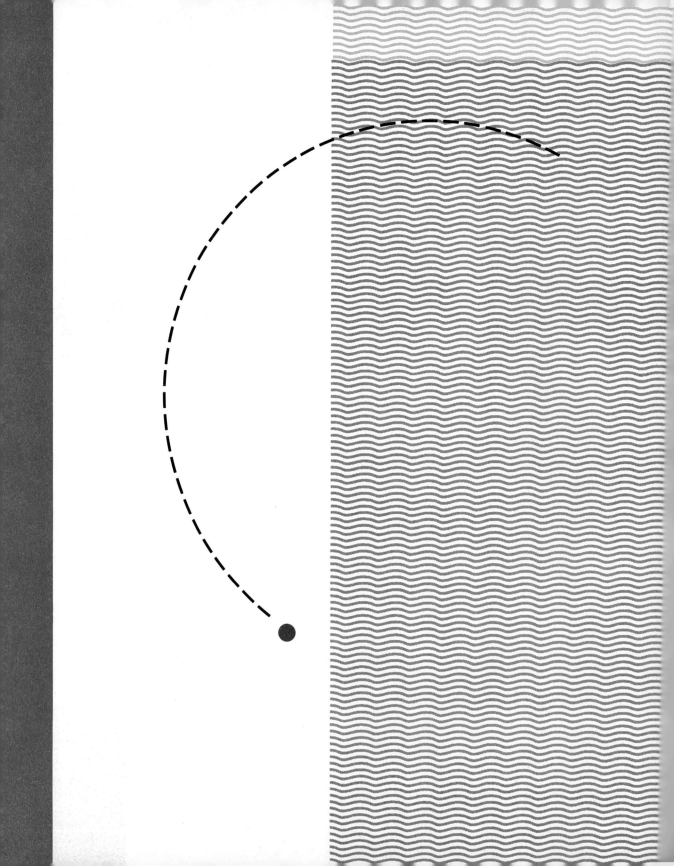

CHAPTER 4

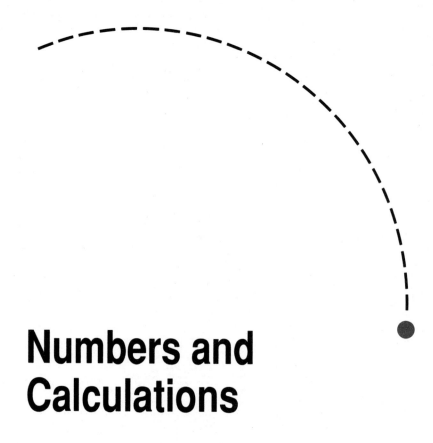

Numbers and Calculations

Numeric operators and assignment statements can be thought of as the heart of a computer program. This is where the figuring is done. All of the rest of the program is devoted to communications—with the user, the disk storage, or the printer. In actuality, because a personal computer uses a microprocessor to execute commands and binary data, numeric operations are performed throughout a program, not just in the program segment that performs the calculations to produce the numbers of interest.

All data stored in a computer—whether numbers, text, or commands—are stored as binary numbers. This is because data are stored in a set of electronic switches, with each switch storing one bit of the data. A switch, or bit, has two states, on and off. If the switch is on, it's a binary 1; if it's off, it's a binary 0. The switches, or bits, are grouped into sets of eight, called bytes. It takes one byte to store a single character in memory.

This chapter will cover

- The different types of numbers used in GW-BASIC
- Variables for storing numbers and strings
- Assignment statements
- Numeric operations
- Array variables

The programs PMT.BAS and PMT2.BAS, two versions of a loan-payment calculator, will be used to illustrate these points. The first version, PMT.BAS, calculates the value of a loan payment based on a single interest rate. The second version, PMT2.BAS, uses arrays to calculate a table of payments and interest rates.

Using Different Types of Numbers

You will generally find three types of numbers useful in GW-BASIC:

- Integers
- Single-precision floating-point numbers
- Double-precision floating-point numbers

The type and precision needed depend on the particular problem being solved. There are two other types of numbers available in GW-BASIC: octal (base 8), and hexadecimal or hex, base 16. The last two, however, are generally used only by advanced programmers.

Using Integer Numbers

Integers are whole numbers. That is, they are numbers with no decimal points and no fractional parts. Examples of integers include

10   0   −31358   96   −34

In GW-BASIC, integers can range in value from −32,768 to +32,767 in steps of 1. (The reason for the odd numbers representing the upper and lower bounds of this range is that the integers are stored as two-byte [16-bit] binary numbers. One bit is used for the sign of the integer [0 for +, 1 for −]; the remaining 15 bits are used for the number. A binary number with n bits can represent 2^n numbers minus one for the value 0, and $2^{15}-1$ is 32,767.) The primary use of integers is for counters and for indices that must not have a fractional part. Integers are also the most economical in terms of storage, taking up only two bytes of memory per number, and the most efficient for performing numeric calculations. As you continue to write programs, you may find yourself using many variables where the numbers they represent do not have fractional parts. Storing them as integers will save about 50 percent of your memory compared with storing them as the default type, single-precision floating-point numbers.

Using Single-Precision Floating-Point Numbers

Single-precision floating-point numbers—real numbers with up to seven digits —are the default numeric type in GW-BASIC. *Real numbers* have an integer part, a decimal point, a fractional part, and an optional exponent. Examples of single-precision floating-point numbers are

    0.0287   37.895   126.7321E+12 32!

Single-precision numbers range between

    ±0.00000000000000000000000000000000002938736
    and
    ±170141200000000000000000000000000000000.0.

These are shown as $\pm 2.938736 \times 10^{-39}$ to $\pm 1.701412 \times 10^{+38}$ in scientific notation or, in computer notation, ±2.938736E−39 to ±1.701412E+38.

The number to the right of the *E* in the computer notation is the *exponent*, which is the power of 10 to multiply times the number. It also shows the number of character positions to move the decimal point. For example,

1.234E−04 = 0.0001234

5.4321E+06 = 5432100.0

The number to the left of the *E* is the *mantissa* of the number. It can contain up to seven digits plus the decimal point, although only six digits may be accurate. Round-off errors and an inability to store a mantissa value greater than 8,388,608 can contribute to inaccuracies in the seventh digit.

Single-precision numbers require four bytes of storage, twice as many as do integers. You can force a number to be stored as a single-precision number by appending an exclamation mark to it. For example, the number 1246! would normally be stored (without the !) as an integer. The ! causes it to be stored as a single-precision number.

Using Double-Precision Floating-Point Numbers

Double-precision numbers are also real numbers with exactly the same range as single-precision numbers (the exponent for double-precision numbers is stored in exactly the same number of bits as is that for single-precision numbers). The difference is that the mantissa can contain up to 17 digits, with 16 of them accurate. Some examples are

32785912.88576   32.56#   5.97863289D+7

Double-precision numbers are used when the accuracy of a single-precision number is inadequate. This is often the case when dealing with dollar amounts. For example, $140,895.21 should be stored as a double-precision number because it contains more than seven digits. If stored as a single-precision number, it will be truncated or rounded to seven digits. You can force an integer or single-precision number to be stored as a double-precision number by appending a pound sign to the number or the variable name used. Double-precision numbers require eight bytes of storage, twice as much as needed by single-precision numbers.

*B*eware the Range of Floating-Point Numbers

While 10^{38} is probably more than adequate for most financial calculations, it can be seriously limiting for some scientific calculations. If an intermediate calculation generates an underflow (a number less than 2.938736×10^{-39}, or you assign a value less than this to a variable), the number is replaced with zero. If there is a numeric overflow (a number greater than $1.701412 \times 10^{+38}$), the number is replaced with the largest possible real number ($1.701412 \times 10^{+38}$). There may be no error messages, and in both cases the program continues to run using the replacement values instead of the true values. These replacements can cause later calculations to be erroneous.

*U*sing Variables and Numbers

One of the most powerful features of a programming language is the ability to store a number or string of text at some location in memory and to name that location with a meaningful name. By giving storage locations names that are more meaningful than the numbers they represent, you make your program significantly more readable and understandable. Variables are names given to locations in memory where values—numbers or strings of text—can be stored. You create a variable by simply using its name and assigning it a value. That value is then stored in memory. Later in your program, when you use that variable in another statement, its value is retrieved from memory and inserted in the statement.

There are two major types of variables in GW-BASIC—numeric and string. There are three types of numeric variables to match the three types of numbers used by GW-BASIC—integer, single-precision floating-point, and double-precision floating-point—and they are subject to the same constraints as those numbers. String variables, which must end in a dollar sign, are used to store strings of text. To assign a string of text to a string variable, enclose the string in double quotation marks and equate it to the variable name. The quotation marks are not stored in memory. Numeric variables will be discussed in this section, and strings and string variables will be discussed in the next chapter.

Naming Variables

Variable names in GW-BASIC can have up to 40 characters consisting of letters, numbers, and periods. The first character must be a letter, and a variable name cannot be the same as any of the BASIC keywords (OPEN, PRINT, NEW, and so forth), although a keyword can be a part of a variable name. (For example, OPENER can contain the BASIC keyword OPEN and still be a valid variable name.)

You are not, of course, required to use all 40 characters in a variable name, and it is generally better to keep the name both meaningful and as short as possible to decrease the possibility of typos and make program statements more readable. It's common practice to create variable names from a string of words linked together with a period. For example, PRESENT.VALUE is a valid BASIC variable name, as is PRES.VAL or PV. When you select variable names, keep in mind the person who will have to use or modify your program in the future. If you are the only one who will use the program, use the shortest name that has meaning to you. If PV obviously means present value to you, use PV.

On the other hand, if your program is going to be modified by other people who may not understand a shortened variable name, then use one of the longer versions. An alternate convention is to define the variables at the beginning of your program with remark (REM) statements and to then use the shortened names.

Upper- or lowercase is not significant in GW-BASIC variable names. Whatever you type in lowercase appears that way on the screen initially. When you list or edit the program, key words and variables are converted to uppercase.

The type of number that can be stored in a variable is determined by the variable type suffix symbol added to the end of the variable name. Without a symbol, the default variable type is single-precision floating-point—which is sufficient for most applications. Table 4.1 lists the variable type suffix symbols that can be added to variables in GW-BASIC.

The symbol becomes part of the variable name, so that changing the symbol produces a different variable. INTEREST! and INTEREST#, for example, are two distinct variables, and can be used in the same program.

While this is allowed, it is generally not good programming practice. Some examples of variable type suffix symbols are

NUM.PMTS%	Integer
PAYMENT	Single-precision floating-point (default)
INTEREST!	Single-precision floating-point
PV#	Double-precision floating-point
FILE.NAME$	String

Another way to set the type of a variable is to use the DEFINT, DEFSNG, DEFDBL, and DEFSTR statements. These statements declare all variables beginning with a certain letter to be integers, single- or double-precision numbers, or strings. For example, DEFDBL A-C declares all variables beginning with A, B, or C to be double-precision floating-point. (Although some programmers like these statements, I rarely use them because they restrict the choice of variable names.) If used, the variable type suffix symbols override any type declarations made with these statements.

Table 4.1: Variable Type Suffix Symbols Allowed in GW-BASIC

Variable Type	Symbol
Integer	%
Single-Precision	!
Double-Precision	#
String	$

Creating Assignment Statements

Assignment statements give value to variables; we used some simple assignment statements earlier to assign values to some variables before printing them. Assignment statements have a variable name on the left, an equal sign, and a value or formula on the right. (In older versions of BASIC, they also had to begin with the keyword LET. That is rarely the case today, and it is not required in GW-BASIC.) When the statement is executed, the right side is evaluated, or calculated, and its value is assigned to the variable on the left.

The value on the right side can be a simple numeric value or a complex formula that includes values, variables, operators, functions, and parentheses. The following are examples of assignment statements:

```
STOCK.VAL = 136.78
NUM.STOCKS% = 30000
INVESTMENT# = NUM.STOCKS%*STOCK.VAL
NAME$ = "John P. Smith"
NAME$ = "479"
```

Note that in the last example, the numerals are enclosed in quotation marks. This defines the value as a character string rather than as an actual number. Therefore, because 479 is a string, you cannot add, subtract, multiply, or divide it.

Although it is not required, placing a space before and after the equal sign makes a formula more readable. A number of programmers use such spacing with the plus and minus signs (more rarely with multiplication and division signs). The results will be the same with or without the spaces.

*U*sing Mathematical Operators

As mentioned above, equations can consist of values, variable names, operators, functions, and parentheses. Table 4.2 lists the operators (that is, the symbols for—and performers of—mathematical operations) available in GW-BASIC and the order of their precedence. *Precedence* is the order in which an equation is evaluated when more than one operator is present. For example, multiplication is always done before addition or subtraction. Parentheses, however, always take precedence over the other operators, so that any operators within parentheses are calculated first. Inserting parentheses will ensure that an equation is evaluated in the order you want. Otherwise, your answer will vary with the function that is performed first. For example, if you type **A*B + C**, GW-BASIC calculates A*B first and then adds the value of C. If you want the addition to be done first, you must use parenthesis: **A*(B + C)**.

Table 4.2: *Variable Type Suffix Symbols Allowed in GW-BASIC In Order of Precedence*

Operator	Function
^	Exponentiation
−	Unary negation (not subtraction)
*	Multiplication
/	Floating-point division
\	Integer division
MOD	Modulus (remainder of an integer division)
+	Addition
−	Subtraction

Using the Built-in Mathematical Functions

The operators in GW-BASIC are complemented by a good set of built-in mathematical functions. A function returns a value based on the values of its arguments. It consists of a function name followed by parentheses containing the argument(s). The built-in functions, shown in Table 4.3, consist of basic trigonometric and logarithmic functions. Use these functions in conjunction with the operators to construct whatever numeric calculations you need. For example, the formula for a loan payment (PMT) is

$$PMT = I*(FV+PV*(1+I)^N)/(1-(1+I)^N)$$

where PV is the present value, FV is the future value, I is the interest rate per period, and N is the number of periods. Depending on the size of the loan, PV and FV might need to be double-precision, while N is usually an integer.

Table 4.3: Variable Type Suffix Symbols Allowed in GW-BASIC

Function	Operation
ABS(x)	Provides the absolute value of x
ATN(x)	Provides the arctangent of x for x expressed in radians
CDBL(x)	Converts x to a double-precision number
CINT(x)	Rounds x to the next higher integer
COS(x)	Provides the cosine of x for x expressed in radians
CSNG(x)	Converts x to a single-precision number
EXP(x)	Provides the exponential of x (e^x)
FIX(x)	Truncates x to a whole number without rounding
INT(x)	Returns the largest integer less than or equal to x
LOG(x)	Provides the natural logarithm (base e) of x
RND()	Returns a random number between 0 and 1
SGN(x)	Returns 1 with the sign of x
SIN(x)	Provides the sine of x for x expressed in radians
SQR(x)	Provides the square root of x
TAN(x)	Provides the tangent of x for x expressed in radians

Converting Differing Numeric Types

Consider the following statement:

```
60 INTEREST.RATE = 8.75/(1200)
```

In this statement, the single-precision value 8.75 is divided by the integer value 1200, and the result is assigned to the single-precision variable INTEREST.RATE. Since GW-BASIC cannot perform numeric operations on numbers with different types, it converts the numbers to the same type. Type conversion governs the way values are converted before any calculations are performed.

All values to the right of the equal sign are converted to the type of the highest-precision number present. (The lowest-precision number is the integer, followed by single-precision and double-precision.) The expression is calculated, and the result is converted to the type of the variable to the left of the equal sign and assigned to it. In our example, the most precise value is single-precision; the integer value (1200) is therefore converted to single-precision before the division is performed.

The Loan Payment Calculator, PMT.BAS

The loan payment calculator is a simple program that assigns the values of an interest rate, a present value, a future value, and the number of payments to some variables. It then calculates the amount of the periodic payment needed to pay off the loan and prints that value. Clear memory, type, and save (using **RUN 10**) the program shown in Listing 4.1.

Running the loan payment calculator in Listing 4.1 produces the following output:

```
RUN
Loan Payment Calculator
The interest rate per period is .7291667 percent,
or 8.75 percent per year.
The present value is $118,000.00
The future value is      $0.00
The term of the loan is 30 years
The monthly payment is   $928.31
Ok
```

```
1 REM PMT.BAS
2 REM Loan Payment Calculator
8 GOTO 20
9 REM autosave segment
10 SAVE "pmt.bas"
11 END
20 REM start of the program
30 PAYMENTS% = 360
40 PRESENT.VALUE# = 118000
50 FUTURE.VALUE# = 0
60 INTEREST.RATE = 8.75/(1200)
70 PAYMENT = (PRESENT.VALUE#-FUTURE.VALUE#)*INTEREST.RATE/(1-
(1/(1+INTEREST.RATE))^PAYMENTS%)
80 CLS
90 PRINT "Loan Payment Calculator"
100 PRINT "The interest rate per period is";INTEREST.RATE*100;"percent,"
110 PRINT "or";INTEREST.RATE*1200;"percent per year."
120 PRINT USING "The present value is $$#####,.##";PRESENT.VALUE#
130 PRINT USING "The future value is $$#####,.##";FUTURE.VALUE#
140 PRINT "The term of the loan is";PAYMENTS%/12;"years"
150 PRINT USING "The monthly payment is $$###,.##";PAYMENT
160 END
```

Listing 4.1: Loan payment calculator

Lines 1 through 20 are the standard prologue (including remarks); this saves the program with the name PMT.BAS. Line 30 is an assignment statement that assigns the value 360 (the number of months in 30 years) to the integer variable PAYMENTS%. In lines 40 and 50, the double-precision variables PRESENT.VALUE# and FUTURE.VALUE# are assigned the values $118,000.00 and $0.00. Because the dollar values of home loans often contain more than seven digits, these two variables must be double-precision.

Next comes a simple formula in line 60 that converts a yearly interest percentage into the monthly fractional interest rate needed to calculate the loan payment. The yearly interest rate is divided by 1,200—that is, by 100 to convert it from a percentage to a decimal and then divided by 12 to get the monthly interest rate. A single-precision variable is sufficient here, since interest rates (we hope) should never exceed seven digits.

Line 70 is a more complicated equation. It calculates the payment due on the loan from the present value, future value, interest rate, and number of payments. In this case, the most precise value on the right is double-precision, so all the variables will be converted to double-precision before the calculation is performed. At the end, the double-precision value is rounded to single-precision and then stored in PAYMENT.

You can use single-precision numbers here because the loan payment will rarely go over five digits. Then again, if you are involved in high finance, corporate takeovers, or financing the federal debt, your variable, PAYMENT, should also be double-precision.

In a program this small, using double-precision will not significantly affect the storage or run time, so you can use them at will. In large programs with many variables and calculations, however, you may want to be more selective about the use of single- and double-precision variables.

Line 80 clears the screen, line 90 prints the program name, and lines 100 through 140 print the interest rate, present value, future value, and term of the loan. Line 150 prints the calculated monthly payment, and 160 ends the program. An END statement is not really necessary here, because there are no more lines to the program after line 160. In larger programs, however, where you often place other pieces of code, such as subroutines (discussed later), after the main segment, the END statement would be needed.

Understanding and Using Arrays

An array is a data structure, that is, a method of grouping data under a single name. Essentially it is a repeated sequence of numbers or strings of a given size. Placing left and right parentheses immediately after a variable name turns that variable into an array variable. The following are array variables:

```
SALE(1000)  RATE(5)  FUTURE.VALUE#(7)  A(I)
```

An array variable actually represents a listing of memory locations where numbers or strings can be stored. Each item in the list (member) is identified by its individual number. The member is selected by placing its integer index (generally called a subscript) in the parentheses. If you had an array called SALES(), SALES(1) would represent one item, SALES(2) another, and so forth.

This may seem like a great deal of trouble just to define a set of similarly named variables. Although it might be simpler to use a list of names, such as SALES1, SALES2, and so on, it would be far more limiting. Because the index within the parentheses can itself be a variable, you can select the desired member by simply changing the value of the index when you run the program. (If you had a used a list of variables such as SALES1, SALES2, etc., each member of the list would have been fixed and the program would have to be edited to change the values.) The arrays thus allow greater flexibility in manipulating data; they allow you to apply the same equation to several sets of data and to treat many discrete values as a more-or-less coherent group.

*M*ultidimensional Arrays

Arrays can also be multidimensional. That is, you can use several indices separated by commas, with each index adding another dimension to the array. A two-dimensional array can be likened to a spreadsheet, where the first index specifies the row and the second index specifies the column. Together these coordinates, or indices, indicate a cell, or memory location. The following examples show how changing the indices changes the cell (and hence the value) in array A(I,J):

I/J	0	1	2
0	1	2	3
1	4	5	6
2	7	8	9

A(I,J) = (row index 1)

Changing the values of I and J gives us

$$A(2,1) = 8$$
$$A(1,2) = 6$$
$$A(0,1) = 2$$
$$A(1,1) = 5$$

This same analogy can be used for three-dimensional arrays, adding depth to the example above (instead of a grid with each compartment holding a value, we will have a cube). Imagine the cube in Figure 4.1 as representing the three-dimensional array A(I,J,K). The cube is divided into many small cells as shown. Each cell contains a value and is indexed with a unique set of three integers, I, J, and K. Cell A(1,3,2) is marked in the figure.

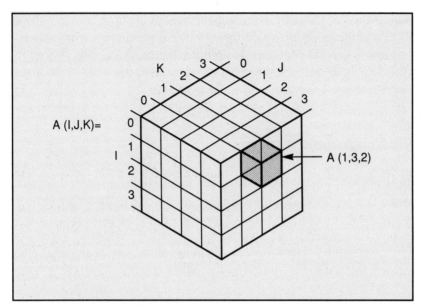

Figure 4.1: A three-dimensional array—A(I,J,K)—with cell A(1,3,2) marked

Higher-dimensional arrays, while difficult to visualize, are created by simply adding more indices, one for each dimension needed. Although GW-BASIC allows up to 255 dimensions, few people use more than three. GW-BASIC also allows up to 32,767 elements per dimension, but you will probably run out of memory long before you get anywhere close to that limit.

Defining Arrays

When you put parentheses and an index (subscript) after a variable name, GW-BASIC automatically creates an array with 11 elements numbered from 0 through 10, for each of up to 4 dimensions. To use more than 4 dimensions or more than 11 elements per dimension (and to avoid a Subscript out of range error) you must specify the size of the array with a DIM statement. For example,

```
10 DIM A(3,20),B(5)
```

creates a two-dimensional array A of single-precision numbers that has 4 rows and 21 columns (elements). It then creates a six-element one-dimensional array of integers B. Variable types are important because arrays can quickly use up a great deal of memory. To avoid confusion, it is usually a good idea to define all arrays with a DIM statement, including those that would be automatically created.

To delete an array so that you can reclaim its memory locations or to reuse the name with a different set of dimensions, use the ERASE statement. For example,

```
100 ERASE A
```

will delete the array A (including the data it contains), and release all the memory it used.

The type of variable stored in an array is determined in exactly the same manner as for single variables. A variable type suffix symbol (see Table 4.1) is placed between the array name and the left parenthesis. For example, A#(5) is element number 5 of a double-precision array, A%(3,7) is the element from row 3 and column 7 of a two-dimensional array of integers, and A$(3) is element number 3 from an array of strings. Note that the variable A and the array variable A(I,J) are different variables, and can both be used in the same program without their values overlapping. While such similar-but-different names are allowed, the high probability of confusion makes their use problematic.

Creating an Array of Loan Payments, PMT2.BAS

As an example of using arrays, we can modify the loan payment calculator program to calculate the payment for three different interest rates (8.75, 9.00, and 9.25 percent). First, edit the program name in line 10 to ensure that you do not overwrite PMT.BAS. Next, add line 25 to cause the variables INTEREST.RATE and PAYMENT to be one-dimensional arrays with four elements each (0, 1, 2, and 3). Since there are fewer than 11 elements and 4 dimensions to these arrays, their dimensions do not need to be explicitly stated in the program. To avoid confusion, however, it is a good practice to use the DIM statement with all array variables.

Modify lines 60 and 70 as shown to make the variables INTEREST.RATE and PAYMENT into array variables. Next, make two copies of line 60 by editing it. Change its line number to 62 and press Enter.

Change the line number to 64, and press Enter again. Change the array indices in lines 60, 62, and 64 to 1, 2, and 3 and the interest rates to 8.75, 9.00, and 9.25, respectively. (Because the array indices and, in general, counting in the programming world start at 0, you could have used 0, 1, and 2; I find it less confusing to start with 1.) Now, edit line 70 to create lines 72 and 74, including all three array indices in each line. Finally, delete lines 100 and 110, replace line 150, and add lines 152, 154, and 156 to print the three different rates. Here is the program, with the changed and added lines in bold.

```
1 REM pmt2.bas
2 REM loan payment calculator number 2
GOTO 20
9 REM autosave segment
10 SAVE "pmt2.bas"
11 END
20 REM start of the program
25 DIM INTEREST.RATE(3),PAYMENT(3)
30 PAYMENTS% = 360
40 PRESENT.VALUE# = 118000.
50 FUTURE.VALUE# = 0.
60 INTEREST.RATE(1) = 8.75/(1200)
62 INTEREST.RATE(2) = 9.00/(1200)
64 INTEREST.RATE(3) = 9.25/(1200)
70 PAYMENT(1) = (PRESENT.VALUE#–FUTURE.VALUE#)*
INTEREST.RATE(1)/(1–(1/(1+INTEREST.RATE(1)))^PAYMENTS%)
72 PAYMENT(2) = (PRESENT.VALUE#–FUTURE.VALUE#)*
INTEREST.RATE(2)/(1–(1/(1+INTEREST.RATE(2)))^PAYMENTS%)
74 PAYMENT(3) = (PRESENT.VALUE#–FUTURE.VALUE#)*
INTEREST.RATE(3)/(1–(1/(1+INTEREST.RATE(3)))^PAYMENTS%)
80 CLS
90 PRINT "Loan Payment Calculator"
120 PRINT USING "The present value is
$$#####,.##";PRESENT.VALUE#
130 PRINT USING "The future value is $$#####,.##";FUTURE.VALUE#
140 PRINT "The term of the loan is";PAYMENTS%/12;"years"
150 PRINT "Rate    Monthly Payment"
152 PRINT USING "##.##%    $$###,.##";
INTEREST.RATE(1)*1200,PAYMENT(1)
154 PRINT USING "##.##%    $$###,.##";
INTEREST.RATE(2)*1200,PAYMENT(2)
156 PRINT USING "##.##%    $$###,.##";
INTEREST.RATE(3)*1200,PAYMENT(3)
160 END
```

Save the program, and then run it.

```
RUN 10
Ok
RUN
Loan Payment Calculator
The present value is $118,000.00
The future value is      $0.00
The term of the loan is 30 years
Rate   Monthly Payment
8.75%    $928.31
9.00%    $949.45
9.25%    $970.76
Ok
```

Most of what this program does is the same as in PMT.BAS; you can refer to that program for more details on each line. Lines 1 through 20 are the standard prologue (here we save the program with the name PMT2.BAS). Line 25 specifies the maximum values for the arrays INTER-EST.RATE() and PAYMENT(). Lines 30 through 50 assign values to PAY-MENTS%, PRESENT.VALUE#, and FUTURE.VALUE#. Lines 60 through 64 assign values to the three elements of the array INTEREST.RATE(). Lines 70 through 74 calculate the payments required for the three interest rates and then assign them to the three elements of the array PAYMENT(). Line 80 clears the screen, and line 90 prints the heading. Lines 120 through 140 print a description of the loan being calculated. Finally, lines 150 to 156 print a table of loan payments and interest rates.

*S*ummary: Numeric Types and Calculations

In this chapter, I discussed numeric calculations in GW-BASIC. There are three different kinds of numbers you will commonly use: integers, single-precision floating-point, and double-precision floating-point.

- Integers are whole numbers ranging from $-32,768$ to $+32,767$. Following a number or variable name with a percentage sign forces its storage as an integer.

- Single-precision floating-point numbers can have up to seven digits, with exponents (powers of 10) that can range from −39 to +38. Variables with an exclamation mark appended to them are stored as single-precision, which is the default numeric type for variables without an appended symbol.

- Double-precision floating-point numbers can have as many as 17 digits, also with exponents ranging from −39 to +38. A number or variable with a pound sign appended is stored as double-precision.

- Most calculations in BASIC are performed using assignment statements, which are used to calculate values and assign them to variables. An assignment statement consists simply of a variable name on the left, an equal sign, and a value or formula on the right. The formula can consist of values, variables, operators, functions, and parentheses. Most of the standard mathematical functions and operators are available in GW-BASIC; they are listed in Tables 4.2 and 4.3.

- Array variables are used to create an arranged group of variables or discrete values, each with its own coordinate(s), the integer index, or subscript. Arrays can have up to 255 dimensions, and 32,767 instances (elements) in each dimension. Arrays with fewer than 4 dimensions and 11 or fewer elements per dimension do not need to be formally defined in GW-BASIC with a DIM statement, but it is wise programming practice to do so.

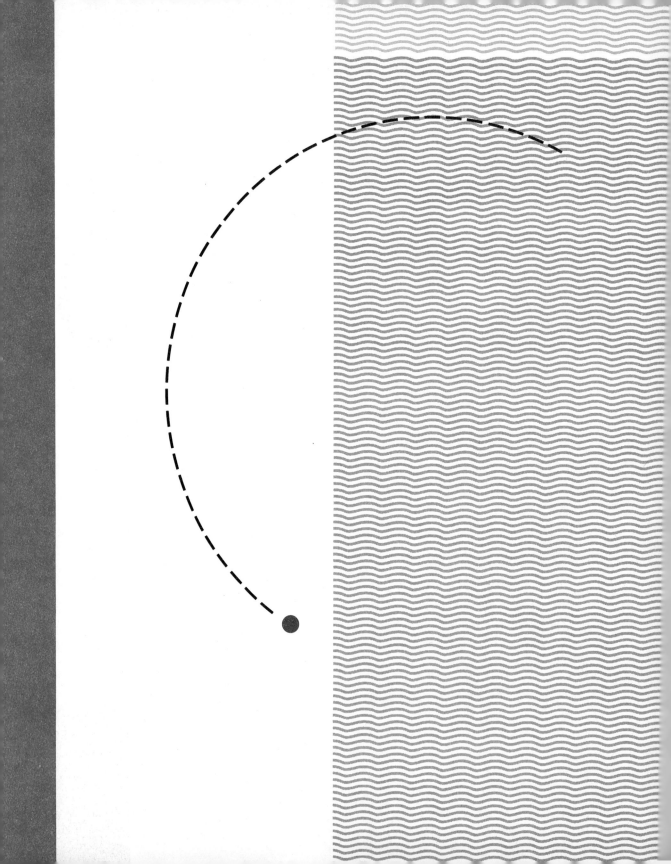

CHAPTER 5

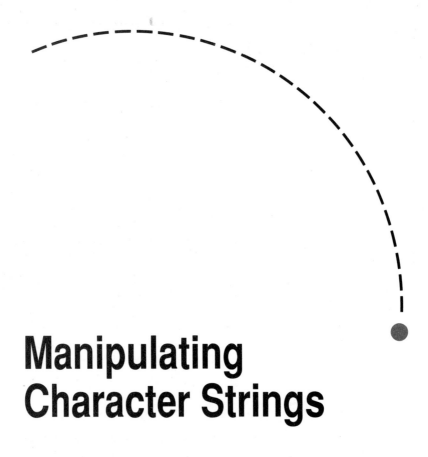

Manipulating Character Strings

Thanks to its powerful string manipulation capabilities, GW-BASIC allows you to create elaborate input and output screens. Using simple functions and statements, you can join (concatenate) two strings and locate, copy, and replace parts of strings or substrings.

This chapter discusses reading and writing strings, storing them in variables, and manipulating them. These functions are used in a simple mail merge program, MMERGE.BAS, that replaces codes in a letter template file with names and addresses from an address file.

Using Strings

A *string* is several (or no) characters, numbers, or symbols. In GW-BASIC, a string is a series of ASCII (American Standard Code for Information Interchange) characters. The ASCII character set consists of all of the normal (IBM) keyboard characters, plus control characters such as backspace and form feed and graphics characters. The last are character-sized symbols that can be combined to make shapes on the screen or printer; ASCII characters 176 through 223 are often used to draw lines and graphs. Figure 5.1 illustrates the range of ASCII characters.

When a string is used in a program, it must be surrounded by double quotation marks. Two double quotation marks in a row ("") denote the empty, or null, string, which is different from a string of spaces (" "). In this book, we've already used strings in PRINT statements to print a series of words on the screen. In general, strings are used in PRINT statements and in assignment statements for string variables.

Storing Strings in Variables

String variables stand for text rather than numbers. Like numeric variables, they also indicate locations in memory. Even though a string variable

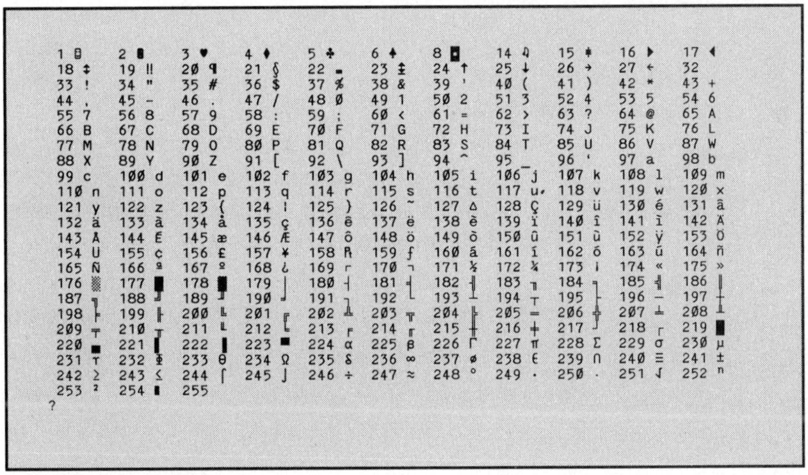

```
1 ☺    2 ☻    3 ♥    4 ♦    5 ♣    6 ♠    8 ◘    14 ♫   15 ☼   16 ►   17 ◄
18 ↕   19 ‼   2Ø ¶   21 §   22 ▬   23 ↨   24 ↑   25 ↓   26 →   27 ←   32
33 !   34 "   35 #   36 $   37 %   38 &   39 '   4Ø (   41 )   42 *   43 +
44 ,   45 -   46 .   47 /   48 Ø   49 1   5Ø 2   51 3   52 4   53 5   54 6
55 7   56 8   57 9   58 :   59 ;   6Ø <   61 =   62 >   63 ?   64 @   65 A
66 B   67 C   68 D   69 E   7Ø F   71 G   72 H   73 I   74 J   75 K   76 L
77 M   78 N   79 O   8Ø P   81 Q   82 R   83 S   84 T   85 U   86 V   87 W
88 X   89 Y   9Ø Z   91 [   92 \   93 ]   94 ^   95 _   96 `   97 a   98 b
99 c   1ØØ d  1Ø1 e  1Ø2 f  1Ø3 g  1Ø4 h  1Ø5 i  1Ø6 j  1Ø7 k  1Ø8 l  1Ø9 m
11Ø n  111 o  112 p  113 q  114 r  115 s  116 t  117 u  118 v  119 w  12Ø x
121 y  122 z  123 {  124 ¦  125 }  126 ~  127 ⌂  128 Ç  129 ü  13Ø é  131 â
132 ä  133 à  134 å  135 ç  136 ê  137 ë  138 è  139 ï  14Ø î  141 ì  142 Ä
143 Å  144 É  145 æ  146 Æ  147 ô  148 ö  149 ò  15Ø û  151 ù  152 ÿ  153 Ö
154 Ü  155 ¢  156 £  157 ¥  158 ₧  159 ƒ  16Ø á  161 í  162 ó  163 ú  164 ñ
165 Ñ  166 ª  167 º  168 ¿  169 ⌐  17Ø ¬  171 ½  172 ¼  173 ¡  174 «  175 »
176 ░  177 ▒  178 ▓  179 │  18Ø ┤  181 ╡  182 ╢  183 ╖  184 ╕  185 ╣  186 ║
187 ╗  188 ╝  189 ╜  19Ø ╛  191 ┐  192 └  193 ┴  194 ┬  195 ├  196 ─  197 ┼
198 ╞  199 ╟  2ØØ ╚  2Ø1 ╔  2Ø2 ╩  2Ø3 ╦  2Ø4 ╠  2Ø5 ═  2Ø6 ╬  2Ø7 ╧  2Ø8 ╨
2Ø9 ╤  21Ø ╥  211 ╙  212 ╘  213 ╒  214 ╓  215 ╫  216 ╪  217 ┘  218 ┌  219 █
22Ø ▄  221 ▌  222 ▐  223 ▀  224 α  225 ß  226 Γ  227 π  228 Σ  229 σ  23Ø µ
231 τ  232 Φ  233 Θ  234 Ω  235 δ  236 ∞  237 φ  238 ε  239 ∩  24Ø ≡  241 ±
242 ≥  243 ≤  244 ⌠  245 ⌡  246 ÷  247 ≈  248 °  249 ∙  25Ø ·  251 √  252 ⁿ
253 ²  254 ■  255
?
```

Figure 5.1: *The ASCII character set*

names the location of up to 258 consecutive bytes of memory that can hold a total of 255 characters, it uses only as much memory as is necessary to hold the actual string (plus three bytes). Defining many short strings therefore does not waste large amounts of memory.

String variable names follow the same rules as numeric variables. A string variable name can be up to 40 characters long, consisting of letters (the first character must be a letter), numbers and a period. A variable name cannot be the same as any of the BASIC keywords, and a string variable name must have the $ character appended to it. The following are all valid string variable names (the last example is an array variable).

```
A$   MY.NAME$   FILENAME$   NAME.LIST$(5,3)
```

A string array can contain one complete 255-character string in each location in the array. You should be aware that in some older versions of BASIC indices after a string variable name may refer to the character location of a single string rather than to a particular string in an array of strings. If you are trying to convert one of those programs to run under GW-BASIC, and it doesn't work correctly, check the string-handling parts.

Creating Strings of Single Characters

There are two string functions—STRING$() and SPACE$()—that are used to create a string containing multiple copies of a single character. The STRING$() function takes an integer and a string or two integers as arguments. It returns a string with the first character of the string argument repeated the number of times specified by the integer argument. For example, type **PRINT STRING$(5,"A")** in direct mode.

```
AAAAA
Ok
```

Further, **PRINT STRING$(5,"RALPH")** produces

```
RRRRR
Ok
```

and letting M$ equal Clyde, **PRINT STRING$(5,M$)** gives us

```
CCCCC
Ok
```

Note that if you use an integer to represent the string argument, it must be the numeric ASCII code of the desired character. As shown in Figure 5.1, each character in the ASCII character set has a numeric equivalent; these standard equivalents allow the exchange of information between dissimilar programs. You can also use them to access the characters within BASIC. Because the letter *A* has the ASCII number 64, **PRINT STRING$(5,65)** produces

```
AAAAA
Ok
```

The SPACE$() function takes one integer argument and returns a string with the number of spaces specified by the integer. For example, typing

WRITE SPACE$(4)

returns four blank spaces.

"   "

*C*onverting ASCII Numeric Codes and Characters

These next two string functions convert ASCII numeric codes to characters and characters to ASCII codes. The function CHR$() takes an integer argument and returns the appropriate character (including control characters). If you use a real number as an argument, it will be rounded before it is converted into a character.

The CHR$() function is most often used to insert control and graphics characters into strings being sent to the screen or printer. The codes of some useful control characters are

7 Bell	11 Vertical tab
8 Backspace	12 Form feed
9 Tab	13 Carriage return
10 Line feed	

Thus, printing CHR$(7) sounds the bell, CHR$(12) ejects the page from the printer, and so forth.

The ASC() function is the opposite of CHR$(). It takes a string as the argument and returns the integer ASCII code of the first character of the string. The ASC() function is often used to identify nonprinting control characters in strings, especially in communications programs where they are used to control terminal characteristics.

Converting Numbers and Strings

The STR$() and VAL() functions are used to convert numeric values into strings and string representations of numbers into numeric values. These functions are used primarily to create elaborate output screens and to convert text into usable numbers. STR$() converts its numeric argument into a string of numeric characters with a leading space or minus sign and no trailing spaces. For example, in

```
PRINT STR$(125)
 125
Ok
```

the result—125—cannot be added, subtracted, multiplied, or divided.

The VAL() function is used to convert string representations of numbers into numeric values that can be used in calculations. VAL() ignores leading blanks or tabs and any trailing characters. If the first character is alphabetic, VAL() returns a zero. For example,

```
PRINT VAL(" 12345abcesd")
 12345
Ok
PRINT VAL("ade1234")
 0
Ok
```

Printing Graphics Characters

In GW-BASIC, the available characters consist of the complete IBM character set of 256 characters. Of those characters, the first 32 are control characters and a few graphics characters, the next 96 are the standard keyboard characters, and the last 128 are graphics and special characters such as foreign characters and mathematical and scientific symbols. The IBM graphics and special characters are generally standard on all monitors—but not necessarily on all printers. The printable IBM character set and the corresponding ASCII characters are shown in Figure 5.1. A fragment of the program used to create that figure follows.

```
1 REM CHARSET.BAS
2 REM Prints the IBM character set
8 GOTO 20
9 REM Autosave segment
10 SAVE "charset.bas",A
11 END
20 REM start of program
30 KEY OFF
40 CLS
50 PRINT 1;CHR$(1);SPACE$(3);2;CHR$(2);SPACE$(3);
 3;CHR$(3);SPACE$(3);
60 PRINT 4;CHR$(4);SPACE$(3);5;CHR$(5);SPACE$(3);
 6;CHR$(6);SPACE$(3);
70 PRINT 8;CHR$(8);SPACE$(3);14;CHR$(14);SPACE$(2);
 15;CHR$(15);SPACE$(2);
 .
 .
 .
850 PRINT 247;CHR$(247);SPACE$(1);248;CHR$(248);
 SPACE$(1);249;CHR$(249);SPACE$(1);
860 PRINT 250;CHR$(250);SPACE$(1);251;CHR$(251);
 SPACE$(1);252;CHR$(252);SPACE$(1);
870 PRINT 253;CHR$(253);SPACE$(1);254;CHR$(254);
 SPACE$(1);255;CHR$(255);SPACE$(1);
880 INPUT X$
890 END
```

Note the use of the CHR$() function to create the character that goes with each ASCII code, and the SPACE$() function to insert different amounts of space. You can insert graphics characters into any string in this way. An alternative method is to type the characters directly into your strings. Do this by holding down the Alt key and then typing the ASCII code on your keypad. When you release the Alt key, the corresponding character is inserted at the cursor.

This program has 90 lines, 81 of them nearly identical. In the next chapter, you will see how to do this same program with only about 20 lines. Because not all printers follow the IBM screen character set, be sure to check your printer's character set when printing graphics and special characters. Some printers also have more than one character set;

if your printer does, refer to the printer manual for information on selecting the one you want.

Reading and Writing Strings

Strings are read from and written to a disk file, the keyboard, and the monitor in much the same manner as numbers are. (The important difference when reading a string is determining where the string begins and ends.) Again as with reading and writing numbers, you must open a disk file before you can use it and close it when you are finished.

Reading Strings

The primary method of reading strings is with the INPUT and INPUT# statements. If an argument of an INPUT statement is a string variable, GW-BASIC skips any leading spaces or tabs and starts reading at the first nonblank character. It continues reading until it encounters a comma, carriage return, line feed, an end-of-file character, or the second of a pair of double quotation marks or when it has read 255 characters. Clear memory with NEW, then type and run the following program:

```
10 OPEN "SCRATCH.TXT" FOR OUTPUT AS #1
20 PRINT #1,"        leading spaces, and a comma"
30 PRINT "        leading spaces, and a comma"
40 CLOSE #1
50 OPEN "SCRATCH.TXT" FOR INPUT AS #1
60 INPUT #1,A$
70 PRINT A$
80 CLOSE #1
90 END
RUN
        leading spaces, and a comma
leading spaces
Ok
```

Lines 10 through 40 create a disk file, write the line "   leading spaces, and a comma" to both the file (line 20) and the screen (line 30), and then close it. Lines 50 through 80 open the file again and try to read that line using an INPUT# statement. Here, when the line of text is read, the leading spaces are skipped by the INPUT# statement in line 60 (which also assigns the line of text to A$), and input terminates at the comma. Thus, the second half of the line is not read.

To include leading and trailing spaces, commas, and line feeds in the string, enclose the string in double quotation marks. If a double quotation mark is the first nonblank character GW-BASIC encounters, reading continues until a second double quotation mark is reached. These marks are not included in the text stored in memory. For example, list the previous example, edit lines 20 and 30 as shown, and then run the program.

```
LIST
10 OPEN "SCRATCH.TXT" FOR OUTPUT AS #1
20 PRINT #1,"     ";CHR$(34);"        double quotes, and a
comma";CHR$(34)
30 PRINT "     ";CHR$(34);"        double quotes, and a
comma";CHR$(34)
40 CLOSE #1
50 OPEN "SCRATCH.TXT" FOR INPUT AS #1
60 INPUT #1,A$
70 PRINT A$
80 CLOSE #1
90 END
Ok
RUN
    "      double quotes, and a comma"
       double quotes, and a comma
Ok
```

Line 20 prints some spaces, a double quotation mark (CHR$(34) must be used to insert double quotation marks into strings), some more spaces, the text double quotes, and a comma, and another double quotation mark. What is actually stored in the file is three spaces, a double quotation mark, six spaces, and the words double quotes, and a comma, followed by a double quotation mark.

When this line is read in line 60, GW-BASIC skips the first spaces and starts reading at the first double quotation mark. It reads the leading spaces and the text (including the comma) and stops at the second double quotation mark.

Reading Lines of Text

The LINE INPUT and LINE INPUT# statements are used specifically for reading strings from the keyboard or a disk file. When executed, they read one complete line of text and store it in a string variable. Reading is terminated by a single carriage return, or after 255 characters have been read, and the carriage return does not become part of the string. If a carriage return is immediately preceded by a line feed character, however, the line feed-carriage return sequence becomes part of the string instead of terminating it. For example, clear memory and type the following short program.

```
10 LINE INPUT A$
20 PRINT A$
```

Run this program and then type anything: text, commas, quotation marks, whatever you wish. Only when you press Enter is input terminated and printed (in line 20).

```
RUN
Hello there, this is a test, " ",,,!!@#$%^ *&^-+=
Hello there, this is a test, " ",,,!!@#$%^ *&^-+=
Ok
```

As another example, clear memory and type the following program and then run it (this program is similar to the two previous examples).

```
10 OPEN "SCRATCH.TXT" FOR OUTPUT AS #1
20 PRINT #1,"Line one";CHR$(10);CHR$(13);"Line two"
30 CLOSE #1
40 OPEN "SCRATCH.TXT" FOR INPUT AS #1
50 LINE INPUT #1,A$
60 PRINT A$
70 CLOSE #1
80 END
RUN
Line one

Line two
Ok
```

In this case, the line feed-carriage return sequence (CHR$(10); CHR$(13)) is read from the file and printed, rather than having the carriage return terminate the input. The input is terminated by the single carriage return at the end of the line. Edit and run the program, changing line 20 as shown, to eliminate the line feed in the center of the line.

```
LIST
10 OPEN "SCRATCH.TXT" FOR OUTPUT AS #1
20 PRINT #1,"Line one";CHR$(13);"Line two"
30 CLOSE #1
40 OPEN "SCRATCH.TXT" FOR INPUT AS #1
50 LINE INPUT #1,A$
60 PRINT A$
70 CLOSE #1
80 END
Ok
RUN
Line one
Ok
```

This time, the single carriage return in the center of the line terminates the input and prevents the second half of the line from being read and printed.

Reading Single Characters

INKEY\$ is different from the other INPUT statements in that it is actually a function instead of a statement. When it is used as A\$ = INKEY\$, the next character in the keyboard buffer is returned and stored in the string variable A\$. In contrast to the INPUT and LINE INPUT statements, which wait for you to enter data, INKEY\$ returns a character only if one is waiting in the buffer. If the buffer is empty, the null string ("") is returned.

The keyboard buffer is an area of memory where all characters entered from the keyboard are stored until they are needed. Whenever you press a key, its character is added to the buffer, and whenever a program needs keyboard input, it removes characters from the buffer. The keyboard buffer is not large—only 15 characters. If the buffer is filled before characters are removed from it, any new characters are lost.

The INKEY\$ function is used to see whether a keystroke has been entered; it can also be implemented (in a loop) to return keyboard input one character at a time.

Reading Everything

The INPUT$() function is used to read a specific number of characters from the keyboard or a disk file. While its use is similar to INKEY$, INPUT$() inputs everything and stores it in a string variable. Nothing terminates the INPUT$ statement until the specified number of characters has been read or Ctrl-Break is pressed. All leading and trailing blanks, tabs, and control characters are read and stored in a string variable. The function is implemented as A$ = INPUT$(5, 1), which would read five characters from disk file number one. To read from the keyboard, omit the comma and file number. The INPUT$() function is often used to read characters from communications channels, where every character can be important and INPUT or LINE INPUT may terminate prematurely.

Writing Strings

As you have already seen, strings can be written on the monitor with the PRINT statement and written to a disk file with PRINT#. You can also use the WRITE and WRITE# statements to accomplish similar tasks. The difference between PRINT and WRITE is the output. PRINT prints the string precisely as it is stored in memory while the WRITE statement separates data items with commas and encloses the string in double quotation marks. (You would rarely use the WRITE statement to write strings on the monitor, because it would be needlessly cluttered with commas and double quotation marks.) The WRITE# statement is used primarily to store data on a disk file that will later be read with an INPUT# statement. By inserting the commas and double quotes, the WRITE# statement makes it possible for the INPUT# statement to separate and read the different data items accurately. In direct mode, type

```
PRINT "some text",5,6,"more text"
some text         5              6                   more text
Ok
WRITE "some text",5,6,"more text"
"some text",5,6,"more text"
Ok
```

*M*anipulating Strings

Strings are manipulated by combining—concatenating—pieces together into larger strings or by copying and replacing substrings (parts of a string).

*C*oncatenating Strings

In the last few examples, we effectively concatenated two strings by printing them side by side to create a longer string on the screen. (The PRINT statement just shown is a good example.) We could just as easily concatenate them into a single string and then print that string. Combining two substrings together into a larger string is as simple as adding two numbers. In fact, the symbol used is the same: the plus sign. Type and run the following example, which combines the string "Bill" and the string "Orvis" into the string "Bill Orvis".

```
10 FIRST.NAME$ = "Bill"
20 LAST.NAME$ = "Orvis"
30 MYNAME$ = FIRST.NAME + SPACE$(1) + LAST.NAME$
40 PRINT MYNAME$

RUN
Bill Orvis
Ok
```

Note that the SPACE$() function inserts a space between the first and last names. I could also have used two double quotation marks separated by a single space or included a space in either of the two strings. Any two or more strings can be combined this way as long as the resulting string doesn't exceed 255 characters.

*G*etting Information about Strings

The next two functions are used to get information about strings. The LEN() function returns the length of a string, and the INSTR() function locates the position of a substring within a string. If INSTR() does not find the substring it returns zero. For example, type the following statements:

```
A$ = "My dog has fleas."
Ok
B$ = "has"
Ok
PRINT LEN(A$),INSTR(A$,B$)
    17          8
Ok
```

LEN() returns the length of the string stored in A$, including the spaces and the period but not the double quotation marks (the quotation marks are not stored as part of the string variable). INSTR() locates the substring has at character position number eight in the string My dog has fleas. The first character position is number one, the second is two, and so on. If an integer argument is inserted in the INSTR() function, the search for the substring starts at that character position and scans to the right. For example, type

```
PRINT LEN(A$),INSTR(9,A$,B$)
    17          0
Ok
```

Here, 9 is the position where the search starts, A$ once again is the string to be searched, and B$ is the substring to be found. This time, the INSTR() function returned a zero because it did not find the substring has to the right of character position nine (the a in has).

Copying and Replacing Substrings

Substrings can be copied or replaced using the LEFT$(), RIGHT$(), or MID$() functions. Both the LEFT$() and RIGHT$() functions take a string and an integer number of characters as arguments. They then extract that many characters from the left or right side of the string. For example, type the following statements:

```
A$ = "My dog has fleas."
Ok
PRINT LEFT$(A$,4)
My d
Ok
PRINT RIGHT$(A$,8)
s fleas.
Ok
```

MID$() can be used in two ways, as a function for extracting or a statement for replacing a substring. The MID$() function takes a string and one or two integers as arguments. The first integer indicates the position of the first character to copy from the string. The second (optional) integer is the number of characters to copy. Thus, in the following example, MID$(A$,4,5), with A$ as the string and 4 and 5 as the integers, MID$ returns a string (from A$) that is five characters long and starts at position four.

```
A$ = "My dog has fleas."
Ok
PRINT MID$(A$,4,5)
dog h
Ok
```

Without the second argument, the entire right half of the string will be copied.

```
PRINT MID$(A$,8)
has fleas.
Ok
```

The MID$ statement is used to replace part of one string with another. It takes a string and one or two integers as arguments and is equated to a second string. Starting at the position in the first string pointed to by the first integer argument, characters from the second string replace those in the first. The single integer in the example MID$(A$,12) = B$ replaces part of the string A$ with all of string B$, starting at the twelfth character:

```
A$ = "My dog has fleas."
Ok
B$ = "ticks."
Ok
MID$(A$,12) = B$
Ok
PRINT A$
My dog has ticks.
Ok
```

The second (optional) integer indicates the number of characters from the second string that are to be inserted into the first string. Thus, in

MID$(A$,4,2) = B$, the statement replaces part of A$ with the first two characters of B$, starting at position four:

```
MID$(A$,4,2) = B$
Ok
PRINT A$
My tig has ticks.
Ok
```

Because the length of the new string cannot exceed that of the original string, you cannot, for example, replace the last three characters in a string with six:

```
MID$(A$,15,6) = B$
Ok
PRINT A$
My tig has tictic
Ok
```

In the last example, note that even though I attempted to insert six characters, only three were actually inserted. Because inserting more than three characters would have exceeded the length of the original string, the additional characters were ignored.

To replace part of a string with a substring that is longer or shorter than the string being replaced, you must extract the left and right sides of the string (excluding the characters to be removed) and then concatenate the left side, the replacement string, and the right side back together. For example, replace the substring "<name>" in the string in TEXT$ with the substring in NAME$.

```
240 LOCATION = INSTR(TEXT$,"<name>")
260 TEXT$ = LEFT$(TEXT$,LOCATION-1)+
NAMES$ +MID$(TEXT$,LOCATION+6)
```

Line 240 locates the position of the first character (<) of the substring "<name>" in the string TEXT$, assigning it to the variable LOCATION. Line 260 extracts the left side of the string up to the character just before < (LOCATION−1) using the LEFT$() function. It extracts the right side of the string in TEXT$ using the MID$() function, starting at the character just after > (LOCATION+6). Finally, line 260 concatenates these two substrings to each side of the string in NAME$. Using this method, you can replace a substring of any length with one of a different length (at least up to the maximum of 255 characters allowed in the final string).

The Mail Merge Program, MMERGE.BAS

The mail merge program, MMERGE.BAS, reads a letter template file like that shown in Figure 5.2, which contains codes (the words surrounded by less than (<) and greater than (>) signs) for replacement of the address and salutation. It also reads a file of names and addresses such as that shown in Figure 5.3. The names and addresses are inserted into the template and the resulting letter is printed. This is a simple mail merge program that does not change the justification of lines after the replacements have been made. Be sure to leave enough room for the longest possible replacement in any line in the template file where a code will be replaced by text.

The file of names and addresses has a specific order: first is the person's name, followed by the street address, city and state, and finally the salutation. After the last salutation, the characters ***done must appear as an end-of-file code. Create these files with a word processor (or EDLIN, the text editor included with the MS-DOS operating system) and save them as text-only files. If they are saved with formatting, the formatting control codes may confuse the program.

Clear memory, type and save the program shown in Listing 5.1.

```
                                        Everyday Insurance
                                        12345 Main Street
                                        Somewhere, USA 12345
        <name>
        <address>
        <citystate>

        Dear <salutation>:

        This letter is to introduce ourselves. We provide a full
        range of business insurance needs, <salutation>, and
        we hope to serve you in the near future.

                                        Sincerely,


                                        Accounts Manager
```

Figure 5.2: A letter template file, LETTER.DOC

```
1 REM MMERGE.BAS
2 REM Mail Merge Program
3 REM This program replaces the following codes in
4 REM a letter file with strings from an address file.
5 REM <name>,<address>,<citystate>,<salutation>
8 GOTO 20
9 REM Autosave Segment
10 SAVE "mmerge.bas",A
11 END
20 REM Beginning of program
30 REM Open the file of addresses
40 OPEN "address.doc" FOR INPUT AS 1
50 REM Open the printer for output. While you are
60 REM developing this program, use SCRN: to print
70 REM on the screen, or a file name to save paper.
80 OPEN "LPT1:" FOR OUTPUT AS 2
90 REM Read the name and see if it is at the end
100 REM then read the address and salutation.
110 LINE INPUT#1,NAMES$
120 IF NAMES$ = "***done" THEN 500
130 LINE INPUT#1,ADDRESS$
140 LINE INPUT#1,CITYSTATE$
150 LINE INPUT#1,SALUTATION$
160 REM open the letter template file.
170 OPEN "letter.doc" FOR INPUT AS 3
180 REM Test for the end of the letter template,
190 REM then read one line from it.
200 IF EOF(3) THEN 430
210 LINE INPUT#3,TEXT$
220 REM Replace the keywords in the letter file
230 REM with the replacements from the address file.
240 LOCATION = INSTR(TEXT$,"<name>")
250 IF LOCATION = 0 THEN 280
260 TEXT$ = LEFT$(TEXT$,LOCATION-1)+NAMES$+MID$(TEXT$,LOCATION+6)
270 GOTO 240
280 LOCATION = INSTR(TEXT$,"<address>")
290 IF LOCATION = 0 THEN 320
300 TEXT$ = LEFT$(TEXT$,LOCATION-1)+ADDRESS$+MID$(TEXT$,LOCATION+9)
310 GOTO 280
320 LOCATION = INSTR(TEXT$,"<citystate>")
330 IF LOCATION = 0 THEN 360
340 TEXT$ = LEFT$(TEXT$,LOCATION-1)+CITYSTATE$+MID$(TEXT$,LOCATION+11)
350 GOTO 320
360 LOCATION = INSTR(TEXT$,"<salutation>")
370 IF LOCATION = 0 THEN 400
380 TEXT$ = LEFT$(TEXT$,LOCATION-1)+SALUTATION$+MID$(TEXT$,LOCATION+12)
390 GOTO 360
400 REM Write the line to the output file.
410 PRINT#2,TEXT$
420 GOTO 200
430 REM Go here when at the end of the letter file.
440 REM Print a form feed.
450 PRINT#2,CHR$(12)
460 CLOSE#3
470 GOTO 110
500 REM Go here when all the addresses are exhausted.
510 CLOSE#1
520 CLOSE#2
530 END
```

Listing 5.1: A mail merge program

When you have created the template and address files shown in Figures 5.2 and 5.3, running the program will create the three letters shown in Figure 5.4.

```
Harry Johnston
12334 Main St.
San Francisco, CA 94123
Mr. Johnston
Ms. Freeda Wilkson
P. O. Box 9999
Alameda, CA  94501
Ms. Wilkson
Wheeling Book Company
1 Wheeling St.
Wherever, IL  60291
Sir
***done
```

Figure 5.3: A name and address file, ADDRESS.DOC

First is the standard prologue in lines 1 through 20. The file of addresses is opened in line 40, and line 80 opens the printer for output like a file. Accessing the printer this way, rather than using LPRINT statements, allows you to direct output easily to the printer, the screen, or a file by changing the file name. If the keywords SCRN:, KYBD:, LPT1:, LPT2:, LPT3:, COM1:, or COM2: are used in an OPEN statement in place of the disk file name, a communications path is opened to the screen, the keyboard, parallel port 1, 2, or 3, or serial port 1 or 2. I did this to save paper while I was developing the program, by using the file name SCRN: to send the printed output to the screen instead of the printer. Once the program was working, I changed the file name to LPT1: to send the final results to the printer.

In line 110, the LINE INPUT# statement reads a line from the address file and assigns the string read to NAMES$. Line 120 uses an IF THEN statement. This statement tests the value of the formula after the word IF. If it is true, the program moves to the line number after the word THEN. Otherwise, it goes on to the next statement. (I will discuss IF THEN statements in more detail later in this book.)

The IF THEN statement in line 120 checks the first line of each address (the <name> field) to see if it is equal to the string ***done. In all cases but the last, the string is different, so the comparison is false and the move is not executed. Since the last line in the file is ***done, the comparison is true when it is read and compared, and the program moves to line 500 and ends. It is important to make sure the program doesn't attempt to read beyond the end of the file. If it does, the program will print an error message and quit.

```
                                    Everyday Insurance
                                    12345 Main Street
                                    Somewhere, USA 12345

        Harry Johnston
        12334 Main St.
        San Francisco, CA 94123

        Dear Mr. Johnston:

        This letter is to introduce ourselves. We provide a full
        range of business insurance needs, Mr. Johnston, and
        we hope to serve you in the near future.

                                    Sincerely,


                                    Accounts Manager
```

```
                                    Everyday Insurance
                                    12345 Main Street
                                    Somewhere, USA 12345

        Ms. Freeda Wilkson
        P. O. Box 9999
        Alameda, CA  94501

        Dear Ms. Wilkson:

        This letter is to introduce ourselves. We provide a full
        range of business insurance needs, Ms. Wilkson, and
        we hope to serve you in the near future.

                                    Sincerely,


                                    Accounts Manager
```

```
                                    Everyday Insurance
                                    12345 Main Street
                                    Somewhere, USA 12345

        Wheeling Book Company
        1 Wheeling St.
        Wherever, IL  60291

        Dear Sir:

        This letter is to introduce ourselves. We provide a full
        range of business insurance needs, Sir, and
        we hope to serve you in the near future.

                                    Sincerely,


                                    Accounts Manager
```

Figure 5.4: Output of the mail merge program, MMERGE.BAS

Lines 130, 140, and 150 read the street address, city, state, and salutation from the address file, assigning the strings to the listed variables. Line 170 opens the letter template file. Line 200 uses a different method—the EOF function—to test for the end of the letter template file, instead of watching for the text ***done as before. In the next character position, just after the last thing written to a disk file, GW-BASIC inserts an invisible end-of-file mark. The function EOF() returns true only if the next character in the disk file is that end-of-file mark.

In line 200, the EOF() function tests the next character in file three, the letter template file. If it is not the end of the file, the IF THEN statement continues with statement number 210, which reads one line from the file. If the next character is the end-of-file mark, the IF THEN statement takes us to line 430. (Again, if the program tries to read an end-of-file mark with an INPUT# statement, it will stop with an error.)

In this program, we are searching for the codes in the letter file and replacing them with the names and addresses read from the address file. Line 210 reads one line of text from the address file, and lines 240 through 270 replace all instances of <name> with NAMES$. Line 240 looks for the code <name>, moving to the next section in line 250 if the code isn't found. Because the replacement string may vary in length from the original, line 260 uses the LEFT$() and MID$() functions rather than the MID$() statement. Line 270 uses the GOTO 240 statement to return the program to line 240 to search for another instance of <name>, and the process repeats until all instances have been found and replaced. (The GOTO statement will be discussed in greater detail later in this book.)

Lines 280 through 390 similarly replace all <address>, <citystate>, and <salutation> codes, and line 410 then prints the line with all its replacements. Line 420 moves back to line 200 and repeats the above steps. When all lines in the letter file have been read and the file is empty, a letter is finished and the program moves to line 430. Line 450 advances the paper in the printer. The program closes the letter file and returns to line 110, where it reads another address from the address file. When the address file is empty, the program moves to line 500, closing the address and printer files in lines 510 and 520 and ending in line 530.

Summary: String Manipulation

This chapter discussed creating and manipulating strings.

- Strings are lists of characters that are enclosed in double quotation marks when they are a part of a program. (Figure 5.1 shows the complete IBM-printable ASCII character set.) Strings are written to or read from the keyboard, monitor, and disk files with the same functions used to read and write numeric variables. They are stored in string variables, in much the same manner as numbers are stored in numeric variables.

- String variables, which follow the same naming conventions as numeric variables, must end in a dollar sign. They hold up to 255 characters. Strings use only three bytes in addition to one byte per character when they are stored in memory, and string arrays hold a complete string in each array location.

- The major difficulty with reading strings is in determining where the string will end. The INPUT and INPUT# statements ignore leading and trailing tabs and blanks and stop reading when they encounter a comma, carriage return, or the second of a pair of double quotation marks. The LINE INPUT and LINE INPUT# statements, on the other hand, input a complete line of text, up to the carriage return, and do not stop at commas. The INKEY$() function is used to input single characters from the keyboard or keyboard buffer, and the INPUT$() function is used to input a specified number of characters, including carriage returns, line feeds, and other control characters, from the keyboard, file, or other source.

- Output is accomplished with PRINT, PRINT#, WRITE, and WRITE#. The difference here is that WRITE separates the data items with commas and encloses strings with double quotation marks, while PRINT does not. Strings and numbers written to disk files with the WRITE# statement are read more accurately with the INPUT# statement than are those written with the PRINT# statement.

- GW-BASIC's string functions include LEN() to provide the length of a string and INSTR() to locate a substring within a string. The functions ASC() and CHR$() convert characters to ASCII codes and ASCII codes to characters. The VAL() function converts a string representation of a number into a numeric value, while the STR$() function converts a numeric value into a string.

- Strings are manipulated by concatenating them with the plus operator, and copying and replacing them with the MID$(), LEFT$(), and RIGHT$() functions. MID$() can be used to copy any substring within a string and to replace a substring with another of equal size. LEFT$() and RIGHT$() are subsets of MID$() that copy substrings from the left or right side of a string. To replace a substring with one of a different size, you must copy the substrings to the left and right of the substring you want to replace and then concatenate them with the replacement string in the middle.

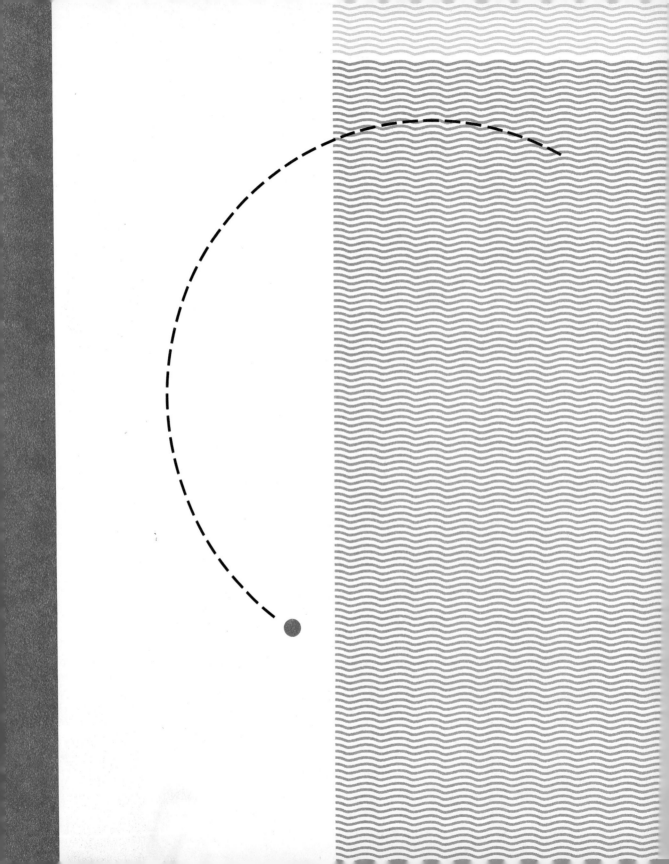

CHAPTER 6

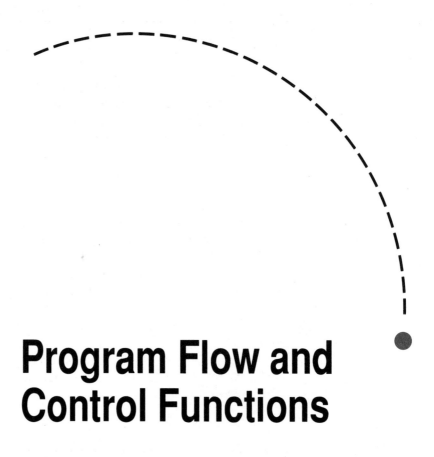

Program Flow and Control Functions

So far in this book, we have looked at relatively linear programs, that is, those that proceed from the beginning to the end as an uninterrupted sequence of statements. Programs in general, however, do not follow such a simple structure.

- Programs have *loops* that execute a single segment of code over and over again to perform a repetitious task.

- Programs have *jumps* that move the point of execution. At a jump in a program, the next statement to be executed is not the statement that follows immediately but a statement elsewhere in the program.

- Programs have *branches*, where the execution can take one of several paths. A branch is the combination of one or more jumps and a value or logicial expression. The value or expression determines which, if any, jump is to be taken. (A *logical expression* is a mathematical formula in which two or more values are compared, or logically combined, with a result of true or false.)

You have already run into jumps and branches in previous chapters of this book, as it is nearly impossible to write a program of any consequence without them. They provide greater flexibility in programming and greater control in program execution. The IF THEN statement, for example, performs a logical test of some sort and then, depending on the result of that test, continues with the next statement or with a statement elsewhere in the program, while the GOTO statement causes an immediate jump to a different location.

This chapter discusses counted loops with FOR/NEXT, logical loops with WHILE/WEND, jumps with GOTO, and branching with ON GOTO and IF THEN statements. It also discusses logical values and expressions.

Using Loops and Counters

When writing computer programs, you will often run into a situation that requires executing a set of statements more than once, with different data at each execution. You could, of course, make several copies of the statements, change the variables in each set, and place the sets one after the other. The program CHARSET.BAS that we used to print the complete ASCII character set used just that technique. Shown again here is part of that program:

```
1 REM CHARSET.BAS
2 REM Prints the IBM character set
8 GOTO 20
9 REM Autosave segment
10 SAVE "charset.bas",A
11 END
20 REM start of program
30 KEY OFF
40 CLS
```

```
50 PRINT 1;CHR$(1);SPACE$(3);2;CHR$(2);SPACE$(3);3;CHR$(3);
SPACE$(3);
60 PRINT 4;CHR$(4);SPACE$(3);5;CHR$(5);SPACE$(3);6;CHR$(6);
SPACE$(3);
70 PRINT
8;CHR$(8);SPACE$(3);14;CHR$(14);SPACE$(2);15;CHR$(15);
SPACE$(2);
        .

        .

        .
850 PRINT 247;CHR$(247);SPACE$(1);248;CHR$(248);SPACE$(1);
249;CHR$(249);SPACE$(1);
860 PRINT
250;CHR$(250);SPACE$(1);251;CHR$(251);SPACE$(1);252;CHR$(252)
;SPACE$(1);
870 PRINT
253;CHR$(253);SPACE$(1);254;CHR$(254);SPACE$(1);255;CHR$(255)
;SPACE$(1);
880 INPUT X$
890 END
```

The program has 94 statements, 83 of them nearly identical, and each of the 83 has three nearly identical parts. For example, in line 50 the arguments of the PRINT statement could be broken into the following three parts:

```
1;CHR$(1);SPACE$(3);
2;CHR$(2);SPACE$(3);
3;CHR$(3);SPACE$(3};
```

As you can see, the three segments are identical except for the codes and symbols being printed. The codes are printed first, sequentially, and then the symbol is printed using the CHR$() function.

All computer languages use loops to allow you to execute the same set of statements repetitively without having to put many copies of them into your code. GW-BASIC uses the FOR/NEXT and WHILE/WEND loops. The difference between these two types of loops is in how they determine when to stop looping. The FOR/NEXT loop executes a set of statements a specified number of times and terminates when a counter (which counts the number of iterations) reaches the predetermined value. The WHILE/WEND loop executes the statements and terminates when the value of the specified conditions becomes false.

Counted Loops with FOR/NEXT Statements

The simplest loops are counted loops that use FOR/NEXT statements. The loop starts with a FOR statement and ends with a NEXT statement. All the statements between the FOR and NEXT statements are repetitively executed until the specified ending value is reached. For example, clear memory and type and run the following program:

```
10 FOR I = 1 TO 10 STEP 2
20 PRINT I
30 NEXT I
40 PRINT "All done"
50 END
RUN
 1
 3
 5
 7
 9
All done
Ok
```

Line 10 is the FOR statement. It contains the loop variable (I), the starting value of the loop variable (1), the ending value (10), and the amount to change the loop variable (the step size) each time the loop is executed (STEP 2). If the step is an increment of one (the default condition), you can omit the STEP 1 at the end of the statement.

When the FOR statement is encountered, the loop variable is set equal to the starting value and compared to the ending value. If it is less than or equal to the ending value, all statements down to the NEXT statement are executed. In the example, the PRINT statement, which prints the value of the loop variable (I) each time the loop is executed, is the only statement in the loop. When the NEXT statement is encountered, execution jumps back to the FOR statement. The STEP value is added to the loop variable and it is again compared to the ending value. The loop continues to be executed until the loop variable exceeds the ending value. Execution of the program then continues with the statement after the NEXT statement; here it is PRINT "All done".

If the starting value exceeds the ending value, none of the statements between the FOR and NEXT statements will be executed unless the step value is negative. In this case, the loop continues until the loop variable is less than the ending value. Thus, FOR/NEXT loops can count down as well as up, as shown in the following example:

```
10 FOR I = 10 TO 1 STEP -2
20 PRINT I
30 NEXT I
40 PRINT "All done"
50 END
RUN
 10
 8
 6
 4
 2
All done
Ok
```

You can use the value of the loop variable for a number of purposes. It is often used as a counter or as an index to indicate the data to which statements are being applied during each loop. Beware of changing the value of the loop variable, however. If you do change it, the loop will continue, but it will use the new, changed value, and your results will probably not be what you intended. There may be occasions where you want to do this—forcing the loop to terminate early or to skip some specified values—but it is usually better to leave the loop variable alone.

Logical Loops with WHILE/WEND Statements

A second type of loop is created with WHILE/WEND statements, which are used like FOR/NEXT statements—without a loop variable. The statements between the WHILE and WEND statements are continually executed until the termination condition becomes false. For example, to constantly check the keyboard for a keystroke, you could write and run the following:

```
10 PRINT "Press any key"
20 KEYVAL$ = ""
30 WHILE KEYVAL$ = ""
40 KEYVAL$ = INKEY$
50 WEND
60 PRINT "Got key ";KEYVAL$
70 END
```

RUN
Press any key
Got key l
Ok

Line 10 prints the request to Press any key. Line 20 initializes the string variable KEYVAL$ to the null string so that the loop is executed at least once. Line 30 is the top of the loop, where KEYVAL$ is tested to see whether it is equal to the null string. If that is true, the loop is executed. Line 40 checks for any key presses and returns the null string if there are none; otherwise, it returns the key that was pressed. Line 50 is the bottom of the loop. Whenever it is reached, execution jumps back to line 30 where the value of KEYVAL$ is tested. This loop continues to execute until you press some key. Pressing the l key causes the test in line 30 to be false. The execution then jumps to line 60, and the result is printed.

*P*rinting the Character Set with CHARSET2.BAS

As you have probably already realized, the 94-line program used to print the character set can be significantly shortened by using loops. While the following program will also produce Figure 5.1, it is only 25 lines long. Clear memory, type the program, save it, run it, and compare the result with Figure 5.1.

```
1 REM CHARSET2.BAS
2 REM Prints the IBM character set
8 GOTO 20
9 REM Autosave segment
10 SAVE "charset2.bas",A
11 END
20 REM start of program
30 KEY OFF
40 CLS
50 FOR I = 1 TO 6
60 PRINT I; CHR$(I);SPACE$(3);
70 NEXT I
80 PRINT 8;CHR$(8);SPACE$(3);
90 FOR I = 14 TO 27
100 PRINT I;CHR$(I);SPACE$(2);
```

```
110 NEXT I
120 FOR I = 32 TO 99
130 PRINT I;CHR$(I);SPACE$(2);
140 NEXT I
150 FOR I = 100 TO 255
160 PRINT I;CHR$(I);SPACE$(1);
170 NEXT I
180 PRINT
190 INPUT X$
200 END
RUN 10
Ok
```

The first few lines are the standard prologue. Line 30 turns off the function key labels that GW-BASIC normally prints across the bottom of the screen, and line 40 clears the screen. Lines 50, 60, and 70 form the first loop, and print the characters 1 through 6. In line 60, the code is printed, followed by the character for that code and three spaces generated with the SPACE$() function. Line 80 prints code 8 and its character. Lines 90 through 170 make up two loops that print the characters from 32 through 255. I broke this into two loops so that the number of spaces for codes greater than 99 could be decreased, making them line up with the codes already printed. Line 190 prevents the information from scrolling off the top of the screen until you press Enter.

Jumping with GOTO Statements

Perform a jump with the GOTO statement when your program is executing one piece of code and you want it to move to a different place and begin executing there. When a GOTO statement is encountered, execution of the program immediately switches to the line number that follows the word GOTO. For example clear memory and type and run the following:

```
10 PRINT "Line 10"
20 GOTO 40
30 PRINT "Line 30"
40 PRINT "Line 40"
50 END
RUN
```

```
Line 10
Line 40
Ok
```

Line 10 prints the words Line 10. The GOTO statement in line 20 causes execution of the program to skip line 30 and continue at line 40, which prints Line 40.

While you can jump to any location in your code, it is usually not a good idea to jump too far. If you do, you may lose track of how the code's execution reached a particular statement. A good rule of thumb is to stay within one or two screen pages of code. If you must jump a long distance, and it is not obvious where you jumped from, insert remark statements at the new location to indicate where you jumped from.

*B*ranching with ON GOTO Statements

The ON GOTO statement is called a computed GOTO; that is, it lets you select one of several branches according to an index value. ON and GOTO are separated by an index (if the index is not an integer, it will be rounded). GOTO is followed by a list of line numbers (as many as 255 can be used). If the index is one, execution moves to the first line number; if the index is two, it branches to the second, and so forth. If the index is zero or greater than the number of line numbers in the list, execution continues with the statement after ON GOTO. Negative values of the index cause an error. Use the following program to experiment with the ON GOTO statement. Clear memory and type and run it.

```
10 PRINT "Input a number";
20 INPUT NUM
30 ON NUM GOTO 60,80,100,120
40 PRINT "At line 40"
50 END
60 PRINT "At line 60"
70 GOTO 10
80 PRINT "At line 80"
90 GOTO 10
100 PRINT "At line 100"
110 GOTO 10
120 PRINT "At line 120"
130 GOTO 10
```

```
RUN
Input a number?2
At line 80
Input a number?1
At line 60
Input a number?5
At line 40
Ok
```

Line 10 prints the string Input a number, and line 20 waits for you to type one in. The first time, I typed 2, and the ON GOTO statement in line 30 branched to the second line number, 80. Line 80 prints At line 80. In line 90, the GOTO statement causes the code to jump back to line 10, where it again asks for a number. This time, I typed 1, which caused a branch to line 60. Line 60 prints At line 60 and line 70 branches back to line 10. The third time, I typed 5. Since there are only four line numbers in the ON GOTO statement, the 5 causes a drop through to line 40, printing At line 40. Line 50 then ends the program. Here, use of a zero or any number greater than four causes a drop through to line 40. A number less than zero or greater than 255 causes an error.

Using Logical Expressions

A logical expression is a formula that evaluates to true or false. In statements that require a logical expression as one of the arguments, a function that evaluates to zero is equivalent to false and nonzero to true. In addition, if you use a logical expression that requires a numeric value, false evaluates to 0 and true evaluates to −1.

Understanding Relational Operators

The relational operators (listed in Table 6.1) are used to determine the relationship between two values or strings. Placing a relational operator between two formulas compares the values of those formulas, with the comparison returning either true or false. For example,

Formula	Returns
5 = 5	true
4 = 7	false
5 + 3 = 8	true
2 + 1 > 3 + 6	false
1 <> 2	true
"AB" = "ab"	false
"A"+"B" =""AB"	true

Understanding Logical Operators

The relational operators compare two values or strings and return a logical value; the logical operators combine logical values to produce more complex logical expressions. The following list shows these operators, in order of precedence:

NOT   Reverses the truth value of a logical expression, so that a false expression becomes true and a true one becomes false.

Table 6.1: Relational Operators

OPERATOR	RELATIONSHIP
=	Equals
<>	Not equal to
<	Less than
>	Greater than
<=	Less than or equal to
>=	Greater than or equal to

AND   Connects two logical expressions; the resulting compound expression is true only when both expressions are true.

OR   Connects two logical expressions, creating a compound expression that is true if either or both of the individual expressions are true.

XOR   Connects two logical expressions, creating a compound that is true only when one (not both) of the original expressions is true.

EQV   Connects two logical expressions; the resulting compound is true when both conditions have the same truth value.

IMP   Connects two logical expressions; the resulting compound expression is always true except when the first condition is true and the second false.

Table 6.2 is a truth table showing the logical operators and the result of their operations.

Because of the order in which logical operators are executed, you must use parentheses in complex logical operations to ensure that the correct comparisons are made. For example,

Formula	Result
False AND true OR true	true
(False AND true) OR true	true
False AND (true OR true)	false

In the first and second cases, because logical operators are executed left to right, the expression false AND true evaluates to false, and false OR true is true. In the third case, true OR true is calculated first, which gives true; false AND true then returns false.

If you want to use the words TRUE and FALSE for logical values in a program, define them at the beginning with the following statements:

```
TRUE = -1
FALSE = 0
```

Table 6.2: Logical Operators Truth Table

A	B	NOT A	A AND B	A OR B	A XOR B	A EQV B	A IMP B
T	T	F	T	T	F	T	T
T	F	F	F	T	T	F	F
F	T	T	F	T	T	F	T
F	F	T	F	F	F	T	T

Branching with IF THEN Statements

The IF THEN statement combines a logical expression and a branch to provide logical control of program execution. (We have already used IF THEN statements in several of the programs developed so far in this book.) Placing a logical expression after IF and a line number after THEN causes a branch to that line number if the expression is true. If it is false, execution continues with the next line after the statement. For example,

```
        .
        .
        .
10 IF A = B THEN 90
20 PRINT "A is not equal to B"
        .
        .
        .
90 PRINT "A equals B"
        .
        .
        .
```

If the expression A = B is true, execution branches to line 90; otherwise, it continues with line 20. Actually, you are not limited to branching with the IF THEN statement. Any valid statement placed after THEN is executed if the logical expression is true. In fact, you can place several statements separated by colons after THEN; they will be executed only if the logical expression is true. For example,

In this case, if A and B are equal, A is set to 5 and B is set to 6. If A and B are not equal, their values are not changed.

*T*he Computer-Usage Report Generator

The computer-usage report generator reads the file created by the computer-usage journaling programs developed earlier. It then categorizes all the entries, calculates total time used for each entry, and prints a report of the different types of computer usage. In addition, it checks for problem entries, such as forgetting to run LO.BAS to insert the closing entry or perhaps running it twice. Logical expressions and IF THEN statements are used to do this testing.

The computer-usage report generator is a bit longer than most of the programs you have seen so far in this book, but most of that length is remark statements. While it may look more complicated at first, if you examine it section by section you will see that it is not. The rows of asterisks between sections make the sections easier to locate. Clear memory and type the program shown in Listing 6.1.

```
1 REM REPORT.BAS
2 REM Computer-Usage Report Generator.
3 REM This program reads the computer-usage files,
4 REM sorts them by type and totals the usage for each
5 REM type.
8 GOTO 20
9 REM Autosave Segment
10 SAVE "report.bas",A
11 END
15 REM ******************************
20 REM Beginning of program.
30 OPEN "c:\usage.txt" FOR INPUT AS 1
40 OPEN "scrn:" FOR OUTPUT AS 2
50 DIM USES$(100),USED.TIME(100)
60 BAD.LINES = 0
70 NUM.TYPES = 0
80 TOTAL.USE = 0
```

Listing 6.1: Computer-usage report generator

```
 90 REM ******************************
100 IF EOF(1) THEN 590
110 LINE INPUT#1,LINE1$
120 IF EOF(1) THEN 590
130 LINE INPUT#1,LINE2$
140 REM ******************************
150 REM Extract the ending category and be sure it is STOP.
160 USE$ = MID$(LINE2$,21)
170 IF USE$ = "stop" THEN 240
180 REM If it is not stop then we forgot to run LO.BAS
190 LINE1$ = LINE2$
200 BAD.LINE = BAD.LINE + 1
210 GOTO 120
220 REM ******************************
230 REM Extract the two dates, two times, and the category.
240 DATE1 = VAL(MID$(LINE1$,4,2))
250 TIME1 = VAL(MID$(LINE1$,12,2))+VAL(MID$(LINE1$,15,2))/60
260 USE$ = MID$(LINE1$,21)
270 DATE2 = VAL(MID$(LINE2$,4,2))
280 TIME2 = VAL(MID$(LINE2$,12,2))+VAL(MID$(LINE2$,15,2))/60
290 REM ******************************
300 REM Same day.
310 IF DATE1 <> DATE2 THEN 350
320 TIME.USED = TIME2-TIME1
330 GOTO 440
340 REM ******************************
350 REM Next day or first of month.
360 IF ((DATE1 + 1) <> DATE2) AND (DATE2 <> 1) THEN 400
370 TIME.USED = TIME2 + 24 - TIME1
380 GOTO 440
390 REM ******************************
400 REM Non-fitting values go here.
410 BAD.LINE = BAD.LINE + 2
420 GOTO 100
430 REM ******************************
440 REM See if this category already exists.
450 FOR I = 1 TO NUM.TYPES
460 IF USE$ = USES$(I) THEN 550
470 NEXT I
480 REM ******************************
490 REM Add a new category to the list.
500 NUM.TYPES = NUM.TYPES + 1
510 USES$(NUM.TYPES) = USE$
520 USED.TIME(I) = 0
530 REM ******************************
540 REM Add the time used to this category.
550 USED.TIME(I) = USED.TIME(I) + TIME.USED
560 TOTAL.USE = TOTAL.USE + TIME.USED
570 GOTO 100
580 REM ******************************
590 REM print the report.
600 CLS
610 PRINT#2,CHR$(10),CHR$(10)
620 PRINT#2,"Computer-usage report"
630 PRINT#2,
640 PRINT#2,"Usage","Hours","Percent"
650 FOR I = 1 TO NUM.TYPES
660 PRINT#2,USES$(I),USED.TIME(I),100*USED.TIME(I)/TOTAL.USE
670 NEXT I
680 PRINT#2,"----------","----------","----------"
690 PRINT#2,"Total Used: ",TOTAL.USE,100
700 PRINT#2,
710 PRINT#2,"Total lines skipped:";BAD.LINE
720 CLOSE #1
730 CLOSE #2
740 END
```

Listing 6.1: Computer-usage report generator (Continued)

Running the program using one of my computer-usage journaling files produced the following result:

Computer-usage report

Usage	Hours	Percent
disk sale	77.81668	15.37677
book	359.216	70.9821
personal	18.88334	3.731394
business	36.68334	7.248718
maintenance	7.150002	1.412858
game	2.766667	.5467003
bok	3.549999	.7014886
-------------------	---------------	--------------
Total Used:	506.0666	100

Total lines skipped: 7
Ok

As you can see, I misspelled the category book one day when I typed it, and the program made bok a separate entry. I can correct that either here, by adding the figures to the correct category with a calculator and a pencil, or in the file usage.txt with a text editor and then rerun REPORT.BAS. Note also the message that seven lines were skipped. This is caused by the data's being inconsistent. The most obvious problem is forgetting to run LO.BAS just before shutting down, so that the ending entry is missing. This report generator looks at lines in pairs and skips a line when the second line does not contain the word stop in the category field. (This allows the program to filter out obvious mistakes.)

If you have been using the computer-usage journaling programs for your own work, you already have a data file that can be used to try out this program. If not, run the journaling programs a few times to create one. While your results will have the same format, the categories and numbers will be different, reflecting your needs.

Lines 1 through 20 are the standard prologue. Lines 30 through 80 open the data file usage.txt for input and the screen for output. They then assign zero to the three numeric variables BAD.LINES, NUM.TYPES, and TOTAL.USE.

Line	Result
1–20	Saves the program with the correct name when you type **RUN 10**.
30	Opens the file usage.txt for reading as file number 1.
40	Opens the screen for output by using SCRN: instead of a file name. You can easily switch the output to a file by replacing SCRN: with a file name.
50	Dimensions the two arrays USES() and USED.TIME() to 101 elements each (the numbering of elements starts with zero).
60	Sets the variable BAD.LINES to zero.
70	Sets the variable NUM.TYPES to zero.
80	Sets the variable TOTAL.USE to zero.

Lines 100 through 130 read two lines from the data file, testing for the end-of-file marker each time before attempting to read a line. If the end-of-file marker is reached, the IF THEN statements branch to the subroutine that begins in line 590, which prints the report. The variable LINE1$ should contain the starting date, time, and category. LINE2$ should contain the ending date and time and the word stop for the category.

Line	Result
100	Sees whether the next record in usage.txt is the end-of-file marker. If it is, branches to line 590 to print the report; otherwise, advances to line 110.
110	Reads a complete line of text from usage.txt and stores it in LINE1$.
120	Tests again for the end-of-file marker in usage.txt.
130	Reads a complete line of text from usage.txt and stores it in LINE2$. This line should be a stop record.

Lines 160 through 210 extract the category from LINE2$ and store it in the variable USE$. The category should be stop. If it isn't, the data in LINE2$ is moved into LINE1$, one is added to the variable BAD.LINE, and execution goes back to line 120 to read a new string for LINE2$. If USE$ is stop, execution advances to line 170 and jumps to line 240.

160   Assigns USE$ the contents of the category field in LINE2$. The category field starts at character number 21 and continues to the end of the string.

170   Tests the category to see if it is the word stop. If it is, execution branches to line 240; otherwise the program continues with line 190.

190   This line is reached if there is a problem. Assigns LINE1$ the value of LINE2$.

200   Increments the variable BAD.LINE by one.

210   Jumps back to line 120 to read another line for LINE2$.

Lines 240 through 290 extract the starting and ending dates and times and the usage category. The dates and times are extracted from the string variables LINE1$ and LINE2$ using the MID$() function. The string values extracted by MID$() are then converted to real numbers with the VAL() function. For the date, I extract only the day and ignore the rest. This is a valid omission because there are only three reasonable possibilities for the starting and ending dates:

1. They are the same.

2. If you work past midnight, the ending date will be one more than the starting date.

3. If you start on the last day of the month and work past midnight, the ending day will be the first of the next month.

Line   Result

240   Assigns DATE1 the day of the month extracted from LINE1$ with the MID$() function and converted to a number with the VAL() function. The day starts in character position four of LINE1$ and is two characters wide.

Line	Result
250	Assigns TIME1 the time (in hours) extracted from LINE1$ with the MID$() function and converted to a number with the VAL() function. The hours field starts at character number 12 in LINE1$ and is two characters wide. The minutes field starts at character number 15 in LINE1$ and is two characters wide. Divides the number of minutes by 60 before adding it to the number of hours.
260	Assigns USE$ the contents of the category field in LINE1$.
270	Assigns DATE2 the day of the month extracted from LINE2$.
280	Assigns TIME2 the time (in hours) extracted from LINE2$.

DATE1 now contains the number of the starting day, DATE2 contains the number of the ending day, and USE$ contains the category for these entries. The next three sections test for the possible date combinations described above. Lines 310 and 320 test to see whether the starting and ending day are the same. If they are, then the number of hours used is simply the difference between the ending time and the starting time.

Lines 360 and 370 test to see whether the ending day is the next day. They do this by seeing if the ending day is one more than the starting day or if it is equal to one (the beginning of the next month). Because DOS uses a 24-hour clock, if the ending day is the next day the number of hours used is the difference between the ending time and the starting time plus 24 hours.

If the two dates do not fit the possible situations, something is wrong with them. Lines 410 and 420 discard the dates, add two to BAD.LINE, and then jump back to line 100 to read two new lines. If the starting and ending days do fit one of the rules, then the program branches to line 440.

Line	Result
310	Compares the two days to see whether they are not equal. If they are unequal, execution branches to line 350; otherwise the program continues with 320.

Line	Result
320	Assigns TIME.USED to the difference between TIME2 and TIME1.
330	Jumps to 440.
360	Tests to see if DATE2 is one more than DATE1 or if it is equal to one. If neither is true, execution branches to line 400; otherwise it continues with line 370.
370	Assigns TIME.USED to the difference between TIME2 and TIME1 plus 24 (because the ending day is the day after the starting day).
380	Jumps to 440.
410	Increments BAD.LINE by two because the data is bad.
420	Jumps back to line 100 to get two new lines of data.

Lines 450 through 470 search the array USES$() (which contains all of the categories found so far) for a category that matches the one in USE$. If a matching category is found, then line 460 branches to line 550. If a match is not found, the loop completes normally, and the program continues with line 490.

Line	Result
450	Starts a FOR/NEXT loop that loops for the number of categories found so far (NUM.TYPES).
460	Compares USE$ with the contents of each element of USES$(). If a match is found, execution branches out of the loop to line 550.
470	The bottom of the loop.

Lines 500 through 520 add a new category. First, the number of categories, stored in NUM.TYPES, is incremented by one; then the current category stored in USE$ is added to the array USES$(). Each category has a corresponding element in the array USED.TIME(). When a new category is added, the corresponding element in USED.TIME() is zeroed. Note that when the loop in lines 450 through 470 ends, the value of I is equal to one + NUM.TYPES if the loop completes normally or to the array location of the matching category if the loop terminates with the IF THEN statement in line 460. This information is used in line 520.

Line	Result
500	Increments the value of NUM.TYPES by one.
510	Assigns the new category to a location in the array USES$(). The location is determined by the value of NUM.TYPES.
520	Assigns the element of USED.TIME() associated with the new category to zero.

Lines 550 through 570 add the current time used to the array variable USED.TIME() for either the new category or the matching category and also to the total time used in TOTAL.USE. The program then branches back to line 100 to get two new lines.

Line	Result
550	Increases the value of USED.TIME() associated with the current category by TIME.USED.
560	Increases TOTAL.USE by TIME.USED.
570	Jumps back to line 100 to input two new lines.

When the last line has been read from the data file, the program branches to line 590 to print the report. Lines 600 through 640 clear the screen and print some blank lines and the headings. Lines 650 through 670 print each category, the time used, and the percentage of the total time used. Lines 690 through 710 print the totals and the number of lines skipped, and lines 720 through 740 close the files and end the program.

Line	Result
600	Clears the screen.
610	Prints two line feeds and a carriage return.
620	Prints Computer-usage report.
630	Prints a blank line.
640	Prints the headings Usage, Hours, and Percent.

Line	Result
650	Starts a FOR/NEXT loop that loops over each of the categories found.
660	For category number I, prints the category name (USES$(I)), the number of hours used (USED.TIME(I)), and the percentage of the total usage (100*USED.TIME(I)/TOTAL.USE).
670	Bottom of the loop.
680	Prints three lines.
690	Prints Total Used:, then prints the value of the total usage TOTAL.USE and the number 100 (percent).
700	Prints a blank line.
710	Prints Total lines skipped: and the value of BAD.LINE.
720	Closes file number 1.
730	Closes file number 2.
740	Ends the program.

Summary: Program Flow and Control Functions

This chapter has discussed counted loops with the FOR/NEXT statements, logical loops with WHILE/WEND statements, jumps with the GOTO statement, and branches with the ON GOTO and IF THEN statements—in addition to logical values and expressions.

- FOR/NEXT loops (counted loops) set up the counter and number of iterations with the FOR statement and end the loop with the NEXT statement.

- WHILE/WEND loops start with a WHILE statement and a logical expression and end with a WEND statement. The loop is repeated until the logical expression is false.

- Jumps in GW-BASIC are performed with the GOTO statement, which causes execution of a program to jump immediately to the line number used as an argument. While branches are similar to jumps, there is more than one location to jump to at a branch. The ON GOTO statement uses an index number to select a statement to branch to; the index selects the chosen line from a list of line numbers included as arguments.

- Logical branches are performed with the IF THEN statement. A logical expression is calculated, and the branch is taken if the expression is true. If it is false, execution continues with the statement following the IF THEN statement. A statement rather than a line number can also follow the word THEN. In that case, the statement is executed if the logical expression is true and ignored if it is false.

- Logical values are true and false, with a numeric value of −1 (true) or 0 (false). Logical expressions are made up of combinations of numeric or string expressions, relational operators, and logical operators. To ensure execution in the proper order, be sure to use parentheses in any logical expression.

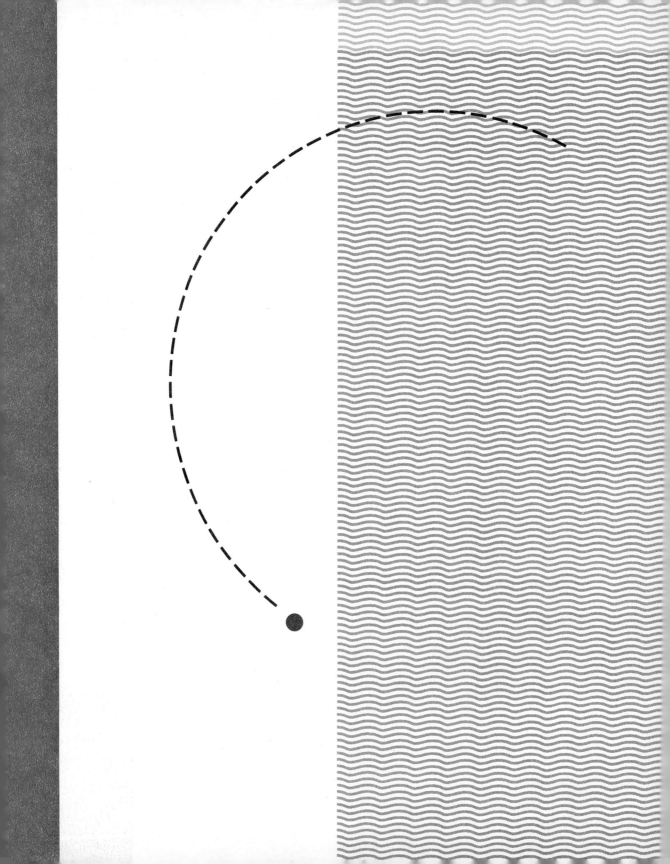

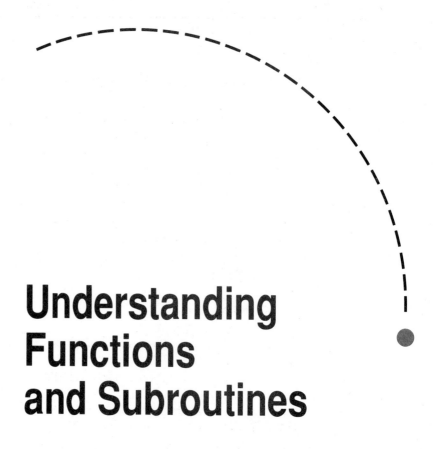

CHAPTER 7

Understanding Functions and Subroutines

In the last chapter, we broke the programming example into several distinct blocks of code, with each block performing a specific, well-defined task. In this way, execution of the program passes from one block to the next as each block's task is completed. Breaking a program into blocks this way makes it much simpler to understand, to validate (that is, determine that it does what it is supposed to do), and to debug.

Functions and subroutines are structures within a program that also help break a program into functional blocks. A second asset is that they make those blocks of code reusable. Often when writing a program, you will need the same or a similar block (or line) of code in several places. Rather than use multiple copies of the code, you can turn it into a function or subroutine that can then be used wherever and whenever it is needed.

Functions and subroutines formally define blocks of code that perform specific tasks. Once defined, they can be called from anywhere in a program. A function consists of a single line of code and is called by its name, while a subroutine contains as many lines (statements) as necessary to perform its task and is called by its first line number.

This chapter discusses creating and using user-defined functions. It also discusses creating and using subroutines to both block-structure a program and to collect common functions into central locations. Our examples calculate and print a straight-line depreciation table and an amortization table.

Creating User-Defined Functions

A function consists of a name and a single line of code and returns a single value. User-defined functions are used much like the built-in mathematical functions. The difference is that you must create, or *define*, them before you can use them.

User-defined functions are created with the DEF FN statement. The function name, which must be a legal BASIC name, is placed after the letters FN. This combination (of FN and the name) then becomes a BASIC keyword. The name is followed by one or more arguments, enclosed in parentheses and separated by commas, an equal sign, and an expression that defines the value of the function. The following example is a user-defined function to calculate yearly depreciation using the straight-line method:

```
30 DEF FNSL(COST,SALVAGE,LIFE) = (COST-SALVAGE)/LIFE
```

Here, FNSL is the name of the function. COST is the initial cost of the asset, SALVAGE is its salvage value, and LIFE is its lifetime. Whenever the function FNSL is later used, or *called*, the numbers used as arguments are inserted into the formula and the result calculated. Let's say, for example, that you want to calculate a table of straight-line depreciations for varying lifetimes and a fixed cost and salvage value. Clear memory and type and save the program in Listing 7.1.

```
1 REM sltable.bas
2 REM Straight-Line Depreciation Table
8 GOTO 20
9 REM autosave segment
10 SAVE "sltable.bas",A
11 END
20 REM start of the program
30 DEF FNSL(COST,SALVAGE,LIFE) = (COST-SALVAGE)/LIFE
40 INITIAL = 24000
50 FINAL = 1800
60 CLS
70 PRINT "Straight-Line Depreciation Table"
80 PRINT
90 PRINT USING "Initial value = $######,";INITIAL
100 PRINT USING "Final value = $######,";FINAL
110 PRINT
112 PRINT "Lifetime    Depreciation per year"
120 FOR YEARS = 5 TO 50 STEP 5
130 PRINT USING "###      $$######,";YEARS,FNSL(INITIAL,FINAL,YEARS)
140 NEXT YEARS
150 END
```

Listing 7.1: Straight-line depreciation program

When the program runs, it produces the following output.

```
Straight-Line Depreciation Table

Initial value = $ 24,000
Final value = $  1,800

Lifetime        Depreciation per year
  5            $4,440
 10            $2,220
 15            $1,480
 20            $1,110
 25             $888
 30             $740
 35             $634
 40             $555
 45             $493
 50             $444
Ok
```

The first few lines are the standard prologue. Line 30 defines the function FNSL (it must be defined before it can be used in the program). Lines 40 and 50 define the cost (INITIAL) and salvage value (FINAL) of the asset. Lines 60 through 112 print some headings and the initial and final values of the asset used in creating the table. Lines 120 and 140 form a FOR/NEXT loop, incrementing the loop variable YEARS in 5-year steps from 5 to 50. Line 130 first prints the current value of YEARS, then calls the function FNSL using the fixed values of INITIAL and FINAL and the current value of YEARS as arguments. FNSL uses these arguments and the definition in line 30 to calculate the straight-line depreciation and returns that value to line 130 where it is printed. The entire program is summarized below.

Line	Result
1-11	Saves the program with the correct name when you type RUN 10.
30	Defines the function FNSL(), which has local variables COST, SALVAGE, and LIFE.
40	Assigns $24,000 to the variable INITIAL.
50	Assigns $1,800 to the variable FINAL.
60	Clears the screen.
70	Prints Straight-Line Depreciation Table.
80	Prints a blank line.
90	Prints Initial value = $ and adds the value of the variable INITIAL.
100	Prints Final value = $ and the value of the variable FINAL.
110	Prints a blank line.
112	Prints the table headings Lifetime and Depreciation per year.
120	Starts a FOR/NEXT loop that loops the variable YEARS over the numbers 5 to 50 in steps of 5.
130	Prints the formatted values of the variable YEARS and the number returned by the user-defined function FNSL(). FNSL() is called with the variables INITIAL, FINAL, and YEARS as arguments.
140	Bottom of the loop.
150	Ends the program.

Note that when FNSL is called in line 130, the names of the arguments do not have to be the same as those in the definition in line 30. When the function is called in line 130, the value of INITIAL is substituted for the first argument (COST) in line 30. FINAL is substituted for the second argument (SALVAGE), and YEARS is inserted for the third (LIFE). In fact, the variable names COST, SALVAGE, and LIFE used in the definition can also be used elsewhere in the program for other purposes, and changing the names of the variables within the definition will not affect the variables with the same names outside the definition.

Defining Local and Global Variables

If you have programmed before in a language other than BASIC, you've already run into local and global variables, where the variables used in subroutines are usually local and have no effect on variables with the same name outside the subroutine. In GW-BASIC, however, nearly all the variables, including those within subroutines, are global. The only local variables are the arguments of one-line user-defined functions. Local variables are defined *locally*, within a function definition and have no effect on identically named variables outside the definition. You can think of them as placeholders for the values that will actually be used when the function is called.

If a variable used in a function definition is not one of the arguments of the function, its current value outside the definition is used. Variables of this type are known as *global variables*, and their values are accessible anywhere in a program. That is, their value can be used or changed in any block, subroutine, or function.

Using Subroutines

Subroutines are blocks of code that perform specific tasks and then return to the statement that called them. They are usually separated from the main program, but are usable wherever they are needed. The program branches to a block of code using GOSUB or ON GOSUB, executes the statements within the subroutine, and jumps back (returns) to the next statement after the one that called the subroutine.

*C*alling Simple Subroutines With GOSUB

The GOSUB statement works much like GOTO, with a major difference in that GOSUB remembers where it was called. When a subroutine completes its assigned task and a RETURN statement is encountered, program execution jumps back to the statement after the GOSUB statement. Consider the Straight-Line Depreciation Table program created at the beginning of this chapter. While a program this short would not normally be broken into so many different subroutines, we can, as an example, break it into blocks and make each block a subroutine. (You can type the program in Listing 7.2 if you wish; its results, however, are identical to those for SLTABLE.BAS.)

```
1 REM sltable1.bas
2 REM Straight-Line Depreciation Table
8 GOTO 20
9 REM Autosave segment
10 SAVE "sltable1.bas",A
11 END
20 REM start of the program
30 REM Set initial values
40 GOSUB 400
50 REM Print the headings
60 GOSUB 500
70 REM Print the table
80 GOSUB 600
90 END
100 REM ****************************************
400 REM Initialization subroutine
410 DEF FNSL(COST,SALVAGE,LIFE) = (COST-SALVAGE)/LIFE
420 INITIAL = 24000
430 FINAL = 1800
440 RETURN
450 REM ****************************************
500 REM Heading subroutine
510 CLS
520 PRINT "Straight-Line Depreciation Table"
530 PRINT
540 PRINT USING "Initial value = $######,";INITIAL
550 PRINT USING "Final value = $######,";FINAL
560 PRINT
570 PRINT "Lifetime   Depreciation per year"
580 RETURN
590 REM ****************************************
600 REM Table printing subroutine
610 FOR YEARS = 5 TO 50 STEP 5
620 REM Print the depreciation
630 GOSUB 700
640 NEXT YEARS
650 RETURN
660 REM ****************************************
700 REM Depreciation subroutine
710 PRINT USING "###      $$######,";YEARS,FNSL(INITIAL,FINAL,YEARS)
720 RETURN
730 REM ****************************************
```

Listing 7.2: Straight-line depreciation program with subroutines added

Lines 1 through 100 are the main program (including our usual prologue). Each major block of code is identified, and a subroutine is called
to perform its task. Note that this is much more readable compared with
the earlier version of this program. As you read the main program, you
can clearly see each step that is taken when the program runs.

In line 40, the subroutine starting in line 400 is called and execution
immediately jumps to line 400. Lines 400 through 430 define the FNSL
function and initialize the variables INITIAL and FINAL. When the
RETURN statement in line 440 is encountered, the program jumps back
to line 50, the next statement after GOSUB. In line 60, execution jumps to
the subroutine starting in line 500. Lines 500 through 570 print the headings, and then the RETURN in line 580 causes the program to jump back
to line 70.

In line 80, the program now moves to the subroutine starting in line
600. Lines 610 and 640 form a FOR/NEXT loop with the loop variable
YEARS. Here, in line 630, we have a subroutine call within another subroutine. This is known as the *nesting* of subroutines. The number of
nested subroutines is limited only by the amount of memory available to
store all the lines to return to, since each GOSUB is paired with a RETURN
statement. Thus, when you have multiple nested subroutines, the first
RETURN statement executed causes a return to the last GOSUB statement
executed. The next RETURN returns to the next-to-last GOSUB and so forth
until execution has moved back to the main program.

Line 630 calls the subroutine starting in line 700. Line 710 prints the
current value of YEARS and then calculates and prints the depreciation
using the user-defined function FNSL. The RETURN in line 720 causes a
jump back to line 640, the bottom of the loop. Each time the loop is
executed, the subroutine in line 700 is executed again. When the loop
is completed, the RETURN in line 650 causes a jump back to line 90 and
the program ends. The END statement is essential here. If you omit
it, the program will continue running and trying to run the subroutines
as though they were part of the main program.

Since subroutines are separate blocks of code, they are often placed at
the end of a program (in the higher line numbers). It is also common
practice to start different subroutines on even hundreds, and to group
them according to function. While none of these are required, such prac-
tices do make things more readable, especially in larger programs.

As shown in the example, it is a good practice to place a remark just before each GOSUB statement, indicating the name or task of the subroutine to which you are jumping. Without the remark, it can be very hard to tell what a program is doing without looking up every subroutine as it is called.

Selecting a Subroutine with ON GOSUB

Like the ON GOTO statement, the ON GOSUB statement allows you to use an index number to select one of several listed subroutines. The statement consists of ON, the index number (rounded if it is not an integer), GOSUB, and a list of line numbers. A subroutine is selected from the list according to the value of the index. If the index is equal to one, the first subroutine is selected, if it's equal to two, the second is selected, and so forth. If the index is zero or greater than the number of subroutines in the list, the ON GOSUB statement will continue with the next line in the program. If the index value is negative or greater than 255, an error results, as shown in the following example:

```
10 A = 2
20 ON A GOSUB 100,200,300
30 PRINT B
40 END
100 B = 5
110 RETURN
200 B = 6
210 RETURN
300 B = 7
310 RETURN
```

Running this program produces the following:

```
 6
Ok
```

Line 10 sets A equal to two. Using A as the index value, line 20 selects the second subroutine in the list, the one starting in line 200. In line 200, B is set to six. The RETURN in line 210 causes a jump back to line 30, the first line after GOSUB. Line 30 prints the value of B, and line 40 ends the program.

*U*sing Special Variable Names with Subroutines

Variable names must be used with care when accessing subroutines. Since in BASIC there are no local variables other than those in functions, you must be careful that you do not reuse a variable name that is already in use elsewhere and that you did not intend to change.

This is not usually a problem in small programs. In larger programs, however, you will need to develop some conventions concerning the names of variables used only in a subroutine—and what happens to them if another subroutine is called. Note that this applies only to variables used exclusively within a subroutine and not to variables whose values you want to pass from one routine to another. So that they won't accidentally be reused, variables that pass values between routines should have more formal names (PRESENT.VALUE, for example). Some programmers define a set of variable names that will be used only in first-level subroutines and a different set that can be used in second-level subroutines. Second-level subroutines are those that are called by another subroutine. For example, all variable names used in first-level subroutines might end with the number 1, and all second-level subroutines end with 2, and so forth. When such differentiation is necessary, use the convention that makes the most sense to you.

*T*he Amortization Table Program, AMORT.BAS

An amortization table is a table of the principal and interest payments for a loan or an annuity. It is typically used to calculate monthly loan payments. With slight modifications, however, it can also be used to calculate the increase in value of a fixed-rate annuity, such as a savings account. The program AMORT.BAS in Listing 7.3 calculates a table of the interest and principal paid each month on a 30-year, $118,000 loan at 8.75 percent interest. It also shows the total interest and principal paid as well as a running total of the principal balance.

The program is designed to print on the screen or on a printer; it uses ON GOSUB statements to switch between the blocks of code that drive those two output devices. The subroutines for the printer are grouped together in lines 1000 to 1999, and the equivalent subroutines for the screen are in lines 2000 to 2999.

```
1 REM AMORT.BAS
2 REM Amortization Table Program
8 GOTO 20
9 REM Autosave Segment
10 SAVE "amort.bas",A
11 END
20 REM Beginning of program
30 REM Define the payment function
40 DEF FNPMT#(PRINC#,INTR,PMTS) = PRINC#*INTR/(1-
(1/(1+INTR))^PMTS)
50 REM Define the round function
60 DEF FNROUND#(NUMB#) = FIX(.5 + NUMB#*100)/100!
70 REM Initialize the variables
80 REM Interest rate per period
90 RATE = 8.75/1200
100 REM Number of periods
110 PERIODS = 360
120 REM Beginning principal
130 PRINCIPAL# = 118000
140 REM The payment
150 PMT# = FNPMT#(PRINCIPAL#,RATE,PERIODS)
160 REM Select the output medium
170 GOSUB 700
180 REM Print the headings
190 ON OUT.DEV GOSUB 1000,2000
200 REM Zero the cumulative interest and principal
210 CUM.INT# = 0
220 CUM.PR# = 0
230 REM calculate and print the table
240 FOR PERIOD = 1 TO PERIODS
250 REM Calculate the data
260 GOSUB 500
270 REM Print the data on the selected device
280 ON OUT.DEV GOSUB 1200,2200
290 REM Count the number of lines printed and end a page
300 LINES = LINES + 1
310 IF LPP = LINES THEN ON OUT.DEV GOSUB 1300,2300
320 NEXT PERIOD
330 REM Finish the table
340 ON OUT.DEV GOSUB 1400,2400
350 END
499 REM ***************************************************
500 REM calculate the interest and principal
510 REM Interest in this payment
520 INTEREST# = FNROUND#(RATE*PRINCIPAL#)
530 REM On the last payment, adjust for an over/under payment of
principal
540 IF PERIOD = PERIODS THEN PMT# = INTEREST# + PRINCIPAL#
550 REM Principal in this payment
560 PR# = PMT# - INTEREST#
570 REM Decrease the principal by the amount paid
580 PRINCIPAL# = PRINCIPAL# - PR#
590 REM Sum the cumulative principal and interest
600 CUM.INT# = CUM.INT# + INTEREST#
610 CUM.PR# = CUM.PR# + PR#
620 RETURN
699 REM ***************************************************
700 REM Select the output medium
710 CLS
720 PRINT "Amortization Table Printing Program"
730 PRINT
740 INPUT "Output to printer (1) or screen (2)";OUT.DEV
750 IF (OUT.DEV = 1) OR (OUT.DEV = 2) THEN 780
760 PRINT "Input out of range, press 1 or 2"
770 GOTO 740
780 RETURN
999 REM ***************************************************
1000 REM For the printer: Print the headings
```

Listing 7.3: Amortization table program

```
1010 LPRINT STRING$(6,13);
1020 LPRINT "          Amortization Table"
1030 LPRINT USING "          Beginning Principal =
$$###,###.##";PRINCIPAL#
1040 LPRINT USING "          Interest rate = ##.##%";RATE*1200
1050 LPRINT USING "          Payment = $$###,.##";PMT#
1060 LPRINT
1070 LPRINT "     Period        Interest
Principal          Balance"
1080 LPRINT "               Paid      Cumulative     Paid
Cumulative"
1090 LPRINT "     --------------------------------------------
----------------------"
1100 LPRINT USING "
$$###,###.##"; PRINCIPAL#
1110 LPP = 54
1120 LINES = 9
1130 RETURN
1199 REM ****************************************************
1200 REM Print a line
1210 LPRINT USING "          ###    $$###,.##  $$###,###.##
$$###,.##  $$###,###.## $$###,###.##";
PERIOD,INTEREST#,CUM.INT#,PR#,CUM.PR#,PRINCIPAL#
1220 RETURN
1299 REM ****************************************************
1300 REM At the end of a page: Start new page
1310 LINES = 0
1320 LPRINT CHR$(12),STRING$(6,13);
1330 RETURN
1399 REM ****************************************************
1400 REM At the end of the table: Kick out last page
1410 LPRINT USING "        The last payment was: $$###,.##";PMT#
1420 LPRINT CHR$(12)
1430 RETURN
1999 REM ****************************************************
2000 REM For the Screen: Print the headings
2010 KEY OFF
2020 CLS
2030 PRINT "Amortization Table"
2040 PRINT USING "Beginning Principal = $$###,###.##";PRINCIPAL#
2050 PRINT USING "Interest rate = ##.##%";RATE*1200
2060 PRINT USING "Payment = $$###,.##";PMT#
2070 PRINT "Period        Interest              Principal
Balance"
2080 PRINT "          Paid      Cumulative    Paid
Cumulative"
2090 PRINT USING "
$$###,###.##"; PRINCIPAL#
2100 LPP = 23
2110 LINES = 7
2120 RETURN
2199 REM ****************************************************
2200 REM Print a line
2210 PRINT USING " ###    $$###,.##   $$###,###.## $$###,.##
$$###,###.## $$###,###.##";
PERIOD,INTEREST#,CUM.INT#,PR#,CUM.PR#,PRINCIPAL#
2220 RETURN
2299 REM ****************************************************
2300 REM At the end of a page: Pause
2310 LINES = 0
2320 PRINT "Press any key to continue";
2330 WHILE INKEY$ = ""
2335 WEND
2340 PRINT
2350 RETURN
2399 REM ****************************************************
2400 REM At the end of the table
2410 PRINT USING "The last payment was: $$###,.##";PMT#
2420 KEY ON
2430 RETURN
2999 REM ****************************************************
```

Listing 7.3: Amortization table program (Continued)

The output devices have different requirements to generate good-looking output. When printing on the screen, you generally want to print flush left and stop at the bottom of each page. On a printed page, you may want to specify top, bottom, left, and right margins and have the printer move to the top of the next page when the bottom of a page is reached. To see how this is done, clear memory, type, save, and run the program in Listing 7.3.

When you run this program, it clears the screen, prints the following heading, and asks you which output device you want. Typing 1 selects the printer; 2 selects the screen.

Amortization Table Printing Program

Output to printer (1) or screen (2)? **2**

If you select the screen, the table shown in Figure 7.1 appears, and the program pauses for you to pess a key. Press any key to print the next page and so on until the whole table has been shown on the screen. If you select the printer, the whole table is printed without any pauses.

Lines 1 through 350 are the main program. First is the standard prologue, then lines 40 and 60 define two user-defined functions. The first calculates the payment on a loan, given the principal, interest rate per

```
Amortization Table
Beginning Principal =  $118,000.00
Interest rate =  8.75%
Payment =    $928.31
Period      Interest                 Principal              Balance
         Paid        Cumulative    Paid      Cumulative
                                                         $118,000.00
    1     $860.42       $860.42    $67.89        $67.89   $117,932.11
    2     $859.92     $1,720.34    $68.39       $136.27   $117,863.73
    3     $859.42     $2,579.76    $68.89       $205.16   $117,794.84
    4     $858.92     $3,438.68    $69.39       $274.55   $117,725.45
    5     $858.41     $4,297.09    $69.90       $344.44   $117,655.56
    6     $857.91     $5,155.00    $70.40       $414.84   $117,585.16
    7     $857.39     $6,012.39    $70.92       $485.76   $117,514.24
    8     $856.87     $6,869.26    $71.44       $557.19   $117,442.81
    9     $856.35     $7,725.61    $71.96       $629.15   $117,370.85
   10     $855.83     $8,581.44    $72.48       $701.63   $117,298.37
   11     $855.30     $9,436.74    $73.01       $774.63   $117,225.37
   12     $854.77    $10,291.51    $73.54       $848.17   $117,151.83
   13     $854.23    $11,145.74    $74.08       $922.25   $117,077.75
   14     $853.69    $11,999.43    $74.62       $996.86   $117,003.14
   15     $853.15    $12,852.58    $75.16     $1,072.02   $116,927.98
   16     $852.60    $13,705.18    $75.71     $1,147.73   $116,852.27
              Press any key to continue
```

Figure 7.1: Output from amortization program

period, and total number of payments. The second function rounds a double-precision number to two significant digits.

Line	Result
1-20	Saves the program with the correct name when you type RUN 10.
40	Defines the function FNPMT#() with the arguments PRINC#, INTR, and PMTS. The function calculates the payment on a loan. The pound sign in the function name makes it return a double-precision value.
60	Defines the function FNROUND#() with argument NUMB#. The function returns a double-precision number rounded to two places after the decimal.

Lines 90 through 220 set the values for the interest rate, number of periods, loan principal, and loan payment (changing the values in these lines makes a table for a different loan). The interest rate in line 90 is divided by 1200 to change it to the monthly interest in decimal form. The 360 periods equal 30 years of monthly payments. The payment is calculated in line 150 using the user-defined function FNPMT#(). Line 170 branches to the subroutine starting in line 700, which asks the user to select the output medium. The number OUT.DEV contains the number of the medium that was selected. OUT.DEV is used to select the subroutine that prints the headings on the selected medium. Finally, the variables that hold the cumulative interest (CUM.INT#) and principal (CUM.PR#) are set to zero.

Line	Result
90	Assigns RATE the value of 8.75 divided by 1200. This is the monthly interest in decimal form.
110	Assigns PERIODS the value 360, which is 30 years times 12 months per year.
130	Assigns PRINCIPAL# the value $118,000.00. This is the beginning balance of the loan.
150	Assigns PMT# the value of the payment calculated with the user-defined function FNPMT#().

Line	Result
170	Branches to the subroutine starting in line 700. The output device number is stored in OUT.DEV (1 = printer, 2 = screen).
190	Branches to the subroutine starting in line 1000 or 2000, depending on the value of OUT.DEV. These subroutines print the table headings.
210	Assigns the value zero to CUM.INT#.
220	Assigns the value zero to CUM.PR#.

Lines 240 through 320 form a FOR/NEXT loop that prints one line of the table during each pass. Line 260 calls the subroutine that begins at line 500 to calculate the values of the principal and interest. In line 280, the value of OUT.DEV again selects the subroutine to use to print the data. The line counter (LINES) is incremented and tested to see if the current table entry is on the last line of a page. If it is, the page-ending subroutines are called. When the loop ends, line 340 selects the subroutine to complete the table.

Line	Result
240	Starts a FOR/NEXT loop that loops PERIOD over the total number of periods in the loan (PERIODS).
260	Branches to the subroutine starting in line 500 to calculate the principal and interest.
280	Branches to the subroutine starting in line number 1200 or 2200 (depending on the value of OUT.DEV) to print the data.
300	Increments the line counter LINES by one.
310	Tests for the bottom of a page and branches to the page-completion routine. When the number of lines printed (LINES) equals the number of lines per page (LPP) the subroutine starting in line 1300 or 2300 is called, depending on the value of OUT.DEV.
320	Bottom of the loop.

Line	Result
340	Branches to the routine starting in line 1400 or 2400 to finish the table.
350	Ends the program.

The subroutine in lines 500 through 620 calculates the principal. The interest is calculated by multiplying the interest rate times the principal. The result is then rounded to the nearest cent using the user-defined function FNROUND#(). In line 540, the program tests for the last iteration of the loop from which this subroutine was called by comparing PERIOD (the loop counter) with PERIODS (the length of the loan). Since the calculated payment is rarely accurate to the penny, the last payment may make the loan slightly overpaid or underpaid. This line changes the last payment to pay off the loan completely by making it equal to the sum of the interest and the remaining principal. In line 560, the principal paid with this payment PR# is calculated, and the principal is decreased by the amount paid. Next, the cumulative interest and principal paid are totaled, and the RETURN in line 620 causes execution to jump back to line 270.

Line	Result
520	Assigns to INTEREST# the interest in this payment calculated by rounding the result of RATE*PRINCIPAL# with the user-defined function FNROUND().
540	Tests for the last period and adjusts the payment to completely pay off the loan.
560	Assigns the principal paid in this payment to PR#.
580	Reduces the principal (PRINCIPAL#) by subtracting the principal paid (PR#).
600	Increases the cumulative interest (CUM.INT#) by the interest paid (INTEREST#).
610	Increases the cumulative principle (CUM.PR#) by the principal paid (PR#).
620	Returns to the calling routine (line 270).

The subroutine starting in line number 700 asks the user to specify the output medium. The screen is cleared, some headings are printed, and the question Output to printer (1) or screen (2)? is printed. The number you type is stored in the variable OUT.DEV. Lines 750 through 770 test that number to see whether it is 1 or 2. If it is neither, an error message appears and the program jumps back to line 740; otherwise it returns to the calling routine.

Line	Result
710	Clears the screen.
720	Prints Amortization Table Printing Program.
730	Prints a blank line.
740	Prints Output to printer (1) or screen (2)? and stores the number typed by the user in OUT.DEV.
750	Tests OUT.DEV to see if it is 1 or 2. If it is, execution branches to line 780; if not, the program prints the error message in line 760.
760	Prints Input out of range, press 1 or 2.
770	Branches back to line 740 so you can try again.
780	Returns to the calling routine (line 180).

The subroutine starting in line 1000 sets up the page format. The page has top and bottom margins of six lines and an eight-character left margin. First the headings are printed, then the initial values of the loan are printed, and finally, the table headings. Each line has eight blanks inserted on the left side to create the left margin.

Line	Result
1010	Prints six carriage returns.
1020	Prints eight blanks and Amortization Table.
1030	Prints eight blanks, Beginning Principal = and the formatted value of the variable PRINCIPAL#.
1040	Prints eight blanks, Interest rate =, and the formatted value of the variable RATE times 1200.
1050	Prints eight blanks, Payment =, and the formatted value of the variable PMT#.

Line	Result
1060	Prints a blank line.
1070	Prints the table headings Period, Interest, Principal, and Balance.
1080	Prints the second line of the table headings, which contains the headings Paid, Cumulative, Paid, Cumulative.
1090	Prints a line across the page.
1100	Prints the value of the starting principal in PRINCIPAL#.
1110	Assigns LPP the number of lines to be printed on a page (54). This creates the bottom margin of six lines (assuming there are a total of 66 lines on a page, 66 minus 6 [for the top margin] minus 54 leaves 6 lines for the bottom margin).
1120	Assigns LINES the number of lines already printed on the page (nine), not including the top margin.
1130	Returns to the calling routine (line 200).

The subroutine starting in line 1200 prints a formatted line on the printer.

Line	Result
1210	Prints eight blanks and the formatted values of the variables PERIOD, INTEREST#, CUM.INT#, PR#, CUM.PR#, and PRINCIPAL#.
1220	Returns to the calling routine (line 290).

The subroutine starting in line 1300 is called to end a page on the printer. A page feed is printed, the number of lines printed is zeroed, and the six blank lines that make the top margin are printed.

Line	Result
1310	Assigns LINES the value zero.
1320	Prints a page feed (CHR$(12)) and six blank lines.
1330	Returns to the calling routine (line 320).

The subroutine starting in line 1400 finishes a table on the printer. The size of the last payment is printed, then the page is ejected by printing a page feed.

Line	Result
1410	Prints eight blanks, The last payment was:, and the formatted value of the variable PMT#.
1420	Prints a page feed (CHR$(12)).
1430	Returns to the calling routine (line 350).

The subroutine starting in line 2000 sets the screen format (these lines parallel those starting in line 1000). Lines 2000 through 2090 turn off the key descriptions along the bottom of the screen, clear the screen, and print the pertinent loan payment information (such as the amount, the interest, and the payment). The screen format is 23 printable lines and no margins. Note that the extra blank line in line 1060 and the line of dashes in line 1090 are not used for the screen. These lines are for the printer only because the screen has fewer viewable lines.

Line	Result
2010	Turns off the key codes printed along the bottom of the screen.
2020	Clears the screen.
2030	Prints Amortization Table.
2040	Prints Beginning Principal = and the formatted value of the variable PRINCIPAL#.
2050	Prints Interest Rate = and the formatted value of RATE*1200.
2060	Prints Payment = and the formatted value of the variable PMT#.
2070	Prints the table headings Period, Interest, Principal, and Balance.
2080	Prints the second line of the table headings Paid, Cumulative, Paid, Cumulative.

Line	Result
2090	Prints the value of the starting principal (PRINCIPAL#).
2100	Assigns LPP the number of lines to be printed on a page (23).
2110	Assigns LINES the number of lines already printed on the screen (seven).
2120	Returns to the calling routine (line 200).

The subroutine starting in line 2200 prints a formatted table entry on the screen.

Line	Result
2210	Prints the formatted values of the variables PERIOD, IN-TEREST#, CUM.INT#, PR#, CUM.PR#, and PRINCIPAL#.
2220	Returns to the calling routine (line 290).

The subroutine starting in line 2300 is called to end a page on the screen. The message Press any key to continue is printed, and the routine then waits for the user to press a key. This is to create a pause at the end of a page so that the user can read the values. Otherwise the printed values would scroll off the top of the screen faster than a user could read them.

Line	Result
2310	Assigns LINES the value zero.
2320	Prints Press any key to continue.
2330	Start of a WHILE/WEND loop. The function INKEY$ is continually tested to see if it is the null string. If it is, the loop continues. If not, the user has pressed a key and execution continues with line 2340.
2335	End of the loop.
2340	Prints a blank line.
2350	Returns to the calling routine (line 320).

The subroutine starting in line 2400 finishes a table on the screen. The value of the last payment is printed, and the key descriptions along the bottom of the screen are turned back on.

Line	Result
2410	Prints The last payment was:, and the formatted value of the variable PMT#.
2420	Turns the key codes along the bottom of the screen back on.
2430	Returns to the calling routine (line 350).

Summary: Functions and Subroutines

This chapter has described user-defined functions and subroutines. A function is a single line of code that returns a single value and is called by name. User-defined functions are defined with the DEF FN statement. The function name, with its arguments in parentheses, is placed immediately after the FN, followed by an equal sign and a formula, or expression, that defines the value of the function.

A subroutine can include any number of statements; it can change the value of any variable and is called by its line number and the GOSUB or ON GOSUB statement. The number of the subroutine's first line is placed after GOSUB. ON GOSUB is an indexed subroutine-calling statement; an index number is placed between the ON and GOSUB, which is followed by a list of subroutines. This number determines which subroutine is selected. When a subroutine is called, GW-BASIC remembers where it was called so that a RETURN statement returns execution to the statement that follows the GOSUB statement.

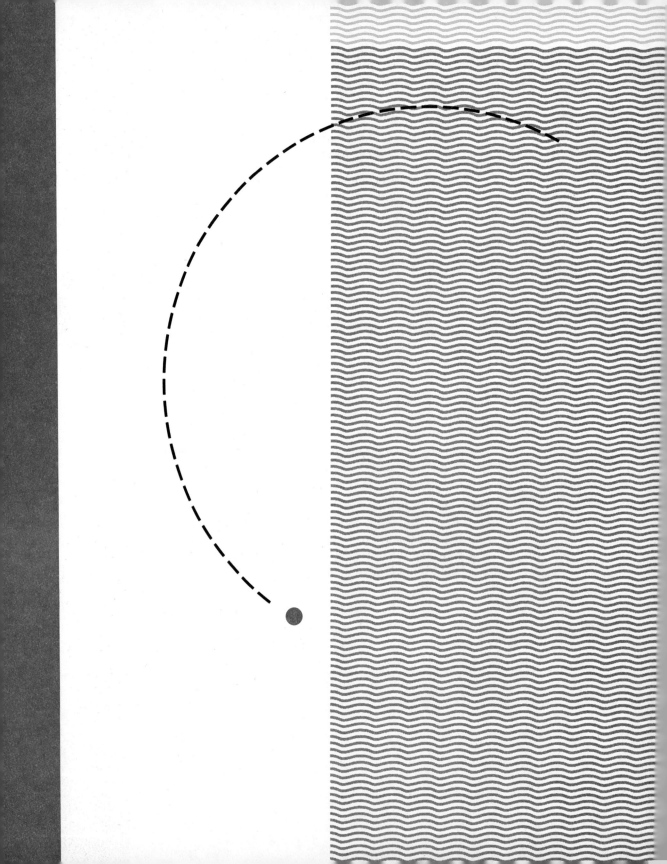

CHAPTER 8

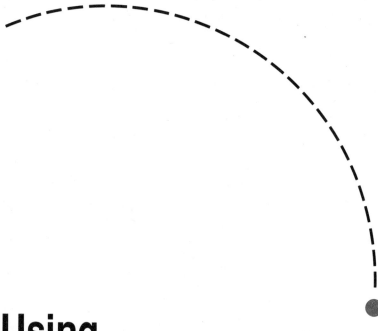

Using
Random-Access Files

Disk files can be accessed in one of two ways: sequentially or random-ly. As discussed in Chapter 3, sequential files are accessed in a linear fashion, from the beginning to the end, much like printing on the screen. The first thing written to a sequential file is thus placed at the beginning, the second thing is written next, and so on. While you can add more data to the end of a sequential-access file, you cannot directly add or change data in the middle. To change or insert data in the middle of a sequential file, you must start a new file, copy the beginning of the old file into it, add the new or changed data, then copy the remainder of the old file into the new file.

Data in random-access files, as the name indicates, are read or written in any order. Random-access files are broken into a numbered series of fixed-length pieces, called *records*. Any individual record in a random-access file can thus be read or written at any time, independent of the other records. This makes random-access files useful for data records and accounts (sequential-access files are useful for text or correspondence).

This chapter examines file storage using random-access files. Our example is a simple inventory maintenance program that uses a random-access file to store the various items in the inventory. The program also reviews most of the topics discussed in this book. Subroutines are used extensively to break the program into small, manageable modules. The example creates and modifies a random-access disk file and uses and manipulates strings, numeric values, and string and numeric functions.

When to Use Random-Access Files

Which type of file to use to store your data depends, of course, on whether the data are sequential, that is, linear in nature. The text of a letter is sequential data, as is a journal of expenses; a general ledger is not. If the amount of data that must be accessed randomly is not large, it can be stored in a sequential-access file and read into an array when needed. The elements of the array are then randomly accessed. The limitation of this method is that the whole array must fit into memory along with the program. A benefit is that access is much faster because the program does not have to read the disk whenever you need a data item. For example, consider the following:

```
10 DIM A(100)
20 OPEN "MYDAT.DAT" FOR INPUT AS #1
30 FOR I = 1 TO 100
40 INPUT #1,A(I)
50 NEXT I
```

Here, line 10 causes the array A to have 101 elements (there are 101 because the array starts at 0). Line 20 opens the file MYDAT.DAT as a sequential-access file for input as file number 1. Lines 30 and 50 loop the value of I from 1 to 100, and line 40 reads the data items into the elements of the array A. After line 50, the program can directly access any of the data items by accessing the element of the array A() that contains it. If you change any elements, just write the array back out to the sequential file before you quit.

This method will not work for large data bases with many items or large amounts of data per item because the data will not all fit into memory at the same time. Here is where you should use random-access files, where only one element is in memory at any one time and the rest of the elements are stored on disk. Thus, the size of the data base is limited, not by the amount of memory, but by the amount of disk storage available.

Using the OPEN Statement

You must first open your file (as with any disk file) before you can access it. The OPEN statement for random-access files is only slightly different from that for sequential-access files. Instead of opening a file FOR INPUT or FOR OUTPUT, you open random-access files FOR RANDOM:

```
30 OPEN "INVENT.DBF" FOR RANDOM AS #1 LEN=32
50 ITEMS! = LOF(1)/32
```

One additional piece of information that is specified when opening random-access files is the record length in bytes. In the example above, the record length is set to 32 bytes by placing LEN=32 at the end of the OPEN statement. Although the record length can range from 1 to 32,767, you must use the /S: switch when starting GW-BASIC to use lengths greater than 128 bytes. If the specification LEN= is omitted, the record length defaults to 128 bytes. Each record in a file is consecutively numbered starting with one. Access to a particular record is gained by using its number in a GET or PUT statement.

The LOF() function indicates the number of bytes in a disk file. To find out how many records there are in a file, divide the file length returned by LOF() by the record length specified in the OPEN statement. In line 50 above, the length of file number 1 is returned by LOF(1) and the record length specified in the OPEN statement is 32 bytes, so the total number of records in the file is LOF(1)/32.

A random-access file can be opened more than once at the same time in a program. Each OPEN statement has a different file number and can independently read or write the file's records.

Defining the Record Buffer with FIELD

In GW-BASIC, each random-access file has a *record buffer* in memory, where data are stored before being written to the disk file. When you read a record from a random-access file using the GET statement, the requested record is transferred from the disk to the buffer. When you write a record to a random-access file using the PUT statement, the contents of the record buffer are then written to the requested record on the disk. Note that changing the contents of the record buffer does not change anything in the disk file until you write the contents of the buffer to disk with the PUT statement.

The locations of data items in the record buffer are assigned with the FIELD statement. This statement breaks the buffer into *fields*, which are named with string variable names. The following is a FIELD statement for the 32-byte record buffer defined in line 30 (above):

```
40 FIELD #1, 2 AS ITEM.NO$, 28 AS ITEM.NAME$, 2 AS UNITS$
```

First comes the word FIELD, followed by a pound sign and the number (#1) of the file to which this FIELD statement applies and a list of field lengths and string variable names delimited by commas. In this case, the first 2 bytes of the buffer are defined as ITEM.NO$, the next 28 as ITEM.NAME$, and the last 2 as UNITS$. Note that the sum of the field widths equals 32 bytes, the length of the buffer. A FIELD statement can define fewer than the total number of bytes in the buffer, but not more. Because FIELD statements do not replace existing field definitions, multiple statements for the same file are all in force when the file is accessed.

Writing Records with PUT

Once you fill the record buffer with data (which you'll learn shortly), it's stored on disk using the PUT statement, as in the following:

```
2050 PUT #1,3
```

This statement writes the contents of the record buffer for file number 1 to record number 3 of that file on the disk. The data contained in the record buffer are not changed; a copy is just made of the contents in the specified record on disk.

While these are random-access files, it's a good idea to write the records sequentially the first time you write them. After that, you can read or write them in any order. If you don't write them sequentially, the records that lie between those you have written will have undefined values. Essentially, they get whatever data were left over the last time a file occupied that space on the disk. For a program that always adds new records to the end of the file, this is no problem. With a program that starts out writing to random records, however, they should first be initialized by putting something known into each of them. The most common way to initialize a file of random-access records is to insert blank records by looping over a PUT statement with the loop variable used for the record number.

Reading Records with GET

To read a record from a random-access file, use the GET statement. The GET statement is the reverse of the PUT statement. For example,

    2090 GET #1,3

This statement gets the contents of record number 3 in file number 1 on disk and puts it into the record buffer for that file. The fielded variables immediately have the values contained in that record.

Storing Data in Record Buffers

The variables defined (or fielded) in a FIELD statement always reference the fields in the record buffer. Changing the value of any of these variables changes the corresponding bytes in the record buffer (but not on the disk file). Their length is fixed by the number of bytes assigned to them in the FIELD statement. Be sure that you never change the value of a variable defined in a FIELD statement with an assignment (=) statement, a LET statement, or any of the INPUT statements. If you do, the variable will be redefined as a standard string variable and will no longer access the contents of the field in the record buffer. To assign values to a fielded variable, use the LSET and RSET statements.

Storing Strings with LSET and RSET

The LSET and RSET statements left- or right-justify a string in a fielded string variable (these statements have no meaning for normal string variables, which are always left-justified). Since a fielded variable has a fixed length specified by the FIELD statement, left or right justification of a string is possible, as long as the string is shorter than the number of bytes in the variable. For example, clear memory, then type and run the following program:

```
10 OPEN "SCRATCH.DOC" FOR RANDOM AS #1 LEN=10
20 FIELD #1, 10 AS A$
30 B$ = "123"
40 LSET  A$ = B$
50 WRITE A$
60 RSET  A$ = B$
70 WRITE A$
80 CLOSE #1
90 END
RUN
"123       "
"       123"
Ok
```

First, line 10 opens a random-access scratch file with a record length of ten bytes. In line 20, a FIELD statement defines those ten bytes as the string variable A$. In line 30, B$ is defined as the string "123"; in line 40, the contents of B$ are left-justified into A$. Since A$ points to a ten-byte-long field, the remaining bytes are filled with blanks. In line 50, A$ is printed using the WRITE statement. As you can see by the first printed result, the three-character string is inserted at the left side of the ten-character field. This is a useful application of the WRITE statement—because it surrounds a printed string with quotation marks, you can easily see where the string begins and ends.

In line 60, the contents of B$ are right-justified in A$, and A$ is printed in line 70. In the second printed result, the three-character string is now on the right side of the ten-character field.

Storing Numbers with MKI$(), MKS$(), and MKD$()

All the fields in a FIELD statement *must* be defined as string variables. To store numeric variables, you must change them into strings or stringlike variables. There are two ways to make numeric values look like strings. The first is to use the STR$() function to turn a numeric value into a string of numbers and then to store that string. While this will work, it can be really wasteful of disk memory. A string representation of an integer can use seven or more bytes of memory; on the other hand, an integer stored in binary form uses only two bytes. Thus, if we could write the binary number, instead of the string, to the disk file, we would need only one-third of the disk space.

In the second, more comon way to store numeric values, binary values are inserted directly into the fielded string variables. The MKI$(), MKS$(), and MKD$() functions make integer, single-precision, and double-precision numeric values appear to be strings. Only the variable type maintained by GW-BASIC is changed; the binary values are not. An integer still occupies only two bytes when it is converted with MKI$(); GW-BASIC just considers it a two-byte string. Once converted with these functions, the numeric values are inserted into fielded string variables using the LSET statement. The field must contain at least the number of bytes necessary to store the variable in memory (two bytes for integers, four for single-precision, and eight for double-precision); for example, the OPEN and FIELD statements in our previous example define space for three string variables.

```
30 OPEN "INVENT.DBF" FOR RANDOM AS #1 LEN=32
40 FIELD #1, 2 AS ITEM.NO$, 28 AS ITEM.NAME$, 2 AS UNITS$
```

These fields are filled with values with the following statements:

```
2020 LSET ITEM.NO$ = MKI$(ITEM.NO%)
2030 LSET ITEM.NAME$ = INAME$
2040 LSET UNITS$ = MKI$(UNITS%)
```

In line 2020, the value of the integer ITEM.NO% is made to look like a string using MKI$(); it is then left-justified into the two-byte fielded variable ITEM.NO$. (Since an integer needs two bytes of storage, this field is just the right size.) Note that because ITEM.NO% and ITEM.NO$ are two separate variables you can store the actual integer in one and its string version in the other. Because they are both holding the same value, this is generally the only situation where you can justify using two variables with the same name but different types.

In line 2030, the string in INAME$ is left-justified into the fielded variable ITEM.NAME$. If INAME$ is longer than the 28 bytes reserved for ITEM.NAME$ with the FIELD statement, it is truncated to 28 characters by removing the excess from the right side.

In line 2040, a second integer is stored in a two-byte fielded variable using MKI$(). Single- and double-precision variables are stored in exactly the same manner, except that MKS$() and MKD$() are used instead, and the fielded variables must be four or eight bytes wide.

Retrieving Data from Record Buffers

Strings are extracted directly from the fielded variables, but string representations of numeric values must first be converted back into numbers with the CVI(), CVS(), and CVD() functions. These three functions are the reverse of the MKI$(), MKS$(), and MKD$() functions:

```
2100 ITEM.NO% = CVI(ITEM.NO$)
2110 INAME$ = ITEM.NAME$
2120 UNITS% = CVI(UNITS$)
```

In line 2100, the fielded string representation of an integer (ITEM.NO$) is converted back into an integer (ITEM.NO%) using the CVI() function. In line 2110, the string is extracted from the fielded string (no conversion is necessary), and in line 2120, another integer (UNITS$) is extracted using the CVI() function. Single- and double-precision floating-point variables are extracted in exactly the same way using the CVS() and CVD() functions.

The Inventory Maintenance Program, INVENT.BAS

INVENT.BAS is a simple inventory maintenance program. Inventory records are stored in a random-access file called INVENT.DBF in 32-byte records. Each record stores an item number (stock number), the item name, and the number of those items in stock. The program has five modules that perform the tasks related to maintenance of an inventory:

- Adding a new item
- Adding or subtracting units
- Printing a single item's record
- Printing the whole inventory
- Modifying the description of an item

Entering and Running the Program

The program is a little more than 100 lines long, though its length is mostly due to remark statements. It illustrates both random-access files and much of what we have done so far in this book. Clear memory, then type the program shown in Listing 8.1 and save it.

```
1 REM INVENT.BAS
2 REM Inventory Maintenance Program
8 GOTO 20
9 REM Autosave Segment
10 SAVE "invent.bas",A
11 END
20 REM Beginning of program
30 OPEN "invent.dbf" FOR RANDOM AS #1 LEN=32
40 FIELD #1, 2 AS ITEM.NO$, 28 AS ITEM.NAME$, 2 AS UNITS$
50 ITEMS% = LOF(1)/32
60 SKIP.REC% = 0
65 REM **************************************************
70 CLS
75 KEY OFF
80 PRINT "Inventory Maintenance Program"
90 PRINT
100 PRINT "1 - Add a new item to the inventory."
110 PRINT "2 - Add or subtract units from an item."
120 PRINT "3 - Print an item."
130 PRINT "4 - Print the inventory."
140 PRINT "5 - Modify an item."
150 PRINT "6 - Quit."
160 PRINT
170 INPUT "Input a number: ";ACTION%
180 IF (ACTION% > 0) AND (ACTION% < 7) THEN 210
190 PRINT "Invalid selection, try again."
200 GOTO 170
210 ON ACTION% GOSUB 270,420,510,620,720,240
220 INPUT "Press any key to continue";Z$
230 GOTO 70
239 REM **************************************************
240 REM Quit the program
```

Listing 8.1: Inventory maintenance program

```
245 KEY ON
250 CLOSE #1
255 REM SYSTEM
260 END
269 REM ****************************************************
270 REM Add a new item to the inventory
272 CLS
274 PRINT "Add a new item."
276 PRINT
280 REM Get the new item number, name, and number of units
290 GOSUB 1000
300 REM Check for an existing item with the same item number
310 GOSUB 1090
320 IF ITEM.EXISTS% = 0 THEN 350
330 PRINT "That item already exists."
340 RETURN
350 ITEMS% = ITEMS% + 1
360 ITEM.NO% = NEW.ITEM.NO%
370 INAME$ = NEW.ITEM.NAME$
380 UNITS% = NEW.UNITS%
390 REM store values
395 REC% = ITEMS%
400 GOSUB 2010
410 RETURN
419 REM ****************************************************
420 REM add or subtract units
430 REM print an item
440 GOSUB 510
442 IF ITEM.EXISTS% = 0 THEN RETURN
450 REM Get amount to change units
460 GOSUB 1280
470 UNITS% = UNITS% + CHANGE.UNITS%
480 REM Save record
482 GOSUB 2010
490 REM Print item values
494 GOSUB 585
500 RETURN
509 REM ****************************************************
510 REM Print an item
515 CLS
520 REM get an item number
530 GOSUB 1200
540 REM find the item
550 GOSUB 1090
560 IF ITEM.EXISTS% = -1 THEN 590
570 PRINT "No such item."
580 RETURN
585 REM Print only entry point
590 REM Print table heading
592 GOSUB 1330
594 REM Print the record
600 GOSUB 1240
610 RETURN
619 REM ****************************************************
620 REM Print inventory
630 CLS
632 PRINT "Inventory"
634 REM Print the table heading
636 GOSUB 1330
640 FOR REC% = 1 TO ITEMS%
650 REM Get a record
660 GOSUB 2080
670 REM Print a record
680 GOSUB 1240
690 NEXT REC%
710 RETURN
719 REM ****************************************************
720 REM Modify item
730 REM Print an item
740 GOSUB 510
750 REM Get new values
760 GOSUB 1000
```

Listing 8.1: Inventory maintenance program (Continued)

```
770 REM test for an existing record
780 REC.SAVE% = REC%
790 SKIP.REC% = REC%
800 GOSUB 1090
810 REC% = REC.SAVE%
820 SKIP.REC% = 0
830 IF ITEM.EXISTS% = 0 THEN 860
840 PRINT "That item already exists."
850 RETURN
860 ITEM.NO% = NEW.ITEM.NO%
870 INAME$ = NEW.ITEM.NAME$
880 UNITS% = NEW.UNITS%
890 REM store values
900 GOSUB 2010
902 REM Print the new values
904 GOSUB 585
910 RETURN
999 REM ****************************************************
1000 REM Get the new item number, name, and number of units
1010 INPUT "Item number: ";NEW.ITEM.NO%
1020 LINE INPUT "Item name (28 characters max):";NEW.ITEM.NAME$
1030 IF LEN(NEW.ITEM.NAME$)<29 THEN 1060
1040 PRINT "Item name must be less than 28 characters."
1050 GOTO 1020
1060 INPUT "Number of units of the item";NEW.UNITS%
1070 RETURN
1080 REM ****************************************************
1090 REM Check for an existing item with the same item number
1100 FOR REC% = 1 TO ITEMS%
1105 IF REC% = SKIP.REC% THEN 1140
1110 REM get a record
1120 GOSUB 2080
1130 IF ITEM.NO% = NEW.ITEM.NO% THEN 1170
1140 NEXT REC%
1150 ITEM.EXISTS% = 0
1160 RETURN
1170 ITEM.EXISTS% = -1
1180 RETURN
1190 REM ****************************************************
1200 REM get an item number
1210 INPUT "Item number: ";NEW.ITEM.NO%
1220 RETURN
1230 REM ****************************************************
1240 REM Print item values
1250 PRINT USING " ######         \                    \      #######";
ITEM.NO%,INAME$,UNITS%
1260 RETURN
1270 REM ****************************************************
1280 REM Get amount to change units
1290 CHANGE.UNITS% = 0
1300 INPUT "Input the amount to change the units (return for 0)";
CHANGE.UNITS%
1310 RETURN
1320 REM ****************************************************
1330 REM Print the table heading
1340 PRINT
1350 PRINT "Item Number    Name                        Number of Units"
1360 PRINT STRING$(57,"-")
1370 RETURN
2000 REM ****************************************************
2010 REM Save a record
2020 LSET ITEM.NO$ = MKI$(ITEM.NO%)
2030 LSET ITEM.NAME$ = INAME$
2040 LSET UNITS$ = MKI$(UNITS%)
2050 PUT #1,REC%
2060 RETURN
2070 REM ****************************************************
2080 REM Get a record
2090 GET #1,REC%
2100 ITEM.NO% = CVI(ITEM.NO$)
2110 INAME$ = ITEM.NAME$
2120 UNITS% = CVI(UNITS$)
2130 RETURN
```

Listing 8.1: Inventory maintenance program (Continued)

Run the program by typing RUN, and you will see the menu shown in Figure 8.1. Type a 1 and press Enter. When you are asked for the item number, type **4079** and press Enter. Next you are asked for the item name and the number of items. Type **Drawer - Keyboard** for the item name and **75** for the number of items. Your screen should now look like Figure 8.2.

```
Inventory Maintenance Program

1 - Add a new item to the inventory.
2 - Add or subtract units from an item.
3 - Print an item.
4 - Print the inventory.
5 - Modify an item.
6 - Quit.

Input a number: ?
```

Figure 8.1: Menu screen of the Inventory Maintenance Program

```
Add a new item.

Item number: ? 4079
Item name (28 characters max):Drawer - Keyboard
Number of units of the item? 75
Press any key to continue? _
```

Figure 8.2: Adding a new item

Table 8.1: Sample Inventory for the Inventory Maintenance Program

Item Number	Name	Number of Units
4079	Drawer - Keyboard	75
9949	Floppy Disk, DSDD 3.5"	1000
9951	Floppy Disk, SSDD 3.5"	1200
9925	Floppy Disk, DSDD 5 1/4"	525
9940	Floppy Disk, DSHD 5 1/4"	575
4489	Chair, Posture	5
4803	CRT Stand, Small	50
6675	Battery, AT Replacement	150
8000	T-Switch, 2 input	25
8214	Surge Protector	37
4613	Printer Paper, 24# Cartons	300
4596	Printer Paper, 20# Cartons	60

Pressing any key returns to the menu (Figure 8.1). Select 1 again from the menu and add the rest of the items listed in Table 8.1 to the inventory.

Now that you have some data to work with, try the rest of the commands in the menu. Select 2 (Add or subtract units from an item.) from the menu and when you are asked for the number of the item to change, type item number 4079. The item's record is printed, and you are asked for the number of units to add or subtract from the inventory. Let's assume that we sold seven units and need to remove them from the inventory. Type **-7**, and the screen will look like Figure 8.3. Pressing any key (here or at the completion of another command) returns you to the menu.

When you select 3 (Print an item.) from the menu and you are asked which item to print, type 4079 and the screen will look like Figure 8.4, showing the record for item 4079.

Select 4 (Print the inventory.) from the menu and the whole inventory is printed on the screen as shown in Figure 8.5. If you press Ctrl-PrtSc before selecting 4 from the menu, the inventory will also be printed

```
Item number: ? 4079

Item Number    Name                              Number of Units
----------------------------------------------------------------
   4079        Drawer - Keyboard                      75
Input the amount to change the units (return for 0)? -7

Item Number    Name                              Number of Units
----------------------------------------------------------------
   4079        Drawer - Keyboard                      68
Press any key to continue?
```

Figure 8.3: Changing the number of units

```
Item number: ? 4079

Item Number    Name                              Number of Units
----------------------------------------------------------------
   4079        Drawer - Keyboard                      68
Press any key to continue?
```

Figure 8.4: Printing the record of an item

```
    Inventory

    Item Number    Name                          Number of Units
    ------------------------------------------------------------
        4079       Drawer, Keyboard                      68
        9949       Floppy Disk, DSDD 3.5"              1000
        9951       Floppy Disk, SSDD 3.5"              1200
        9925       Floppy Disk, DSDD 5 1/4"             525
        9940       Floppy Disk, DSHD 5 1/4"             575
        4489       Chair, Posture                        5
        4803       CRT Stand, Small                     50
        6675       Battery, AT Replacement             150
        8000       T-Switch, 2 input                    25
        8214       Surge Protector                      37
        4613     / Printer Paper, 24# Cartons          300
        4596       Printer Paper, 20# Cartons           60
    Press any key to continue?
```

Figure 8.5: Printing the inventory

(echoed) on the printer. Press Ctrl-PrtSc again to stop the echoing of the screen to the printer.

The next-to-the-last command on the menu, 5 (Modify an item.), lets you change the item number, description, and number of items. Use it to correct the item number or name or to delete an item by changing the name to Unused or something similar. Select 5, and when you are asked which item to change, type 4079. The program prints the item's record and then asks you for the new item number. Don't change the item number; simply type 4079 again. Make the name of the item consistent with the rest of the items by changing it to Drawer, Keyboard (change the hyphen to a comma). Don't change the number of units of the item; type 68. The screen should now look like Figure 8.6.

To leave the program, select 6 (Quit.) from the menu.

The program INVENT.BAS consists of a main program and 14 subroutines. Figure 8.7 shows the main program and the subroutines. The main program opens the inventory file and displays a menu. When a function is selected from the menu, the main program selects and executes the subroutine that performs that function. The subroutines are broken into two groups. Those in the center column of the figure implement the functions selected from the main menu, while those on the right perform simple tasks that are used by the other subroutines.

```
Item number: ? 4079

Item Number    Name                              Number of Units
----------------------------------------------------------------
     4079       Drawer - Keyboard                     68
Item number: ? 4079
Item name (28 characters max):Drawer, Keyboard
Number of units of the item? 68

Item Number    Name                              Number of Units
----------------------------------------------------------------
     4079       Drawer, Keyboard                      68
Press any key to continue?
```

Figure 8.6: Modifying an item

The Main Program

The first block of code is the main program. It opens the disk file, prints a menu on the screen, and after the user makes a selection, directs the execution of the program to the subroutine that performs the desired function. Note that although we refer to subroutines as starting on specific line numbers, those lines are usually remarks that describe the function to be performed rather than instructions to be executed.

Line	Result
1-20	The standard prologue. Lines 10 and 11 save the program with the correct name when you type RUN 10.
30	Opens the random-access data base file as file number 1 with 32-byte records.
40	Divides (with the FIELD statement) the record into three string fields: a 2-byte field for the string version (ITEM.NO$) of the integer item number (ITEM.NO%), a 28-byte field for the item name (ITEM.NAME$), and a 2-byte field for the string version (UNITS$) of the integer number of units (UNITS%).

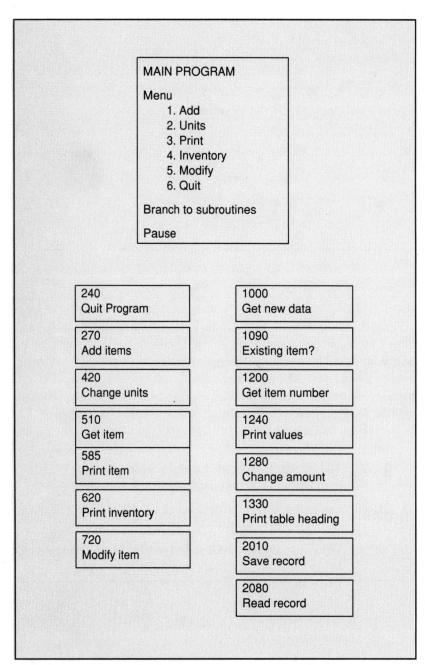

Figure 8.7: Main program and subroutines

Line	Result
50	Calculates the number of records, or items (ITEMS%), in the file by dividing the length of the file returned by LOF(1) by the record length set in the OPEN statement (32).
60	Initializes the variable SKIP.REC% to zero.
70	Clears the screen.
75	Turns off the key codes along the bottom of the screen.
80	Prints Inventory Maintenance Program
90	Prints a blank line.
100	Prints 1 - Add a new item to the inventory.
110	Prints 2 - Add or subtract units from an item.
120	Prints 3 - Print an item.
130	Prints 4 - Print the inventory.
140	Prints 5 - Modify an item.
150	Prints 6 - Quit.
160	Prints a blank line.
170	Prints Input a number:? and then stores the number typed by the user in the variable ACTION%.
180	Checks ACTION% to see whether it is in the range 1 through 6. If it is, branch to line 210; if not, print the error message in line 190.
190	Prints Invalid selection, try again.
200	Jumps back to line 170 so you can try again.
210	Branches according to the value of ACTION% to the subroutine that carries out the function selected from the menu.
220	Returns here after function is completed. Prints Press any key to continue and waits for user input. The variable Z$ is a dummy variable to receive the key pressed by the user so that the screens do not disappear as soon as the functions are completed.

Line	Result
230	Jumps back to line 70 and redisplays the menu.

Main Menu Subroutines

Add a New Item

If you select 1 (Add a new item.) from the menu, you invoke the series of subroutines shown in Figure 8.8. Line 210 calls the subroutine starting in line 270, which controls adding a new item to the inventory.

Line	Result
270	Introduces the subroutine to add new items.
272	Clears the screen.
274	Prints Add a new item.
274	Prints a blank line.
290	Branches to the subroutine starting in line 1000 (described in detail later), which gets and returns the new item number (NEW.ITEM.NO%), the new item name (NEW.ITEM.NAME$), and the new number of units (NEW.UNITS%) from user input.
310	Branches to the subroutine starting in line 1090 (also described later), which checks all records in the data base to see whether an item already exists with the new item number. If it finds an item with that item number, the integer ITEM.EXISTS% is set to -1 (true); otherwise it is set to 0 (false).
320	Tests the value of ITEM.EXISTS%. If it is zero, branches to line 350; otherwise prints the error message in line 330.
330	Prints That item already exists.
340	Returns to the calling routine in line 220.
350	Increments the total number of items (ITEMS%) by one.

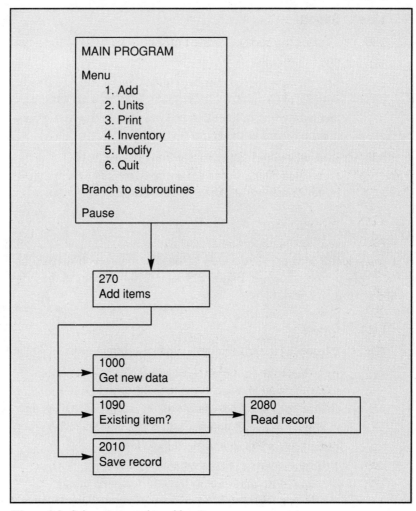

Figure 8.8: Subroutines used to add an item

Line	Result
360	Equates the current item number (ITEM.NO%) to the new item number (NEW.ITEM.NO%).
370	Equates the current item name (INAME$) to the new item name (NEW.ITEM.NAME$).

Line	Result
380	Equates the current number of units (UNITS%) to the new number of units (NEW.UNITS%).
395	Sets the new record number (REC%) to be equal to the number of items (ITEMS%). Since ITEMS% was just incremented by one in line 350, it is pointing to the first unused record at the end of the disk file.
400	Branches to the subroutine starting in line 2010 (described later), which saves the contents of the record buffer in record number REC%.

Add or Subtract Units

If you select 2 (Add or subtract units.) from the menu, you invoke the series of subroutines shown in Figure 8.9. Line 210 branches to the subroutine starting in line 420.

Line	Result
420	Introduces the subroutine to add or subtract units.
440	Branches to the subroutine beginning in line 510 (described later), which first gets the item number to change and then finds and prints its record. If it finds an item with that item number, integer ITEM.EXISTS% is set to -1 (true); otherwise it is set to 0 (false).
442	Tests the value of ITEM.EXISTS%. If it is zero, the item does not exist, and the routine returns to the menu. (There is no need to print an error message here because the subroutine has already printed one in line 570.) If the item does exist, the routine continues with line 460.
460	Branches to the subroutine starting in line 1280 (also described later), getting the amount to change the number of units in inventory (CHANGE.UNITS%).
470	Changes the number of units of the current item by adding CHANGE.UNITS% to it.

Line   Result

482   Branches to the subroutine starting in line 2010
         (described later), which saves the contents of the record
         buffer in record number REC%.

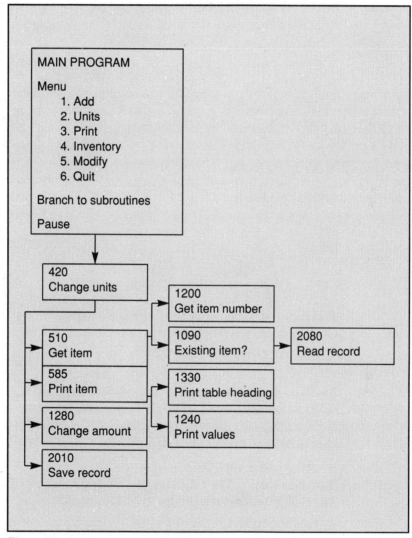

Figure 8.9: Subroutines used to add or subtract units

Line   Result

494   Branches to the entry point at line 585 in the subroutine starting in line 510; this is the point at which the current record is printed.

500   Returns to the calling routine, line 220.

Print an Item

If you select 3 (Print an item.) from the menu, you invoke the series of subroutines shown in Figure 8.10. Line 210 branches to the subroutine starting in line 510, which has two parts: to get an item and to print an item. (This subroutine is also used by function 2 in the menu to get and print the item that needs its units changed, and by function 5 in the menu to get the item that needs editing.) The subroutine is also a demonstration of the use of multiple entry points in a subroutine. Routines that need to get, check, and print an item number branch to line 510. A routine that already has an item and just needs to print it branches to line 585.

Line   Result

510   Introduces the subroutine to print an item.

515   Clears the screen.

530   Branches to the subroutine starting in line 1200 (described later), which gets the item number (NEW.ITEM.NO%) of the item to print. Returns to 540 and continues with 550.

550   Branches to the subroutine starting in line 1090, which searches for the record containing item NEW.ITEM.NO%. If it finds an item with that item number, the integer ITEM.EXISTS% is set to -1 (true) otherwise it is set to 0 (false).

560   Tests the value of ITEM.EXISTS%. If it is -1, the item exists, and the routine branches to 590. If the item does not exist, the routine continues with line 570.

570   Prints No such item.

580   Returns to the calling routine, line 220.

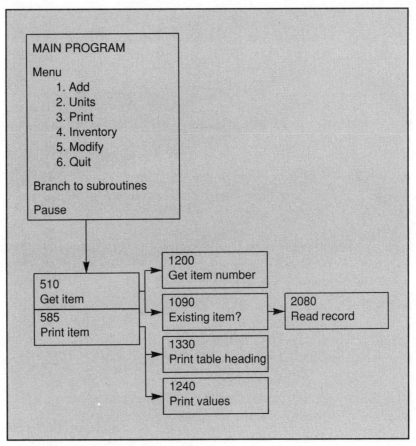

Figure 8.10: *Subroutines used to print an item*

Line	Result
585	Alternate entry point into this subroutine; allows another routine to print the table heading and current record without getting and checking an item number.
592	Branches to the subroutine starting in line 1330 (described later), which prints the table heading.
600	Branches to the subroutine starting in line 1240 (described later), which prints the contents of the current record REC%.

Line	Result
610	Returns to the calling routine, line 220.

Print the Inventory

If you select 4 (Print the inventory.) from the menu, you invoke the series of subroutines shown in Figure 8.11. Line 210 branches to the subroutine starting in line 620.

Line	Result
620	Introduces the subroutine to print the inventory.
630	Clears the screen.
632	Prints Inventory.
636	Branches to the subroutine starting in line 1330, which prints the table headings.
640	Starts a loop, which goes from one to the total number of items in the file (ITEMS%). It uses REC% as the loop variable; this is the record number used by the Read record subroutine starting in line 2080.
660	Branches to the subroutine starting in line 2080 (described later), which reads record number REC% from the data base file.
680	Branches to the subroutine starting in line 1240, which prints the item's values.
690	Bottom of the loop; increments REC% and branches back to 650 if it is less than or equal to ITEMS%.
710	Returns to the calling routine, line 220.

Modify an Item

If you select 5 (Modify an item.) from the menu, you invoke the series of subroutines shown in Figure 8.12, with line 210 branching to the subroutine that begins in line 720.

Line	Result
720	Introduces the subroutine to modify an item.
740	Branches to the subroutine starting in line 10, which gets an item number from the user and then prints its record.
760	Branches to the subroutine starting in line 1000, which gets and returns the new item number (NEW.ITEM.NO%), the new item name (NEW.ITEM.NAME$), and the new number of units (NEW.UNITS%) from the user.

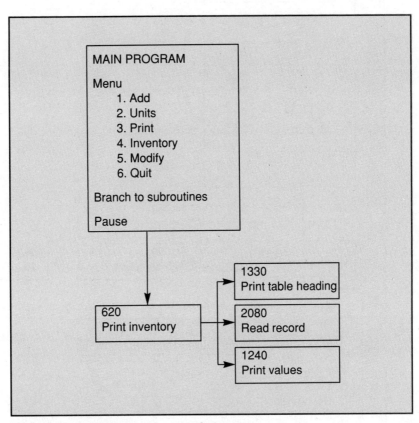

Figure 8.11: Subroutines used to print the inventory

Line   Result

780   Saves the current value of REC%, then checks for an existing item with the same item number. The check is slightly more difficult this time, because we must skip the record we are modifying, which probably does have the same number as the one input (that is all right here since we're going to replace that record anyway).

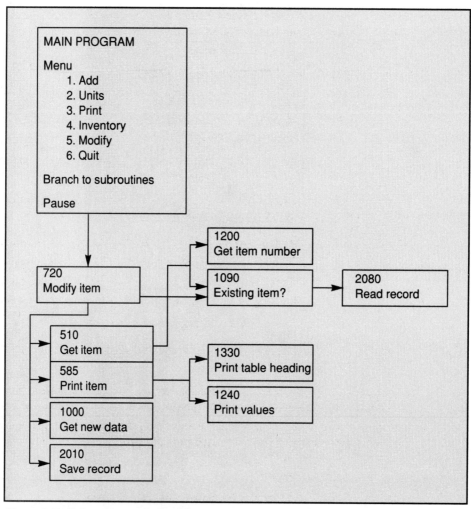

Figure 8.12: Subroutines used to modify an item

Line	Result
790	Sets the value of SKIP.REC% to REC% (the record we are going to skip).
800	Branches to the subroutine starting in line 1090 to check for an existing record, then returns.
810	Restores the original value of REC%.
820	Resets the value of SKIP.REC% to zero.
830	Checks to see whether an existing record was found. If one wasn't found, branches to 860. If one was found, prints the error message in line 840.
840	Prints That item already exists.
850	Returns to the calling routine, line 220.
860	Equates the current item number (ITEM.NO%), to the new item number (NEW.ITEM.NO%).
870	Equates the current item name (INAME$), to the new item name (NEW.ITEM.NAME$).
880	Equates the current number of units (UNITS%), to the new number of units (NEW.UNITS%).
900	Branches to the subroutine starting in line 2010, which saves the record buffer in record number REC%.
904	Branches to the entry point at line 585 in the subroutine starting in line 510, where the current record is printed.
910	Returns to the calling routine, line 220.

Quit the Program

If you select 6 (Quit.) from the menu, you invoke the single subroutine shown in Figure 8.13, with line 210 branching to the subroutine starting in line 240, which turns the key codes along the bottom of the screen back on, closes the inventory file, and ends the program.

Line	Result
240	Introduces the subroutine to quit a program.

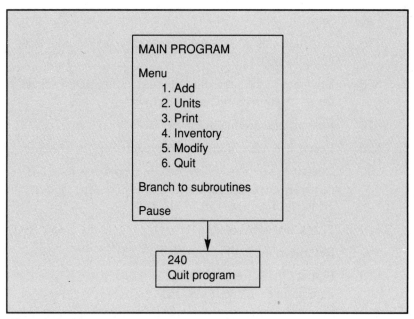

Figure 8.13: Subroutines used to quit the program

Line	Result
245	Turns the key codes back on.
250	Closes the inventory file.
255	Remark. If you edit the REM out of line 255 it becomes a SYSTEM statement, which causes GW-BASIC to quit and return you to DOS, instead of just returning to the GW-BASIC prompt. Don't do this until everything is running correctly; otherwise, you will quit GW-BASIC every time you quit INVENT.BAS.
260	Ends the program.

*S*upporting *Subroutines*

The subroutines in this section do much of the repetitive work required by the menu subroutines (referred to earlier).

Get a New Item Number

The subroutine starting in line 1000 gets a new item number, a new item name, and a new number of units from the user.

Line	Result
1000	Introduces the subroutine to get new item number.
1010	Prints Item number: and stores the result typed by the user in NEW.ITEM.NO%.
1020	Prints Item name (28 characters max): and stores the result typed by the user in NEW.ITEM.NAME$.
1030	Checks the length of the new item name. If it is less than 29 characters, execution branches to 1060; otherwise, it continues with line 1040.
1040	Prints Item name must be less than 28 characters.
1050	Jumps to 1020 so you can try again.
1060	Prints Number of units of the item and stores the result typed by the user in NEW.UNITS%.
1070	Returns to the calling routine in line 300 or 770.

Search for an Item Number

The subroutine starting in line 1090 searches for an item with the same item number as NEW.ITEM.NO%.

Line	Result
1090	Introduces the subroutine to check item numbers.
1100	Starts a loop over record numbers one through the total number of items in the data base (ITEMS%).
1105	Checks to see whether we should skip this record. If so, execution jumps to line 1140 and the loop continues with the next record. If not, it continues with line 1110.

Line	Result
1120	Branches to the subroutine starting in line 2080, which reads the record number (REC%) and extracts the data from the record buffer.
1130	Compares the item number (ITEM.NO%) just read with the new item number (NEW.ITEM.NO%); if they are the same, branches to line 1170. Otherwise, the subroutine continues with line 1140.
1140	Bottom of the loop. REC% is incremented by one, and if it is less than ITEMS%, the loop jumps back to line 1105.
1150	If the loop completes without any of the item numbers matching the new item number, ITEM.EXISTS% is set to zero (false, item not found).
1160	Returns to the calling routine, line 320, 560, or 810.
1170	If the item was found, jumps here and sets ITEM.EXISTS% to -1 (true, item found).
1180	Returns to the calling routine, line 320, 560, or 810.

Four Essential Functions

The following brief subroutines perform four essential functions. The subroutine starting in line 1200 inputs an item number, stores it in NEW.ITEM.NO%, and returns. The subroutine starting in line 1240 prints a record and returns. The subroutine starting in line 1280 inputs the amount to change the units, stores it in CHANGE.UNITS%, and returns. The subroutine starting in line 1330 prints the table heading.

Line	Result
1200	Introduces the subroutine to input item numbers.
1210	Prints Item number: and stores the value typed by the user in NEW.ITEM.NO%.
1220	Returns to the calling routine, line 540.
1240	Introduces the subroutine to print items.

Line	Result
1250	Prints the formatted contents of the current record, ITEM.NO%, INAME$, UNITS%.
1260	Returns to the calling routine, line 610 or 690.
1280	Introduces the subroutine to get the change in units.
1290	Sets CHANGE.UNITS% to zero.
1300	Prints Input the amount to change the units (return for 0) and stores the number input by the user in CHANGE.UNITS%.
1310	Returns to the calling routine, line 470.
1330	Introduces the subroutine to print the table heading.
1340	Prints a blank line.
1350	Prints the table heading Item Number Name Number of Units.
1360	Prints a line of hyphens.
1370	Returns to the calling routine, line 594 or 640.

Write a Record

The subroutine beginning in line 2010 saves the current contents of the record buffer in record number REC%.

Line	Result
2010	Introduces the subroutine to save records.
2020	Makes the integer ITEM.NO% look like a string with MKI$() and left-justifies it into the two-byte fielded variable ITEM.NO$.
2030	Stores the item name in INAME$ in the 28-byte fielded variable ITEM.NAME$.
2040	Makes the integer UNITS% look like a string with MKI$() and left-justifies it into the two-byte fielded variable UNITS$.

Line	Result
2050	Stores the contents of the record buffer in record number REC%. If REC% is one more than the number of records stored on the disk, a new record is created and added to the disk file. If it's an existing record, the data in the record buffer replace the data stored in the record on disk.
2060	Returns to the calling routine, line 410, 490, or 902.

Read a Record

The subroutine beginning in line 2080 reads record number REC% from disk and extracts the data from it.

Line	Result
2080	Introduces subroutine to read records.
2090	Gets the contents of record number REC% on the disk and puts it into the record buffer.
2100	Extracts the integer stored in the two-byte fielded string variable ITEM.NO$ with CVI() and stores it in ITEM.NO%.
2110	Extracts the item name in the fielded string ITEM.NAME$ and stores it in INAME$.
2120	Extracts the integer stored in the two-byte fielded string variable UNITS$ and stores it in UNITS%.
2130	Returns to the calling routine, line 670 or 1130.

Summary: Using Random-Access Files

This chapter has discussed creating and using random-access files, which differ from sequential access files in that any part of the file may be read or written at any time (rather than sequentially from beginning to end). To do this, random-access files are broken up into equal-sized records whose length is specified in the OPEN statement. You open a random-access file with an OPEN statement, indicating a file type of RANDOM and including a record length specifier (LEN=*length*, where *length* is the number of bytes in a record). This defines a record buffer in memory to which the records from the disk file are moved with a GET statement and that is the source of data written to the disk file with a PUT statement.

The contents of the record buffer and access to it are set up with the FIELD statement. The FIELD statement divides the buffer into pieces and assigns a string variable name to each piece.

Since the buffer has fixed-width fields for string variables, you cannot load data into the buffer using standard assignment statements, but must use LSET, RSET, MKI$(), MKS$(), and MKD$(). Use LSET and RSET assignment statements to left- or right-justify the strings in the fields of the buffer. Since the buffer can accept only strings, you use the functions MKI$(), MKS$(), and MKD$() to change integers and single- and double-precision floating-point numbers into string forms. These are not printable strings; they are instead stringlike objects with the same size as the numeric variables they represent.

You can extract string data directly from the buffer with a simple assignment statement, but to extract numeric data stored as strings with MKI$(), MKS$(), and MKD$(), use the CVI(), CVS(), and CVD() functions. These functions change the string forms of the numeric data back into their original numbers.

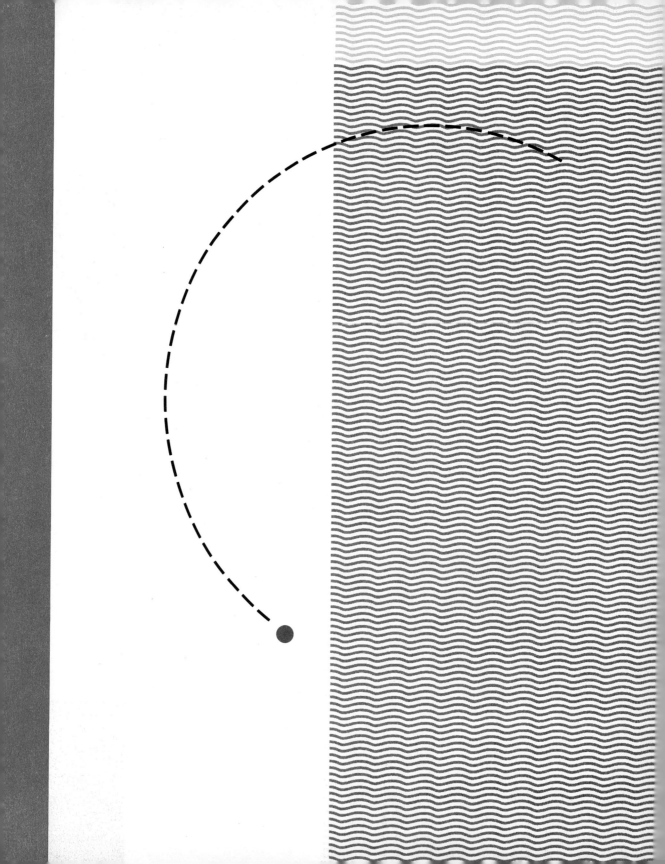

CHAPTER 9

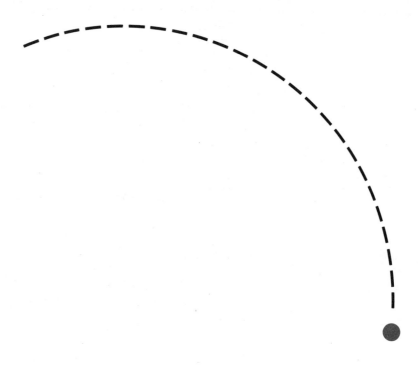

The Art
of Debugging

Up to this point, you have only had to deal with syntax errors in your programs. These errors occur when you type something that GW-BASIC doesn't recognize as a valid statement. When that happens, the program stops and the problem line is presented to you for correction. You fix it and run your program again.

Syntax errors are relatively straightforward to fix, but what do you do when everything runs—but runs wrong? The disks spin, but they store the wrong data; the printer prints, but not what you expected; words appear on the screen, but they are the wrong words. Now what do you do? Somewhere in your code is an error, known as a bug, and you must find it. It could be a typo (a typographical error); that is, you may have typed the wrong variable name or used a plus instead of a minus. It could also be a *logical error*, where the sequence of steps you've written doesn't do what you thought it would. *Debugging* is the art of finding and correcting those errors.

One of the biggest omissions in GW-BASIC is a source-code debugger. A source-code debugger allows you to execute your code one line at a time, displaying each line and the values of pertinent variables at each step. While GW-BASIC does have a trace function, it lacks the ability to move through a program one step at a time.

This chapter discusses the art of debugging code. It is an art, because there is no set series of actions that can guarantee that you'll find the problem. Finding bugs in computer programs is its own form of detective work. You gather all the information about the problem that you can find, and from that information, you must determine where the bug is and how to fix it. This chapter explores the different ways used to gather information about the code—tracing its step-by-step execution, examining variables and printing their values while the code is running, and using software solutions to make up for the lack of a source-code debugger.

Locating the Problem

The most difficult part of debugging a program is locating the source of the problem. The results of the problem are usually obvious—your code does something it wasn't supposed to do. The error that precipitated the problem might just have occurred, or it could have occurred earlier and not been apparent until now. Here is where the detective work comes in: You must use every piece of evidence you can gather to help you discover the perpetrator, that line or segment of code that does what it was written to do, which is really not what you intended it to do.

If you're lucky, the problem will be repeatable, and you can define the sequence of events that led up to your discovery of it. Keep track of what you did, what you typed, which options you selected, and so forth. If you can make the problem happen again, you have a good chance of locating the bug quickly. If the problem is transient, that is, it only happens sometimes, and you cannot discover a definite set of steps that cause it to happen, you have a far more difficult problem. Again, all you can do is to continue to gather evidence about the bug until—eventually—you discover its location.

*E*choing Screen Printing Elsewhere

Because anything printed on the screen can quickly scroll off the top and be lost, one of the first things to do while tracing a bug is to echo the screen output to a more permanent medium. If you have time to examine it, it may give you a clue as to what is going on with your code. There are basically two places to send the contents of the screen—to the printer or to a disk file. Which to use depends largely on what the code does.

If your code prints extensively to the printer, you may not want to mix the screen printing with the normal output. Then again, you might want to do just that, as the mixing of the screen printing with the normally printed output may provide a clue to the problem. If you have a lot of data printed to the screen, you may not want to send it to the printer (which can be very wasteful of paper), but prefer to echo the screen printing to a disk file.

You can echo everything printed or typed on the screen to the printer by pressing Ctrl-PrtSc. Press Ctrl-PrtSc again to turn off the echoing. You can also redirect the printed output by typing a greater than symbol (>) and LPT1: (assuming of course, that your printer is connected to the first parallel port) on the command line when you invoke GW-BASIC:

```
GWBASIC >LPT1:
```

Here, everything entered at the keyboard or printed to the screen with PRINT statements will also be sent to the printer. Things printed to the screen using PRINT# statements will not be sent to the printer. If you use the OPEN statement to open a communications path to the screen by using SCRN: as the file name (see the MailMerge program in Chapter 5), anything you print to the screen using that device will not be echoed to the printer using redirection. Ctrl-PrtSc, however, does echo everything printed on the screen—even lines written with PRINT#—to the printer.

Redirecting screen output to a file is accomplished in the same way as redirecting output to the printer. Use a greater than symbol and a file name in the invocation line for GW-BASIC.

GWBASIC >SDUMP.TXT

In this case, everything printed on the screen, except lines written with PRINT#, will be echoed to the file SDUMP.TXT. You can later either print the file or examine it with your word processor.

Following the Flow of Code Execution

The next thing you can do is follow the flow, or thread, of execution of your code. Does your code really execute the statements you thought it would, and in the order you expected? With more complicated codes, such as the inventory maintenance program, INVENT.BAS, execution threads from subroutine to subroutine and back. Any unexpected break or deviation in the intended path of execution will cause problems. Although, as mentioned previously, GW-BASIC does not have a source-code debugger (which would immensely simplify following the execution of code), that does not mean you cannot trace a code.

Using Trace

The TRON and TROFF statements turn tracing on and off. When tracing is on, GW-BASIC prints on the screen the line number currently being executed, allowing you to track the code's execution. TRON and TROFF statements can either be executed in direct mode before and after you run a short program or they can be used as program statements and inserted just before and after a suspect piece of code. When they are used as program statements, they will print only the line numbers of the statements that are executed between TRON and TROFF statements. Make sure that you have a paper listing of your program while doing a trace so that you can follow the execution as it is being printed on the screen.

One of the difficulties with using TRON and TROFF is that the line numbers can quickly scroll off the top of the screen before you can read them. Here is a good place to use screen echoing. All the line numbers printed in the trace will be preserved on paper or disk, and echoing to the printer can slow the program down slightly so that you can more easily read the line numbers and follow the trace.

A second difficulty with TRON and TROFF is that if your program is printing or drawing on the screen, the trace will mess up the output, and that output will mess up the trace. Unfortunately, there is really little that you can do about this, unless you can divert your screen printing elsewhere.

As an example of using the trace function, type and run the following simple program. The results of listing and running the program are shown in Figure 9.1.

```
20 PRINT "Hello"
25 TRON
30 FOR I = 1 TO 5
40 PRINT I
50 NEXT I
60 FOR I = 1 TO 20
70 J = I*I
80 NEXT I
85 TROFF
90 END
```

When the program is run, it first prints the string Hello in line 20. In line 25, tracing is turned on, and the trace function prints [30][40], indicating that statements 30 and 40 have been executed. Next, the number 1 is printed, which is the result of printing the value of I, the loop

```
Ok
list
20 PRINT "Hello"
25 TRON
30 FOR I = 1 TO 5
40 PRINT I
50 NEXT I
60 FOR I = 1 TO 20
70 J = I*I
80 NEXT I
90 END
Ok
run
Hello
[30][40] 1.
[50][40] 2
[50][40] 3
[50][40] 4
[50][40] 5
[50][60][70][80][70][80][70][80][70][80][70][80][70][80][70][80][70][80][70][80]
[70][80][70][80][70][80][70][80][70][80][70][80][70][80][70][80][70][80][70][80]
[70][80][90]
Ok

1 LIST    2 RUN←   3 LOAD"  4 SAVE"  5 CONT←  6. "LPT1  7 TRON←  8 TROFF←  9 KEY    0 SCREEN
```

Figure 9.1: Using the trace statements TRON and TROFF

variable, in statement 40. A carriage return follows, so printing moves down one line and the trace prints [50][40]. Line 50 is the bottom of the loop, at which point I is incremented and control passes back up to line 40 again to print 2, the next value of I. This continues for the five iterations of the first loop.

In line 60, the program starts to execute the second loop. You can see the execution even though the loop produces no output. Because the loop doesn't print anything, the results of the trace do not move down a line every two steps. Instead they continue to the right side of the screen and then wrap around back to the left (lines 70 and 80 are executed 20 times). As you can imagine, tracing a more complicated program can quickly cover the screen with line numbers from the trace. (As an example, turn on tracing and run the inventory maintenance program from the last chapter.) Note that graphics programs are particularly difficult since they write to all parts of the screen, and the line numbers start printing wherever the cursor happens to be.

Printing Messages to the Screen, the Printer or a File

Another method of following the execution of a program is to insert PRINT, LPRINT, or PRINT# statements at strategic points in the program to print messages to the screen, the printer, or a disk file. (Don't forget to OPEN a disk file to use with the PRINT# statements.) Include a short piece of descriptive text with the PRINT statements so you know where you are. For example,

```
20 LPRINT "At line 20"
80 PRINT "In subroutine 1"
```

Enter the following program:

```
20  PRINT "Hello"
25  PRINT "Starting first loop, line 25"
30  FOR I = 1 TO 5
40  PRINT I
50  NEXT I
55  PRINT "Ending first loop, line 55"
56  PRINT "Starting second loop, line 56"
60  FOR I = 1 TO 20
70  J = I*I
80  NEXT I
```

```
85  PRINT "Ending second loop, line 85"
90  END
```

Running it produces

```
Hello
Starting first loop, line 25
1
2
3
4
5
Ending first loop, line 55
Starting second loop, line 56
Ending second loop, line 85
Ok
```

Signaling with Sounds

In addition to printing text to the screen, you can also use sound to indicate a location. The nice thing about sound is that it doesn't interfere with the printing on the screen or printer. The BEEP statement causes a short system beep (1/4 second, 800 Hz) when the program execution reaches that point. You can also cause the system to beep by using CHR$(7) to print ASCII control character number 7. Unfortunately, stringing several BEEP statements together doesn't create short beeps that could be counted and used as a code to indicate your position. The beeps all blend together into one longer beep whose length is difficult to estimate. Since some printers also beep, you can use combination of both the system's and printer's beeps to create a beep code that indicates where you are. The following causes the system and the printer to beep:

```
20 BEEP
30 PRINT CHR$(7);
40 LPRINT CHR$(7);
50 PRINT CHR$(7);:LPRINT CHR$(7);
```

Note that lines 30, 40, and 50 end in a semicolon to suppress the carriage return. Without the semicolon, you'll be scrolling text off the top of the screen or needlessly kicking paper out of the printer. Line 50 is a compound line, with two statements placed on the same line and separated by a colon. Line 50 is actually the same as the following;

using the colon allows you to place both statements on one, rather than two, lines.

```
50 PRINT CHR$(7);
60 LPRINT CHR$(7);
```

A more versatile statement is the SOUND statement. The word SOUND is followed by two numbers indicating frequency and duration. The first number, frequency in Hertz (Hz), ranges from 37 through 32,767, although most people hear tones only up to about 12,000 Hz. The second number is duration and ranges from 0 through 65,535. A duration of 18.2 causes a one-second tone. A duration greater than 0 but less than 0.02 causes a continuous tone, and a duration of 0 turns off a tone. SOUND statements can be set to produce different tones to indicate where the program is executing. If you have trouble discerning different sounds, you can create an oscillating tone and count the oscillations. The following example produces three distinct tones:

```
20 SOUND 800,4
30 SOUND 600,18.2
40 SOUND 400,18.2
```

The statement in line 20 has the same effect as the BEEP statement, and the statements in lines 30 and 40 produce one-second tones at 600 and 400 Hz. To produce the oscillating tone, insert the following subroutine somewhere out of the way in the program you're testing (it doesn't have to be at line 1000). Set the number of oscillations with the variable BELLS and then call the subroutine. You should use different numbers of oscillations to indicate different locations in a program. When you clear memory and type and run this program, you will hear a two-tone oscillation that oscillates five times, pauses, and oscillates five times again. The loop in lines 1050 and 1060 inserts the short pause so that the two calls to the subroutine don't run together. You can easily create more elaborate sounds by adding more SOUND statements (it can be kind of fun, too).

```
NEW
Ok
10 REM BELLS.BAS
20 BELLS = 5: GOSUB 1000
22 BELLS = 5: GOSUB 1000
30 END
1000 REM Bells subroutine
1010 FOR I = 1 TO BELLS
```

```
1020 SOUND 800,1
1030 SOUND 600,1
1040 NEXT I
1050 FOR I = 1 TO 1000
1060 NEXT I
1070 RETURN
RUN
Ok
```

Examining Variables with the Code Stopped

Now that you've looked at the output and traced your code's execution, you can look at the values of the variables at different points during the execution. First stop the code at an appropriate location, then use direct mode to print the value of any variable. If you type PRINT and the variable's name, the variable's value will be printed. You can print several variables at the same time by separating their names with commas. You can also change the value of a variable by typing an assignment statement in direct mode, but stopping the code at the time you want to make the change is difficult.

Using Control-Break

Although you can press Ctrl-Break to stop program execution, you will almost never stop where you want to be. No matter how fast you are, many statements can be executed in the time it takes your finger to press the keys. When you have finished examining the variables, type CONT in direct mode. As long as you have not changed any program lines, the code will start up again exactly where it stopped. If you change a program line, you cannot restart the program with CONT; you must start it over again with RUN. You can also type GOTO and a line number to start the code running again at a different location.

Using Fixed Breakpoints

If you know where you want to stop your code, you can make it stop at exactly that point with the STOP statement rather than using Ctrl-Break. When this statement is encountered, the program will stop with the message Break in *nnn* (where *nnn* is the number of the line containing STOP), and you can examine or change variables (not program lines), change the point of execution with GOTO, or restart the program at the original point with CONT. The STOP statement consists simply of a line number and the word STOP. STOP, which can be restarted, is thus different from the END statement, which closes files and is not restartable.

Creating a STEP Function

One thing that GW-BASIC lacks is a command or key that would allow you to make your program execute one step at a time and then stop so that you could examine the changes caused by that one step. While I cannot make a step that executes only one line at a time, it is possible to use your software to make the code stop every few lines or so. Clear memory and type and run the following program. Note that the trace is on so that you can follow the execution.

```
1 REM STEP.BAS
10 ON TIMER(1) GOSUB 1000
20 GOSUB 1030
30 FOR I = 1 TO 1000
40 PRINT I
50 NEXT I
60 END
1000 TIMER OFF
1005 TROFF
1010 X$=INPUT$(1)
1020 IF X$ = "s" THEN STOP
1022 IF X$ = "q" THEN 1070
1030 TIMER ON
1040 FOR IIIII = 1 TO 2200
1050 NEXT IIIII
1060 TRON
1070 RETURN
```

Remember that the subroutine starting in line 1000 can be placed anywhere out of the way in the program you're testing. Simply change the GOSUB line numbers in lines 10 and 20 to point to the location. Line 10, which needs to be executed only once near the beginning of the program, prepares for timed event trapping. The argument (1) of the TIMER function causes the subroutine starting in line 1000 to be called once every second. Line 20 starts the stepping, so place this statement near where you want to start examining your program.

Figure 9.2 shows part of the output generated by this code.

Line	Result
10	Sets the subroutine starting in line 1000 as the one to branch to whenever the timer goes off and sets the duration of the timer to one second.
20	Branches to 1030 to turn timed event trapping on.
30	Begins the loop.
40	Prints value of loop counter.
50	End of the loop.
60	Ends the program.
1000	Turns timer off.
1005	Turns trace off.
1010	Waits for input from keyboard, stores the key pressed in X$.
1020	If the input is s, stops execution with a STOP, allowing you to examine or change the variables (in direct mode). Entering CONT restarts the program.
1022	If the input is q, branches to 1070, ending the subroutine and returning you to the program. If you press any other key, the subroutine moves to 1030 and continues.
1030	Turns timer on.

Line	Result
1040–1050	Limits the amount of code that can be executed in the one-second timer interval. Since several statements would normally be executed in one second, this loop wastes time, thereby limiting the executed statements to one or two.
1060	Turns trace on.
1070	Returns to the program.

The longer your computer takes to execute the loop in lines 1040 and 1050, the smaller and more frequent the intervals will be. The value of 2200 produced the results shown in Figure 9.2, using a 12 MHz AT-compatible computer. Slower computers will need smaller values; change the size of the loop in lines 1040 and 1050 so that they work best for you.

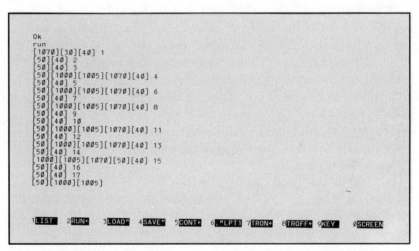

Figure 9.2: *The STEP subroutine, using timed event trapping to step through a program's execution*

Examining Variables with the Code Running

In addition to stopping a code to examine the variables, you can ex-amine them while running by printing them to the screen, the printer, or a disk file. If you know where the problem area is, insert appropriate PRINT statements to print the variables that might shed some light on the problem. Don't forget to include some text in the statement so that you know what and where you are printing. If you combine PRINT and IF THEN statements, you can turn the printing on or off. For example, you can use a statement such as the following to see the value of the variable A:

```
50 IF DEBUG = 1 THEN PRINT "line 50, A =";A
```

To set the value of the variable DEBUG to one, insert the statement DEBUG = 1 in your program or stop your program with STOP or Ctrl-Break and issue the statement in direct mode. Setting DEBUG to zero turns off the printing; use this when you don't wish to see the variable's value.

You can use sound to examine the value of a variable without disturb-ing the contents of the screen or printer. The effectiveness, of course, depends on your ability to distinguish tones. Using the SOUND state-ment, convert the value you are interested in to a number between 37 and about 10,000 and use it for the frequency. The tone will then be proportional to the size of the number. If the value of the frequency gets out of range (37 to 32,767), an error will result. Clear memory and type and run the following short example. You will hear a slowly rising tone controlled by the increasing value of the loop variable. Note that Ctrl-Break will make it stop.

```
10 FOR I = 1 TO 10000 STEP 50
20 SOUND I+37,1
30 NEXT I
```

Summary: Debugging Your Program

Now that everyone around you is looking at you and wondering about the strange sounds coming out of your computer and printer, you can calmly explain that this has been an experiment in advanced debugging techniques. The art of debugging involves detective work; you gather information about the problem—here the operation of the code and the values of its variables—until you can discover its cause.

Because debugging is concerned with gathering and using information, the first step is to redirect screen printing so that it can be examined in detail. Screen printing can be redirected by pressing Ctrl-PrtSc or by invoking GW-BASIC as GWBASIC >LPT1:. Screen printing can also be redirected to a disk file by replacing the LPT1: with a file name.

The next step is to trace the thread of code execution to see which statements are being executed, and in what order. Do this with the TRON and TROFF statements. Although GW-BASIC lacks a built-in function that would move through a program one step at a time, the process can be implemented, at least in part, with an event-trapping subroutine using the ON TIMER(1) GOSUB statement.

While you are following the thread of your code's execution, you can also print the values of different variables to see whether they are correct. Insert PRINT, LPRINT, or PRINT# statements to send the values to the screen, the printer, or a disk file. These three statements can also be combined with an IF THEN statement (IF DEBUG=1 THEN PRINT) so you can turn the printing on and off by changing the value of DEBUG (setting it to 1 turns on printing, and 0 turns printting off).

You can stop execution of the code so that you can examine the variables in your code in more detail with a STOP statement or by pressing Ctrl-Break. You can then examine any variable in direct mode by printing its value. You can also change the value of a variable with a direct-mode assignment statement. As long as you have not changed any of the program statements, you can make your code continue from where it stopped by executing the CONT statement. If you have made changes, you can start the code running again with RUN or at a different location with a direct-mode GOTO statement.

You can use sound in addition to printing variables and messages to determine where you are in a program and what the variables are doing. The BEEP and SOUND statements will signal when you have reached a particular location or indicate the size of a value by the tone.

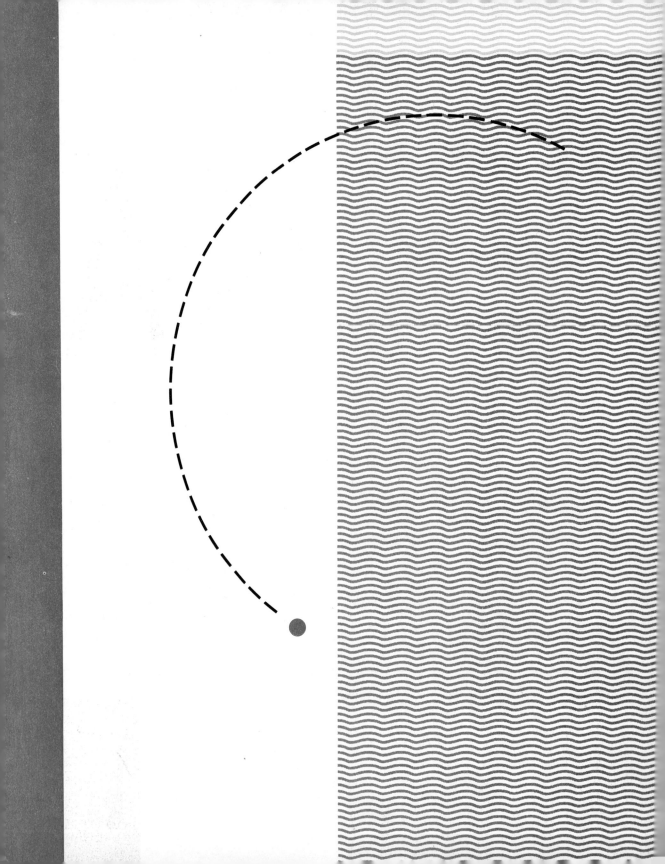

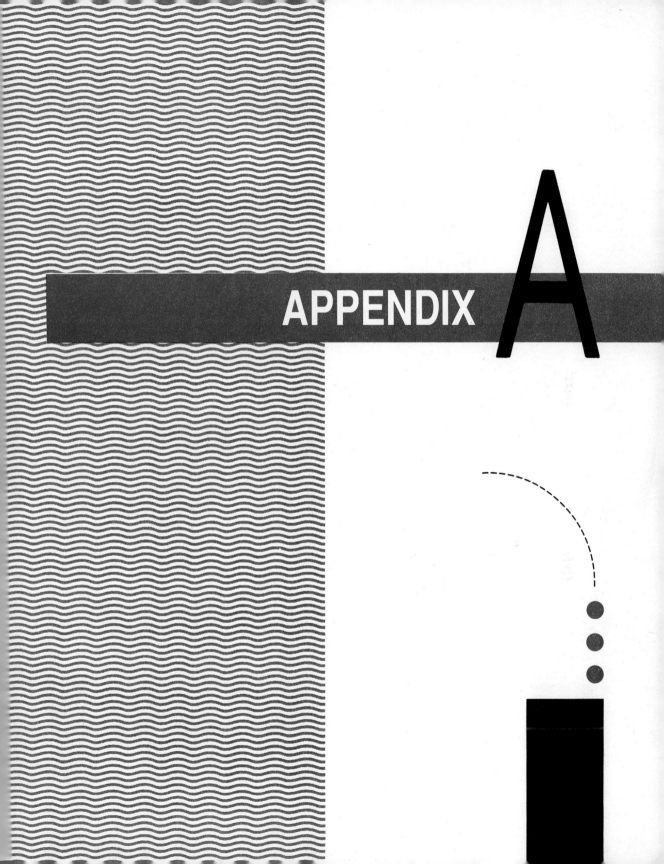

APPENDIX A

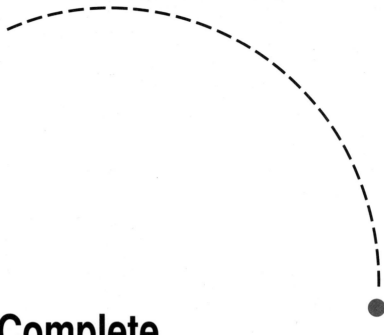

Complete
GW-BASIC Reference

This reference for GW-BASIC contains the invocation command used at the DOS prompt; the numeric, relational, and logical operators; and an alphabetic list of the functions and statements. The entries are presented in the following order:

- The name of the operator, statement, or function
- The syntax
- A description and usage
- A list of related entries or of chapters with more information.

The conventions used in the syntax statements are as follows: All the words and symbols that must be typed exactly as shown are in capital letters. Placeholders for variables or numbers are in italic. Several abbreviations are used in the variable names: *num* for number or number of, *len* for length, and *char* for characters. If a specific type of value or variable is required, the name will have the type suffix symbol appended to it: % for integer, ! for single-precision, # for double-precision, and $ for string. If no symbol is appended, any numeric type is allowed. Except when invoking GW-BASIC—and where specifically noted—numeric place holders can be replaced by numbers, numeric variables, or formulas that evaluate to numbers. String placeholders—also except where noted—can be replaced by quoted strings, string variables, or formulas that evaluate to strings. When you invoke GW-BASIC, you are operating at the DOS prompt, and the rules are different. Use actual values for numbers and strings rather than variables, and do not place quotation marks around strings.

Within the syntax, alternative items are separated with vertical lines, |, and enclosed by square brackets, [], if they are optional and by braces, { }, if they are not. Default values are the values the different options take if new ones are not given. To skip an item in an ordered list of items and use its previous or default value, insert a comma.

All *file_name$* placeholders can contain either a simple file name or a directory path and file name. If only a file name is used, the file is assumed to be in the default directory.

For example,

```
INPUT$(num_char[,[#]file_num])
```

Here, the statement name and the two parentheses, INPUT$(), are required. The integer *num_char* (number of characters) is required. The comma and the integer *file_num* are optional. The pound sign (#) is optional if you use *file_num*.

*I*nvoking GW-BASIC

```
GWBASIC[file_name$][<input_file$][[>]>output_file$]
[/F:num_files%][/I][/S:record_len%][/C:receive_buf_len%]
[/M:[mem_top%][,block_len%][/D]
```

Invoking GW-BASIC without any options or file names starts the interpreter and leaves it in direct mode. If the string *file_name$* is included, the program contained in that file is loaded and run. The file must be a BASIC program file created with the SAVE command or a text file containing a BASIC program. The file name must be a legal DOS file name and if the extension is omitted, it is assumed to be .BAS.

If the string *<input_file$* is included, the contents of the named text file are used as input to GW-BASIC just as though they were typed at the keyboard. If the string *>output_file$* or *>>output_file$* is used, anything printed to the screen by GW-BASIC (error messages, and so forth) and anything printed to the screen using a PRINT, PRINT USING, or WRITE statement is printed in that file. Using one greater than symbol causes a new file to be created. Using two greater than symbols causes the text to be appended to the end of an existing file.

The /F: flag and the integer *num_files%* determine the maximum number of files that can be open at any one time. If they are omitted, the default is three; the /I flag makes GW-BASIC statically allocate space for file operations. The default is to allocate the space dynamically when it is needed. The /S: flag and the integer *record_len%* set the maximum record length allowed for use with random-access files. The range is 1 through 32,767 bytes; the default value is 128 bytes. The /C: flag and the integer *receive_buf_len%* set the size of the receive buffer for serial communications (COM1:, COM2:). The range is 0 to 32,767 bytes, and a value of 0 disables serial communications. The default is 256 bytes for the receive buffer and 128 for the transmit buffer for each installed serial port.

The /M: switch and the integers *mem_top%* and *block_len%* set the highest location that GW-BASIC can use in memory and the maximum block size for use in allocating memory. GW-BASIC attempts to allocate 64K bytes (actually 65,536 bytes since 1K = 1024 bytes) of memory for data. You can reserve space for machine language segments of code by reducing the amount of memory that GW-BASIC can use. The default value is 65,535 bytes. The maximum allocation block size must be specified in multiples of 16 bytes and defaults to *mem_top%*. The /D switch sets the transcendental functions (SIN(), LOG(), and so forth) to return double-precision values. The default is single-precision values.

See also Chapters 1 and 2.

GW-BASIC Arithmetic Operators

The GW-BASIC arithmetic operators are listed here in the order of their precedence, that is, the order in which the different operations take place.

^   (Exponentiation)

number^exponent

The exponential operator calculates *number* raised to the power *exponent*. For example 10^3 returns 1,000.

-   (Unary Negation)

-number

The negation operator returns the negative of *number*.

*   (Multiplication)

number*number

The multiplication operator returns the product of two *number*s.

/   (Floating-Point Division)

dividend/divisor

The division operator calculates the floating point quotient of *dividend* by *divisor*.

\   (Integer Division)

dividend\divisor

The integer division operator calculates the integer quotient of *dividend* by *divisor*. The numbers *dividend* and *divisor* are rounded to integers before the division operation takes place. The resulting *quotient* is truncated to an integer before it is returned.

MOD   (Modulus)

dividend MOD *divisor*

The modulus operator returns the remainder of an integer division of *dividend* and *divisor*. For example,

7.2 MOD 4 returns 3	7.8 MOD 4 returns 0
–7.2 MOD 4 returns –3	–7.2 MOD –4 returns –3

+   (Addition)

number + number
string + string

The addition operator returns the sum of two values, or concatenates two strings.

-   (Subtraction)

number_1 – number_2

The subtraction operator returns the difference between *number_1* and *number_2*.

*G*W-BASIC *Relational Operators*

The relational operators are used to compare two expressions that can be either numeric values or strings. Strings are compared by using the ASCII codes for each character (see Figure 5.1). The results are either true (−1) or false (0).

= (Equality)

expression_a = expression_b

The equality operator returns true (−1) if *expression_a* and *expression_b* are the same and returns false (0) if they are different. Since the equal sign is also used in assignment statements, the context of the expression determines whether it is an assignment or an operator.

<> (Inequality)

expression_a <> expression_b

The inequality operator returns true (−1) if *expression_a* and *expression_b* are different; it returns false (0) if they are the same.

< (Less than)

expression_a < expression_b

The less than operator returns true (−1) if *expression_a* is less than *expression_b*; otherwise, it returns false (0).

> (Greater than)

expression_a > expression_b

The greater than operator returns true (−1) if *expression_a* is greater than *expression_b*; otherwise, it returns false (0).

<= (Less than or equal to)

expression_a <= expression_b

The less than or equal to operator returns true (−1) if *expression_a* is less than or equal to *expression_b*; otherwise, it returns false (0).

>= **(Greater than or equal to)**

expression_a >= expression_b

The greater than or equal to operator returns true (−1) if *expression_a* is greater than or equal to *expression_b*; otherwise, it returns false (0).

*G*W-BASIC *Logical Operators*

The logical operators perform Boolean arithmetic on integer values, and return logical results according to a truth table (see Table 6.2). The logical operators are used to combine other logical relations into more complex logical formulas.

The logical operators actually perform bitwise operations on two operands (one for the NOT operator). That is, each bit in the first operand (A) is paired with its equivalent bit in the second operand (B) to produce the value (0 or 1) of the equivalent bit in the result. Thus, logical operators can be used for bit masking operations as well as for combining logical expressions. The operands are truncated to 16-bit integers before the operation is carried out. For example A% AND &H00FF returns the lower byte of the integer A%, by changing the bits in the upper byte to zero.

NOT **(Logical negation)**

NOT *logical*

The logical negation operator reverses the sense of the logical value *logical*, true becomes false and false becomes true. For bit operations, zero becomes one and one becomes zero.

AND **(Logical AND)**

logical_a AND *logical_b*

The logical and operator returns true if both *logical_a* and *logical_b* are true; otherwise, it returns false. For bit operations, it returns a one for a bit if the corresponding bits in *logical_a* and *logical_b* are both one; otherwise, it returns a zero.

OR   (Logical OR)

logical_a OR *logical_b*

The logical or operator returns true if either *logical_a* or *logical_b* is true; otherwise, it returns false. For bit operations, it returns a one for a bit if the corresponding bit in either *logical_a* or *logical_b* is one; otherwise, it returns a zero.

XOR   (Logical exclusive OR)

logical_a XOR *logical_b*

The logical exclusive or operator returns true only if either (but not both) *logical_a* or *logical_b* is true; otherwise, it returns false. For bit operations, it returns a one for a bit if the corresponding bit in *logical_a* and *logical_b* are different (one and zero, or zero and one); otherwise, it returns a zero.

EQV   (Logical equivalence)

logical_a EQV *logical_b*

The logical equivalence operator returns true if *logical_a* and *logical_b* are the same (both true or both false); otherwise, it returns false. For bit operations, it returns a one for a bit if the corresponding bit in *logical_a* and *logical_b* are the same (one and one, or zero and zero); otherwise, it returns a zero.

IMP   (Logical implies)

logical_a IMP *logical_b*

The logical implies operator returns true if *logical_a* implies *logical_b*; otherwise, it returns false. For bit operations, it returns a one for a bit if a bit in *logical_a* implies the corresponding bit in *logical_b*; otherwise, it returns a zero.

GW-BASIC Functions and Statements

The rest of this appendix covers the GW-BASIC functions and statements. A function returns a value and can be used in a formula like any number or variable. A statement causes some action to take place and does not return a value (all GW-BASIC commands are statements).

ABS( )
Calculates absolute value

ABS(*number*)

The ABS() function calculates the absolute value of *number*. *See also* SGN().

ASC( )
Converts a character into an ASCII code

ASC(*string$*)

The ASC() function returns the ASCII code of the first character of *string$*. See Figure 5.1 for a list of the printable ASCII codes and characters. The unprintable control characters produce the following codes:

Code	Character	Code	Character
0	Null	12	Form feed
7	Bell	13	Carriage return
8	Backspace	28	Cursor right
9	Horizontal tab	29	Cursor left
10	Line feed	30	Cursor up
11	Home	31	Cursor down

Note that code 8 (backspace) produces a symbol rather than a backspace when printed with GW-BASIC.

See also CHR$().

ATN( )
Calculates the arctangent in radians

ATN(*number*)

The ATN() function calculates and returns the arctangent of *number*. The result is a number in radians that ranges between $-\pi/2$ and $+\pi/2$. The result is single-precision unless the /D switch is used when invoking GW-BASIC, which makes it double-precision. The arcsine and arccosine can be calculated using the following formulas:

Arcsine (ASIN())	ATN(*number*/SQR(1$-$*number*^2))
Arccosine (ACOS())	$\pi/2 - $ASIN(*number*)

See also COS(), SIN(), TAN().

AUTO
Automatically generates line numbers

AUTO[*starting_line_number%*|.][,*increment%*|,]

The AUTO command generates a new line number every time you press Enter, making program line-numbering very convenient. If a line already exists with that line number, a * is printed to the right of the line number on the screen. Line numbers are not entered or changed until you press Enter with the cursor still in the line. To quit AUTO mode, press Ctrl-Break or Ctrl-C. The line with the cursor when you press Ctrl-Break or Ctrl-C is not saved.

If *starting_line_number%* is included, automatic line numbering begins with that line. A period used for the starting line number causes the current line number to be used as the starting number. The current line is the last line printed on the screen with LIST or EDIT, or the last line edited with the editing keys. The default starting line number is ten.

The variable *increment%* sets the step between successive line numbers. The default for *increment%* is ten, unless you use only the comma, in which case it defaults to the previous value.

BEEP
Emits a system beep

    BEEP

The BEEP statement causes a quarter-second system beep at 800 Hz. This is equivalent to printing CHR$(7).
See also SOUND(), PLAY.

BLOAD
Loads a memory image disk file

    BLOAD *file_name$[,offset]*

The BLOAD statement loads into memory a binary memory image file saved with BSAVE, without translation or interpretation. This command is for loading machine language programs into memory. The string *file_name$* is a disk file containing the memory image. The file is loaded into the segment defined by the last DEF SEG statement. The number *offset* specifies the distance in bytes from the beginning of the current segment to the point where the image should start loading. The range of *offset* is 0 to 65,535. If *offset* is omitted, the number used is that used when it was saved with BSAVE.
See also BSAVE, CALL, DEF SEG, DEF USR, USR.

BSAVE
Saves a memory image to a disk file

    BSAVE *file_name$,offset,image_size*

The BSAVE statement stores a memory image in a disk file for later reloading with BLOAD. The string *file_name$* must contain a valid DOS file name to receive the image. The number *offset* is the distance in bytes into the segment (defined with DEF SEG) of the beginning of the image, and the number *image_size* is the size of the image in bytes. The range of values for both numbers is 0 to 65,535.

See also BLOAD, CALL, DEF SEG, DEF USR, USR.

CALL
Calls a machine language subroutine

CALL *offset*[(*variable*[,*variable*[,...]])]

The CALL statement executes a machine language subroutine. The number *offset* is the distance in bytes into the segment (defined with DEF SEG) of the beginning of the machine language subroutine. CALL executes a jump to that location and begins executing the code found there. The argument *variable*[,*variable*[,...]] is a list of the variables required by the subroutine and is delimited by commas.

See also BLOAD, BSAVE, DEF SEG, DEF USR, USR.

CDBL( )
Converts a value to double precision

CDBL(*number*)

The CDBL() function converts *number* to a double-precision number. This function is rarely needed, because the current version of GW-BASIC automatically converts numbers to double-precision when necessary.

See also CINT, CSNG.

CHAIN
Loads and runs another program

CHAIN[MERGE] *file_name$*[,[*start_line*]][,[ALL][,DELETE *l_num*[-[*l_num*]]]]]

The CHAIN statement deletes the current program, but not the variables, from memory. It then loads the program in the disk file specified by *file_name$* and begins executing it. Because the new program has access to the deleted program's variables, the two programs are chained together. If the MERGE option is used, the old program is not deleted and the program lines in *file_name$* are merged with those already in memory as if they had been typed at the keyboard. If the MERGE option is used, the program lines in *file_name$* must be ASCII text, such as a program saved with the SAVE command and the ,A switch.

If the optional number *start_line* is included, execution of the chained program starts at that line number. If it is omitted, execution starts at the first line in the program. The ALL option specifies that all the current program's variables are to be preserved and passed on to the chained program. If it is omitted, only those variables specified in a COMMON statement are preserved.

The DELETE option behaves exactly like placing a DELETE statement just before the CHAIN statement. The lines specified in the range are deleted before the chained program is loaded. Note that the DELETE statement is useful only with the MERGE option. The argument *l_num*[-[*l_num*]] is a range of line numbers to delete.

See also DELETE, LOAD, MERGE.

CHDIR
Changes the working directory

CHDIR *directory$*

The CHDIR command sets the working directories on different disk drives. The string *directory$* must be a valid directory path. A directory path consists of a disk letter, followed by a colon and a backslash. This is the root directory of the disk. Adding a list of directory names separated by backslashes moves the working directory to that directory. For example, entering CHDIR C:\SALES\LETTERS will make subdirectory LETTERS (in directory SALES on drive C) the working directory.

See also FILES, KILL, MKDIR, NAMD AS, RESET, RMDIR, SHELL.

CHR$( )
Converts an ASCII code into a character

CHR$(*code*)

The CHR$() function returns a one-character string containing the character that corresponds to the ASCII code in *code*. Figure 5.1 lists the printable ASCII codes and characters. The number *code* must be within the range 0 to 255. Codes 0 through 31 are control characters, although many of them do produce symbols on the screen or a PC-compatible printer. The following codes produce some of the unprintable control characters:

Code	Character	Code	Character
0	Null	12	Form feed
7	Bell	13	Carriage return
8	Backspace	28	Cursor right
9	Horizontal tab	29	Cursor left
10	Line feed	30	Cursor up
11	Home	31	Cursor down

Note that instead of producing a backspace, code 8 (backspace) produces a symbol when printed with GW-BASIC.

See also ASC().

CINT( )
Rounds to the closest integer

CINT(*number*)

The CINT() function converts the single- or double-precision value *number* into an integer by rounding it to the closest integer. For example,

CINT(4.5) returns 5   CINT(−4.5) returns −5

CINT(4.4) returns 4   CINT(−4.4) returns −4

See also CDBL(), CSNG(), FIX(), INT().

CIRCLE

Draws a circle, ellipse or arc

CIRCLE(*center_x,center_y*),*radius*[,[*line_color*][,
[*start_angle*],[*stop_angle*][,*aspect_ratio*]]]

The CIRCLE statement draws a circle, ellipse, or arc on the screen.
The numbers *center_x*, and *center_y* are the *x* and *y* coordinates of the
center of the circle or ellipse, and *radius* is the radius of the circle
or the major axis of the ellipse. The coordinates can be in either screen or
user coordinates, depending on the last call to the WINDOW statement.
Screen coordinates (those that are built into the system) are in pixels; the
origin is in the upper-left corner. The range depends on both the monitor
and the screen mode set with the SCREEN statement. User coordinates
are defined with the WINDOW statement, which maps them onto the
physical screen coordinates.

The optional number *line_color* determines which color to draw the circle
or ellipse. The allowed values are determined by the screen mode set with
the SCREEN statement and the current palette set with the COLOR statement. If *line_color* is omitted, the current foreground color is used.

The two optional numbers *start_angle* and *stop_angle* are the starting
and ending angles for drawing an arc. Drawing proceeds counterclock-
wise, and angle 0 is at 3 o'clock. The angles are in radians (calculated by
multiplying the degrees in the angle by π divided by 180) and must be in
the range -2π through 2π. If either angle is negative, a line is drawn
from the center of the circle to that end of the arc. If both angles are negative, both radii are shown and you get a pie-slice-shaped object. (If your
angles are obtuse enough, you will have a pie with a missing piece.)

The optional number *aspect_ratio* is used to create an ellipse, with
radius as the length of the major (long) axis. Values of *aspect_ratio* equal
to one create a circle. Values greater than one create an ellipse with the
long axis in the vertical direction, and values less than one have the long
axis in the horizontal direction.

See also COLOR, LINE, PSET(), SCREEN, VIEW, WINDOW.

CLEAR
Clears all memory except program memory

CLEAR [,[*mem_top*][,*stack_len*]]

The CLEAR statement clears everything but the program from memory. It clears all variables, including those in COMMON statements; it closes all files, and it turns off all trapping. If the optional number *mem_top* is used, it specifies the upper limit of memory, in bytes, that GW-BASIC can use. This protects all memory above that number through the end of the 65,535-byte (64K byte) segment for other uses, such as machine language programs. The default is the whole 64K-byte segment, unless it has been restricted with the /M: switch when invoking GW-BASIC.

The second optional number *stack_len* specifies the size of stack space. Stack space is where the return addresses for subroutines and user-defined functions are stored. The default size is 512 bytes or one-eighth of available memory, whichever is smaller.

See also the beginning of this Appendix, *Invoking GW-BASIC*; NEW.

CLOSE
Closes any open disk files

CLOSE [[#]*file_num*[,[#]*file_num*[...]]]

The CLOSE statement closes some or all of the communications paths created with the OPEN statement. While most communications paths are to disk files, they can be to the screen, keyboard, printer, or serial ports. If CLOSE is used without any arguments, all open files are closed. If one or more of the optional *file_num* file numbers (assigned with the OPEN statement) are used, only those files are closed, and the file numbers are released for use in another OPEN statement.

See also CLEAR, END, OPEN, RESET.

CLS
Clears the screen

CLS [*clear_what*]

The CLS statement clears the screen. The argument *clear_what* is used to clear selective parts of the screen.

clear_what	**Part of screen to clear**
0	Everything
1	Graphics viewport only
2	Text window only

If CLS is given without an argument, it clears the graphics viewport if that is active (see VIEW), or the text window if it is not (see VIEW PRINT). *See also* SCREEN, VIEW, VIEW PRINT, WIDTH.

COLOR
Selects the display colors from the palette

COLOR[*foreground_color*][,[*background_color*][,*border_color*]]
COLOR[*background_color*][,[*palette*]]

The COLOR statement is used to select the screen colors from the current palette of colors available for the monitor and screen mode selected. The arguments that can be given depend on the current display state set with the SCREEN statement. The optional number *foreground_color* selects the color for both text and graphics on the screen. The optional number *background_color* selects the color for the background. The optional number *border_color* sets the color of a border around the edge of the screen. The optional number *palette* selects a palette of colors to use for the foreground colors of graphics.

Color arguments in GW-BASIC drawing commands are actually numeric codes, called attributes, that are linked to actual colors using the SCREEN and PALETTE statements. The COLOR statement and other drawing statements such as CIRCLE select an attribute, and get the color linked to that attribute.

Screen mode 0 is text mode, with either 40 or 80 columns of text and 25 rows; the number of columns is set with the WIDTH statement. In this mode, you can set the text color, the background color, and the border color, although setting a border color has no effect on some EGA monitors. The foreground color must be in the range of 0 to 31, with the colors for 0 to 15 given below. Adding 16 to the numbers of the first

15 colors gives blinking text in the same color. For example a foreground color of 5 gives magenta while a foreground color of 21 (5 + 16) gives blinking magenta. The default is 7 (white). The background color must be in the range of 0 to 7, with the 0 (black) as the default. The border color must be in the range 0 to 15; 0 is the default.

The attributes and associated colors for screen modes 0, 7, 8, and 9 are listed below.

Attribute	Color
0	Black
1	Blue
2	Green
3	Cyan
4	Red
5	Magenta
6	Brown
7	White
8	Gray
9	Light blue
10	Light green
11	Light cyan
12	Light red
13	Light magenta
14	Yellow
15	Intense white

Screen mode 1 is a medium-resolution graphics mode in which you can set the background color and the palette of foreground colors. The background color must be in the range 0 to 7; 0 (black) is the default. There are three palettes to choose from, each containing three colors, numbered 1, 2, and 3. The default palette is in force when the SCREEN 1 statement is executed. The even and odd palettes are put in force with the COLOR statement by using 0 (or any even number) or 1 (or any odd number) for the *palette* argument. The default colors produced by the palettes in screen mode 1 on a color display are as follows:

Palette	Attribute	Color Number	Color
0 (even)	0	0	Black
0 (even)	1	2	Green
0 (even)	2	4	Red
0 (even)	3	6	Brown
1 (odd)	0	0	Black
1 (odd)	1	3	Cyan
1 (odd)	2	5	Magenta
1 (odd)	3	7	White
Default	0	0	Black
Default	1	11	Light cyan
Default	2	13	Light magenta
Default	3	15	Intense white

Screen mode 2, a high-resolution graphics mode, supports only two colors. The only attributes available in this mode are 0 (black) and 1 (intense white). The COLOR statement generates an error if executed in this mode.

Screen modes 7 and 8, which are enhanced versions of modes 1 and 2 and are for EGA monitors only, support the full 16 colors. Only the *foreground_color* and *background_color* arguments can be specified. The foreground must be in the range 0 to 15, with 15 (intense white) the default. The background must be in the range 0 to 7, with 0 (black) the default.

Screen mode 9 is an enhanced resolution graphics mode for EGA monitors only. It has up to 64 colors assignable to 4 attributes if the EGA has 64K of memory, or to 16 attributes if it has more than 64K of memory. Colors are assigned to the attributes using the PALETTE statement, and selected as with modes 7 and 8. The default palette of 16 colors is the same as that for the other modes.

Screen mode 10 is for an EGA attached to a monochrome monitor, and has 9 pseudo-colors numbered 0 through 8 assignable to 4 attributes. The pseudocolors in screen mode 10 are

Number	Pseudocolor
0	Black
1	Blink—black to white
2	Blink—black to intense white
3	Blink—white to black
4	White
5	Blink—white to intense white
6	Blink—intense white to black
7	Blink—intense white to white
8	Intense white

The four default pseudocolors of screen mode 10 are shown below.

Attribute	Pseudocolor
0	Black
1	White
2	Blink
3	Intense white

If you have a monochrome display and parallel printer adapter, the attributes give the following colors:

Attribute	Color
0	Black
1	White, underlined
2	White
3	White
4	White

Attribute	Color
5	White
6	White
7	White
8	Black
9	Intense white, underlined
10	Intense white
11	Intense white
12	Intense white
13	Intense white
14	Intense white
15	Intense white

See also PALETTE, SCREEN.

COM( ) ON|OFF|STOP
Enables/disables trapping the serial ports

COM(*com_port*) ON|OFF|STOP

The COM() ON statement turns on trapping activity at the serial ports, monitoring either or both for incoming data. Use an ON COM() GOSUB statement to set the subroutine to branch to whenever communications events occur at the indicated serial port. Set the port to be watched with the number *com_port*, which can have a value of 1 or 2 (for serial port COM1 or COM2). Turning on communications event trapping causes GW-BASIC to check the port between the execution of program statements. If communications is detected, the program stops current execution and branches to the set subroutine.

The COM() OFF statement disables communications event trapping, and the port monitoring stops. Communications that arrive with event trapping off will be lost. While the COM() STOP statement disables event trapping, it does not lose communications events. Data that arrive with this statement in force are saved until a COM() ON statement is executed. A COM() STOP is automatically executed whenever a communications event trap takes place, and a COM() ON is automatically executed when you return from the trap subroutine unless a COM() OFF is executed in the trap subroutine.

See also ON COM() GOSUB.

COMMON
Saves variables for a chained program

COMMON *variable_name*[[,*variable_name*][,...]]

The COMMON statement passes the variables *variable_name* to a chained program. When creating an overlay program using the CHAIN statement, you can save all the variables using the ALL option in that statement, or you can select specific variables to save using the COMMON statement. There can be more than one COMMON statement in a program, and all of them will be in force; however, the same variable cannot appear again.

See also CHAIN, MERGE.

CONT
Continues executing a program after a break

CONT

The CONT statement restarts a stopped program. A GW-BASIC program is stopped using a STOP statement or by pressing Ctrl-Break. After a program is stopped, the variables are examined using PRINT statements in direct mode. As long as none of the program lines have been changed, the program can be restarted by executing the CONT statement. A program that has been stopped using the END statement cannot be restarted, and must be rerun with the RUN statement. You can use a GOTO statement in direct mode to restart execution at a specified line.

See also Chapter 9, END, STOP.

COS( )
Calculates the cosine of an angle in radians

COS(*angle*)

The COS() function calculates the single-precision cosine of *angle*. The number *angle* must be in radians. To convert from degrees to radians, multiply degrees by π/180. To get double-precision values of the cosine, use the /D switch when invoking GW-BASIC.

See also ATN(), SIN(), TAN().

CSNG( )

Converts a value to single-precision

CSNG(*number*)

The CSNG() function converts *number* to single-precision. This function is used mostly for compatibility with older versions of BASIC that required all the variables in a statement to be of the same type. GW-BASIC automatically converts any variables when necessary.

See also CDBL(), CINT().

CSRLIN

Gets the number of the row containing the cursor

CSRLIN

The CSRLIN function returns the number of the screen row containing the cursor. The rows are counted from the top of the screen, with the top row as number 1 and the bottom row as number 25.

See also POS(), LOCATE.

CVD( )

Converts an eight-byte string into a double-precision number

CVD(*eight_bytes$*)

The CVD() function converts the double-precision binary numeric value stored in an eight-byte string back into a double-precision number. It is used in random-access files with strings that were converted from numbers with the MKD$() function.

See also Chapter 8, CVI(), CVS(), FIELD, LSET, MKD$(), MKI$(), MKS$(), OPEN.

CVI( )
Converts a two-byte string into an integer

CVI(*two_bytes$*)

The CVI() function converts the integer binary numeric value stored in a two-byte string into an integer. You use it with strings that were converted from integers with the MKI$() function in random-access files.

See also Chapter 8, CVD(), CVS(), FIELD, LSET, MKD$(), MKI$(), MKS$(), OPEN.

CVS( )
Converts a four-byte string into a single-precision number

CVS(*four_bytes$*)

The CVS() function is used in a random access file to convert the single-precision binary numeric value in a four-byte string back to a single-precision number. The function MKS$() is used to store single-precision numbers in strings.

See also Chapter 8, CVD(), CVI(), FIELD, LSET, MKD$(), MKI$(), MKS$(), OPEN, RSET.

DATA
Makes an internal data statement

DATA *data_value*[[,*data_value*][,...]]

The DATA statement defines a list of internal data values. Lists of data can be stored within a program and read with a READ statement. The values *data_value* can be integers, single- and double-precision numbers, or strings, and must be separated by commas. Strings that contain commas, colons, leading spaces, or trailing spaces must be surrounded with double quotation marks. A DATA statement can be reread by executing a RESTORE statement; this causes the READ statement to start again at the first or at a selected DATA statement. Any number of DATA statements can be in a program; they do not have to be contiguous. Reading starts with the lowest-numbered DATA statement and continues to the highest-numbered one.

See also READ, RESTORE.

DATE$
Sets or Gets the current date

DATE$

The DATE$ function returns a ten-character string containing the current date as stored in the system clock. The format of the string is the same as the first example for the DATE$ statement below. Months and days with values less than 10 have a leading 0 (for example, 03 for March).

DATE$ = *new_date_string$*

This DATE$ statement changes the current date as stored in the system clock. To set the date, the string variable *new_date_string$* must contain the new date in one of the following (month-day-year) forms; anything else will cause an error.

12-25-1990   12/25/1990   12-25-90   12/25/90

See also TIME$.

DEF FN
Defines a user function

DEF FN*name*[(*argument*[,*argument*][,...]])] = *formula*

The DEF FN statement is used to create one-line user-defined functions. The function name FN*name* must be a legal variable name beginning with the characters FN and must be of the correct type for the value that will be returned by the formula. To force the type of the result, insert the desired suffix (% for integer, ! for single-precision [the default], # for double-precision, and $ for string) after the function name. The optional arguments *argument* are parameters, that is, the values used in the *formula*, and are supplied whenever the function is called. The *argument* type must be the same as that of the value passed to it. The arguments are completely local to the function, and other variables in a program with the same name will have no effect on them. Any other variables in the formula that are not included as arguments will take on their global values when the function is executed. The DEF FN statement must appear before the function is used.

Once it is defined, a user-defined function is used like any other function in GW-BASIC. Insert the function name followed by parentheses and arguments wherever the result of the function is needed. For example, the arcsine function could be defined with DEF FNASIN(SINX) = ATN(SINX/SQR(1–SINX^2)) and used in some formula as A = FNASIN(0.5). The value of the variable SINX is defined only in the definition and will have no effect on some other variable named SINX elsewhere in the program.

See also Chapter 7, GOSUB.

DEF SEG
Sets the current segment address

DEF SEG [[=]*segment_address*]

The DEF SEG statement sets the segment address for use by the BLOAD, BSAVE, CALL, PEEK, POKE and USR statements. All these statements are used for directly extracting or setting the actual binary values stored in memory. Memory in the INTEL 80xx and 80xxx series of microprocessors is accessed in 64K-byte segments. The DEF SEG statement marks the location in memory of the beginning of the segment used by the statements, each of which then uses an offset into that segment where it will operate. The actual physical address accessed in memory is the sum of the segment address times 16, plus the offset.

If the DEF SEG statement is given without an argument, the segment is set to the beginning of GW-BASIC's data segment. The numeric argument *segment_address* must contain a value between 0 and 65,535. It represents the physical address of the beginning of the segment divided by 16 (the segment address is shifted left by 4 bits before it is combined with the offset). This results in physical addresses up to 1,048,560 bytes (65,535×16) that can be defined as the beginning of a segment. Physical memory can extend to 655,350 bytes, depending on how much memory you have installed, with the system ROMs and screen buffers located above that. For example, the start of the screen buffer for a color graphics display is located at 753,664 bytes (&HB80000 in hexadecimal). To set the start of the segment to the beginning of the screen buffer, use DEF SEG = 47104 (DEF SEG = &HB800 in hexadecimal).

See also BLOAD, BSAVE, CALL, PEEK, POKE, USR.

DEF USR
Sets the starting address for a USR function

DEF USR[*num*] = *offset_address*

The DEF USR statement defines the offset into the current segment for one of the USR machine language functions. There are ten USR functions set with the number *num*, named USR0 through USR9. The number *offset_address* is the offset, in bytes, into the current segment (set with the DEF SEG statement) to where the machine language subroutine starts. The subroutine can then be called with the USR() function. This statement is used primarily for compatibility with older versions of BASIC.

See also CALL, DEF SEG, USR().

DEFDBL
Declares variables as double-precision numbers

DEFDBL *letter*[,*letter*|-*letter*]...

The DEFDBL function defines all variables beginning with the letter *letter* to be double-precision numbers. The arguments can be a list of letters separated by commas or a range of letters separated by hyphens. DEFDBL A,B,D-G would define all variables starting with the letters A, B, D, E, F, and G as double-precision. You can override the definition by using a different variable type suffix.

See also Chapter 4.

DEFINT
Declares variables as integers

DEFINT *letter*[,*letter*|-*letter*]...

The DEFINT function defines all variables beginning with the letter *letter* to be integers. The arguments can be a list of letters separated by commas or a range of letters separated by hyphens. DEFDBL A,W,F-L would define all variables starting with the letters A, W, F, G, H, I, J, K, and L as integers. You can override the definition by using a different variable type suffix.

See also Chapter 4.

DEFSNG
Declares variables as single-precision numbers

> DEFSNG *letter*[,*letter*|-*letter*]...

The DEFSNG function defines all variables beginning with the letter *letter* to be single-precision numbers. The arguments can be a list of letters separated by commas or a range of letters separated by hyphens. DEFSNG H,J,N-P would define all variables starting with the letters H, I, J, N, and P as single-precision. You can override the definition by using a different variable type suffix.

See also Chapter 4.

DEFSTR
Declares variables as strings

> DEFSTR *letter*[,*letter*|-*letter*]...

The DEFSTR function defines all variables beginning with the letter *letter* to be strings. The arguments can be a list of letters separated by commas or a range of letters separated by hyphens. DEFSTR A,C,T-V would define all variables starting with the letters A, C, T, U, and V as strings. You can override the definition by using a different variable type suffix.

See also Chapter 4.

DELETE
Deletes program lines

> DELETE [-]*line_num*[-|-*line_num*]

The DELETE statement removes the specified lines from memory. If only the first line number *line_num* is given, only that line is deleted. If both line numbers are given separated by a hyphen, those line numbers and all the lines between them are deleted. If only the first line number and a hyphen are used, that program line and all program lines with greater line numbers are deleted. Use a single *line_num* preceded by a hyphen to delete all lines up to and including the one specified (DELETE -10, for example).

See also NEW, CLEAR, RENUM.

DIM
Defines array variables

DIM
array_name(sub%[[,sub%][,...]])[,array_name(sub%[[,sub%][,...]])][,...]

The DIM statement is used to set the dimensions of array variables. The strings *array_name* are standard GW-BASIC variable names. Insert a data type suffix (% for integer, ! for single-precision (the default), # for double-precision, and $ for string) between the name and the following parenthesis when it is necessary to set the variable type. The integers *sub%* specify the maximum number of elements in that dimension of the array. The actual number of elements in a dimension is one more than that maximum number since array elements start at zero (unless you change it to one with the OPTION BASE statement). There can be up to 255 dimensions in each array and 32,767 elements in each dimension. It is not necessary to define arrays that use fewer than four dimensions and fewer than 11 elements in a dimension with the DIM statement; the process is automatic the first time they are used.

See also Chapter 4, OPTION BASE.

DRAW
Draws a Graphics Macro Language object

DRAW *gml_picture_string$*

The DRAW statement is used to draw an object using the Graphics Macro Language (GML), which is a series of one-letter commands that are followed by arguments. These commands are stored in the string variable *gml_picture_string$*. The arguments are either integer constants like 30 or variable names prefaced by an equal sign and followed by a semicolon, such as *=variable_name;*. The commands can be separated by semicolons. Only if an argument contains a variable name is the semicolon required, to ensure that the characters in the name are not mistaken for commands.

Movement with the commands is relative to the current position by the number of pixels specified in the argument. If a scale factor has been specified with the S command, the movement is scaled by that factor. See the SCREEN command for the coordinate ranges (numbers of pixels in each direction) for the various screen modes. The origin of the coordinates is the upper-left corner. The commands are as follows:

Command	Effect
U*pixels*;	Draws *pixels* upward.
D*pixels*;	Draws *pixels* downward.
L*pixels*;	Draws *pixels* to the left.
R*pixels*;	Draws *pixels* to the right.
E*pixels*;	Draws *pixels* diagonally up and to the right.
F*pixels*;	Draws *pixels* diagonally down and to the right.
G*pixels*;	Draws *pixels* diagonally down and to the left.
H*pixels*;	Draws *pixels* diagonally up and to the left.
M*x_pixels,y_pixels*;	Draws a line to the absolute screen location *x_pixels, y_pixels* from the current point.
M±*x_pixels,±y_pixels*;	Draws a line to the point ±*x_pixels*, ±*y_pixels* relative to the current position.
B	Preface to a drawing command; makes it move without drawing.
N	Preface to a drawing command; makes it return to the starting location after drawing.

Command	Effect
A*angle*;	Sets the drawing angle, where *angle* is 0 (0 degrees), 1 (90 degrees), 2 (180 degrees), or 3 (270 degrees). Figures rotated to 90 or 180 degrees will be scaled by the standard aspect ratio of 4/3 so they will look the same rotated as they do unrotated.
TA*degrees*;	Rotates by degrees from the current position—clockwise if the angle is less than zero, counterclockwise if it is greater than zero. The argument *degrees* can range from 360 to 360.
C*color_number*,	Sets the color to the *color_number* attribute. See the COLOR command for the valid attributes.
S*scale_factor*,	Sets the scale factor for drawing. The argument *scale_factor* ranges from 1 to 255 and is 4 times the number of pixels to move. The default factor is 4.
X*gml_string$*;	Executes GML commands in another string variable *gml_string$* and returns(this is similar to a subroutine call).
P*color_number*, *outline_color*,	Paints (fills in) the region bounded by the *outline_color* attribute using the color defined by the *color_number* attribute. This follows the same rules as the PAINT statement.

See also COLOR, PAINT, SCREEN.

EDIT
Extracts a program line for editing

EDIT *line_number*|.

The EDIT statement extracts a line for editing. The command first prints the line *line_number*, then places the cursor at the beginning of the line so that you can edit it. If you use the period instead of the line number, the current line—the last line listed with the LIST command or edited with EDIT—is displayed.

See also Chapter 2, LIST.

END

Ends a program and closes all files

    END

The END statement ends a program and closes all files. (Use STOP to stop a program with the files open so that it can be restarted with the CONT statement.) A program stopped with an END statement cannot be restarted; it can be rerun only with a RUN statement. An END statement is necessary only when you want to end a program before you reach the highest-numbered statement. GW-BASIC automatically ends a program when it reaches the last statement.

See also STOP, CONT.

ENVIRON

Adds or changes GW-BASIC's environment string table

    ENVIRON *environ_string$*

The ENVIRON statement is used to set or to add new values in GW-BASIC's environment string table. Initially, the table is equivalent to the DOS environment string table. GW-BASIC's table is separate from DOS's, so any changes will disappear when you quit GW-BASIC. Make changes in or add environment variables by inserting them in the string *environ_string$*. The format for *environ_string$* is *variable_name=value*, where *variable_name* is the name of the environment variable to change or add and *value* is its value. To remove a variable, make *value* equal to a semicolon or the null string. Environment variables are used to change the environment or to send messages to subprocesses started with the SHELL command. The ENVIRON$() function is used to read the contents of the environment string table.

See also ENVIRON$(), the SET command in DOS.

ENVIRON$
Gets strings from GW-BASIC's environment string table

ENVIRON$(*variable_name$|variable_num*)

The ENVIRON$() function returns environment strings from GW-BASIC's environment string table. The string *variable_name$* consists of the name of the variable whose environment string you want. If you use the number *variable_num* instead, GW-BASIC counts down from the top of the list of environment variables by *variable_num* strings, and returns that string. GW-BASIC's environment string table is initially the same as DOS's. Environment strings are created or changed with the ENVIRON statement.

See also ENVIRON, SHELL, the SET command in DOS.

EOF( )
Checks for the end-of-file

EOF(*file_num*)

The EOF() function checks for the end-of-file mark in disk or communications files. The number *file_num* is the file number assigned to the file with the OPEN statement. For a sequential file, EOF() returns −1 (true) if the next record is the end-of-file; otherwise it returns 0 (false). For a random-access file, EOF() returns −1 (true) only if the file buffer is empty (for example, after executing a GET for a record beyond the end-of-file). For a communications path, EOF() returns −1 (true) only if the communications buffer is empty.

See also INPUT#, OPEN.

ERASE
Deletes array variables from memory

ERASE *array_variable*[[,*array_variable*[,...]]

The ERASE statement removes array variables from memory so that the memory can be reused. The arguments are the names of the array variables to erase from memory.

See also CLEAR, DIM, NEW.

ERDEV
Gets a device error number

ERDEV

The ERDEV function returns the device error number. (Devices in the DOS system usually return errors using interrupt &H24.) ERDEV returns a two-byte integer with the error number in the lower eight bits and the upper eight bits of the device header attributes in the upper eight bits. To extract the upper and lower bytes of ERDEV, mask it with &HFF00 and &H00FF using the AND operator. If you attempt to use a printer that is not online, you'll get a device error. To get the error number print ERDEV AND &H00FF, which returns 10.

See also ERDEV$, ERR, ERL, ERROR, EXTERR, ON ERROR GOTO.

ERDEV$
Gets the name of the device with an error

ERDEV$

The ERDEV$ function returns an eight-character string containing the name of the device causing an error. If you attempt to use a printer that is not online, you'll get a device error; ERDEV$ will give you the string LPT1:.

See also ERDEV, ERR, ERL, ERROR, EXTERR, ON ERROR GOTO.

ERL
Gets the line number that caused the last GW-BASIC error

ERL

The ERL function returns the program line number for the most recent GW-BASIC error. This function is usually used along with the ERR function in an error-trapping subroutine defined with the ON ERROR GOTO statement.

See also ERDEV, ERDEV$, ERR, ERROR, EXTERR, ON ERROR GOTO.

ERR
Gets the error code for the last GW-BASIC error

ERR

The ERR function returns the error number for the most recent GW-BASIC error. Use this function along with the ERL function in an error-trapping subroutine that has been defined with the ON ERROR GOTO statement.

See also Appendix B, ERDEV, ERDEV$, ERL, ERROR, EXTERR, ON ERROR GOTO.

ERROR
Simulates a GW-BASIC program error

ERROR *error_number*

The ERROR statement simulates a GW-BASIC error to test error-trapping routines. The number *error_number* must be in the range 1 to 254. If the error number matches any of GW-BASIC's error codes (Appendix B), that error will be simulated and the relevant error message printed. (You can also define your own error code.)

See also ERDEV, ERDEV$, ERL, ERR, EXTERR, ON ERROR GOTO.

EXP( )
Calculates the exponent (base e) of a number

EXP(*number*)

The EXP() function returns the single-precision exponent of *number*. That is, it calculates **e**, the base of the natural logarithm, raised to the power *number*. To get double-precision results, use the /D switch when invoking GW-BASIC.

See also LOG().

EXTERR
Gets extended error information from DOS

EXTERR(*code*)

For versions of DOS later than 3.0, the EXTERR() function returns extended error codes from the operating system. The number *code* must be in the range zero through three. The following values are returned by the codes:

Code	Value
0	Extended error code
1	Extended error class
2	Extended error suggested action
3	Extended error locus

You will need a copy of the *MS-DOS Programmer's Reference* for version 3.0 or later to decipher the values returned.

See also ERDEV, ERDEV$, ERL, ERR, ERROR, ON ERROR GOTO.

FIELD
Defines the contents of a record buffer

FIELD[#]*file_num,bytes* AS *variable*[,*bytes* AS *variable*][,...]

The FIELD statement is used to break the record buffer for random-access files into fields and to name those fields with string variables. The number *file_number* is the file number assigned to the file with the OPEN statement, and the length of the record buffer is defined in the OPEN statement with the LEN=*buffer_length* option. Fields in the record buffer are defined, starting from the left, with the construct *bytes* AS *variable*, which assigns the number of bytes *bytes* to the variable *variable*. Subsequent constructs assign the next *bytes* to the next *variable* until the whole record buffer is accounted for.

Variables assigned this way are not normal string variables but fixed width strings. To change the values of these variables, you must use the LSET and RSET statements. If you use one in a normal assignment statement, a LET statement, or any of the INPUT statements, the string variable will be redefined as a standard string variable and will no longer point to the record buffer. To store numeric values in the record buffer, use the MKI$(), MKS$(), and MKD$() functions. To retrieve numeric values from the record buffer, use the CVI(), CVS(), and CVD() functions.

See also Chapter 8, CVD(), CVI(), CVS(), LSET, MKD$(), MKI$(), MKS$(), OPEN, RSET.

FILES
Lists the files in the current directory

    FILES [*directory_path$*]

The FILES statement lists all the files in the current directory or the directory specified by *directory_path$*. Wildcards are allowed in the directory path in the same manner as in DOS: The ? wildcard stands for any single character, and the * stands for any number of characters.

See also CHDIR, KILL, MKDIR, NAME AS, RESET, RMDIR.

FIX( )
Truncates a number to an integer

    FIX(*number*)

The FIX() function converts the single- or double-precision number *number* into an integer by truncating all digits at the right of the decimal. For example,

    FIX(4.6) returns 4   FIX(-4.6) returns -4

    FIX(4.4) returns 4   FIX(-4.4) returns -4

See also CDBL(), CINT(), CSNG(), INT().

FOR/NEXT
Defines a counted loop

    FOR *loop_counter* = *start_num* TO *end_num* [STEP *step_num*]

NEXT [*loop_counter*][,*loop_counter*]

The FOR/NEXT statements define a counted loop. The statements between the FOR and the NEXT statements are executed the number of times specified in the FOR statement. The *loop_counter* keeps track of the number of times the loop has been executed. When the FOR statement is encountered, the loop counter is set to the value *start_num*. If it is equal to or less than *end_num* the statements between the FOR and NEXT statements are executed. When the NEXT statement is encountered, *step_num* is added to the loop counter. If it is equal to or less than *end_num* the loop is calculated again; otherwise, the loop ends and execution continues with the statement after the NEXT statement. If the step is omitted, it defaults to one. If *step_num* is negative, the loop will count down from *start_num* to *end_num*. The loop counter must be equal to or greater than *end_num* for the loop to execute.

Multiple loops can be nested within each other. If they have the same end point, a single NEXT statement will terminate them all (the code will be clearer, however, if each FOR has its NEXT). The innermost loop starts last and will finish first, and the outermost loop will finish last.

See also Chapter 6, WHILE/WEND.

FRE

Gets the amount of available string memory

FRE(*dummy*)

The FRE() function returns the amount of string memory available. The argument *dummy* is a dummy argument that can be anything, including a null string (FRE("")). It also initiates garbage collection before determining the amount of free string memory. *Garbage collection* is the removal of deleted strings and compaction of the remaining strings to produce the largest possible continuous area of free space.

See also CLEAR, ERASE, NEW.

GET
Copies part of the screen image into a variable

GET (*x_ul,y_ul*)-(*x_lr,y_lr*),*graphics_array*()

The graphics version of the GET statement is used to copy a piece of a screen image and store it in an array. (The PUT statement is used to copy an image from the array variable and put it back on the screen.) The image bounded by the rectangle specified by the *x*, *y* coordinates of the upper-left corner (*x_ul,y_ul*) and the lower-right corner (*x_lr,y_lr*) is copied into the numeric array *graphics_array()*. The rectangle coordinates (*x_ul,y_ul*)-(*x_lr,y_lr*) can be either screen or user units set with the WINDOW statement. (See the LINE statement with the ,B option for an explanation of the options available for selecting the rectangle.) The array can be any numeric array that has been dimensioned large enough to hold the graphic image. To find the size, use the following formula:

$$bytes = 4 + INT ((pix\_wide \times bits\_deep + 7)/8) \times pix\_tall$$

Here, *pix_wide* is the width of the image in pixels; it is the difference between *x_ul* and *x_lr*. The number *pix_tall* is the height of the image in pixels and is the difference between *y_ul* and *y_lr*. Finally, *bits_deep* is the number of bits per pixel. The number of bits per pixel is determined by the number of colors possible on-screen at any one time, which is set with the SCREEN statement. The result is in bytes; to find the length of an array needed, divide by 2 if you use an integer array, by 4 if you use a single-precision array, or by 8 if you use a double-precision array.

See also LINE, PUT, SCREEN, WINDOW.

GET
Reads a disk record into a record buffer

GET[#]*file_num*[,*record_num*]

The file version of the GET statement reads a record from a random-access disk file into the record buffer. (The PUT statement puts the contents of the record buffer into the record on the disk.) The number *file_num* is the file number assigned to the file when it was opened with the OPEN statement. The number *record_num* is the record number of the record on disk to get. Records in the file are numbered sequentially, starting with the first record as number 1, and the number can be as high as 4,294,967,295. If the record number is omitted, the default is the next record in the file after the one retrieved with the last GET statement.

Access to the record buffer is through the string variables created with the FIELD statement, which defines fields in the buffer as string variables. The record buffer can also be read with the INPUT# and LINE INPUT# statements. If the communication path is to a communications port instead of a disk file, the record number is the number of characters to be read from the communications buffer.

See also Chapter 8, CVD(), CVI(), CVS(), FIELD, LSET, MKD$(), MKI$(), MKS$(), OPEN, PUT, RSET.

GOSUB
Initiates a subroutine

    GOSUB *line_number*

The GOSUB statement is used to initiate a branch to a subroutine starting at line *line_number*. When a GOSUB statement is executed, execution immediately moves to the line number specified as its argument. The subroutine then executes normally until it encounters a RETURN statement, at which time it branches back to the statement following the GOSUB statement.

Subroutines can be nested, that is, one subroutine can call another, which calls a third. When the RETURN statements are executed, they will always branch back to the statement after the most recently executed GOSUB statement.

See also Chapter 7, RETURN, GOTO, IF THEN, ON GOSUB.

GOTO
Jumps to a specific program line

    GOTO *line_number*

The GOTO statement initiates an immediate, unconditional jump to line *line_number*. When execution of a program reaches the GOTO statement, it immediately jumps to the line number specified in the argument and begins executing there.

See also GOSUB, IF THEN, ON GOTO.

HEX$()

Converts a number into a hexadecimal string

HEX$(*number*)

The HEX$() function converts the numeric value *number* into a hexadecimal (base 16) string. The number must be in the range −32,768 to 65,535. The numbers 0 through 65,535 are changed into the hexadecimal values 0 through FFFF. The numbers −1 through −32,768 are changed into the two's complement hexadecimal values FFFF through 8000. The &H prefix used to denote hexadecimal values in GW-BASIC is not returned in the string by the function.

See also OCT$(), STR$().

IF THEN

Creates a conditional branch

IF *logical*[,] THEN *t_statement*[[,]ELSE *f_statement*]
IF *logical*[,] GOTO *t_line_number*[[,]ELSE *f_statement*]

The IF THEN statement creates a conditional branch, based on the result of a logical statement. The logical statement *logical* must return a value of zero for false or nonzero for true. If *logical* is true, THEN *t_state-ment* or GOTO *t_line_number* is executed. The argument *t_statement* can be a line number to which the program branches, or one or more state-ments separated by colons; *t_line_number* must be a line number. If *logical* is false, execution continues with either the statement following IF THEN or with *f_statement* if the optional ELSE clause is included. The argument *f_statement* can be a line number to which the program branches, or one or more statements separated by colons. The only restriction is that the ELSE clause must be on the same logical line as the IF statement.

IF THEN statements can be nested; that is, another IF THEN statement can be part of a *t_statement* or *f_statement*. When they are nested, the first ELSE clause encountered is matched with the most recently executed IF THEN.

See also Chapter 6, ON GOSUB, ON GOTO.

INKEY$
Gets one character

INKEY$

The INKEY$ variable checks the keyboard buffer and, if a character is available, returns the first character from it. If no characters are in the keyboard buffer, INKEY$ does not wait for input but immediately returns the null string (""). Characters are not displayed on the screen as they are with the INPUT statements.

For a few special characters, INKEY$ returns a two-character string. These characters (the extended characters) represent keys and combinations of keys that cannot be represented as a single ASCII character. If an extended character is returned as a two-character string, the first character is zero, and the second contains the code for the extended character. In many cases, the extended character code is also the key's scan code (see the KEY statement).

Code	Extended characters
3	NUL
15	Shift-Tab
16 to 25	Alt-Shift-Q,W,E,R,T,Y,U,I,O,P
30 to 38	Alt-Shift-A,S,D,F,G,H,J,K,L
44 to 50	Alt-Shift-Z,X,C,V,B,N,M
59 to 68	F1 to F10 (when disabled as soft keys)
71	Home
72	Up arrow
73	Page up
75	Left arrow
77	Right arrow
79	End

Code	Extended characters
80	Down arrow
81	Page Down
82	Ins (Insert)
83	Del (Delete)
84 to 93	Shift-F1 to F10 (F11 to F20)
94 to 103	Ctrl-F1 to F10 (F21 to F30)
104 to 113	Alt-F1 to F10 (F31 to F40)
114	Ctrl-PrtSc
115	Ctrl-left arrow
116	Ctrl-right arrow
117	Ctrl-End
118	Ctrl-Page Down
119	Ctrl-Home
120 to 131	Alt-1,2,3,4,5,6,7,8,9,0,-,=
132	Ctrl-Page Up

Characters not returned by INKEY$ are

F11 and F12 on an extended keyboard

PrtSc

Scroll Lock

Ctrl-Break

Ctrl-Num Lock

Ctrl-Alt-Delete

Ctrl-PrtSc

Pause

See also Chapter 3, INPUT, INPUT$, LINE INPUT.

INP
Returns a byte from a machine port

INP(*port_num*)

The INP() function returns a byte from machine port number *port_num*. The number *port_num* must be in the range 0 to 65,535 and must be a valid machine port. You will need a technical reference manual for your computer for a list of valid machine ports. The INP() function serves the same function as the assembly language command IN.

See also OUT, WAIT.

INPUT
Gets input from the keyboard

INPUT[;][*prompt$*{;|,}]*variable*[,*variable*[,...]]

The INPUT statement gets input from the keyboard. The listed variable names *variable* receive the data input from the keyboard and are either numeric or string variables.

The prompt string *prompt$* is a quoted string of text rather than a string variable and is printed on the screen before the statement waits for input. If the prompt string is followed by a semicolon, a question mark is printed to its right and the input typed by the user is printed to the right of the question mark. If the prompt string is followed by a comma, the user's input appears to the right of the prompt string, without the question mark. If a semicolon follows the word INPUT, the carriage return typed by the user is not printed on the screen, and any other printed output appears to the right of what the user input.

See also Chapter 3, INKEY$, INPUT#, INPUT$, LINE INPUT, LINE INPUT#, OPEN, PRINT, WRITE.

INPUT#
Gets delimited input from a file

INPUT#*file_num*,*variable*[,*variable*[,...]]

The INPUT# statement is used to get data from a communications path established by the OPEN statement. While this path is normally connected to a disk file, it can be attached to any device, such as the keyboard or serial communications ports (COM1: and COM2:). The number *file_num* is the file number assigned to the communications path by the OPEN statement.

Numeric input, whether entered by the user or read from a disk file, must be separated by commas. Line feeds and leading spaces are ignored, and the first character encountered is assumed to be the initial number. Reading of a number ends at a space, comma, line feed, or carriage return.

String input also ignores leading spaces and line feeds. It begins with the first character and terminates with the first comma, line feed, or carriage return. If the first character (other than blanks or line feeds) is a double quotation mark, reading begins with the next character and continues until another quotation mark or a carriage return is encountered. The reading includes all leading and trailing spaces and commas between the quotation marks. In all cases, reading of a string terminates when 255 characters have been read.

See also Chapter 3, INKEY$, INPUT, INPUT$, LINE INPUT, LINE INPUT#, OPEN, PRINT, WRITE.

INPUT$( )
Gets a specific number of characters

INPUT$(*num_char*[,[#]*file_num*])

The INPUT$() function is used to get a specific number of characters from the keyboard or a communications path established by the OPEN statement and connected to a disk file or device such as the keyboard or serial communications ports (COM1: and COM2:). The file number *file_num* is assigned to the communications path by the OPEN statement. If the optional pound sign and file number are omitted, the characters are gotten from the keyboard. When reading from the keyboard, no characters are echoed to the screen as they are with the INPUT and LINE INPUT statements. The number *num_char* is the number of characters to get from the specified device. The only character that terminates input before the requested number of characters are read is a Ctrl-Break.

See also Chapter 3, INKEY$, INPUT, INPUT#, LINE INPUT, LINE INPUT#, OPEN.

INSTR( )
Locates a substring in a string

INSTR([*start_char*,]*target_string$*,*search_string$*)

The INSTR() function locates a substring within a string. The function returns the location of the substring *search_string$* in the string *target_string$*. The first character in *target_string$* is one, the second two, and so on, and the search starts at the (optional) character number indicated in *start_char*, continuing to the end of the string. If *start_char* is omitted, the search starts at the first character.

See also LEFT$(), LEN(), MID$(), RIGHT$().

INT( )
Rounds down to the next integer

INT(*number*)

The INT() function rounds the number *number* down to the next lower whole number. For example,

INT(4.6)   returns 4

INT(−4.2) returns −5

See also CINT(), FIX().

IOCTL
Sends a control string to a device driver

IOCTL[#]*file_num*,*control_string$*

The IOCTL statement sends a control string to a device driver after a communications path is opened with the OPEN statement, which assigns the file number *file_num* to the path. The string *control_string$* is a string of up to 255 characters to control the device driver. Separate commands within the string can be separated by semicolons.

See also IOCTL$().

IOCTL$( )
Gets a control string from a device driver

IOCTL$([#]*file_num*)

The IOCTL$() function returns a control string from a device driver after a communications path has been opened to the driver using the OPEN statement. The file number *file_num* is assigned to the communications path with the OPEN statement.

See also IOCTL.

KEY
Defines the special function keys

KEY *key_num,key_string$*
KEY ON|OFF|LIST
KEY *user_key_num*,CHR$(*modifier_code*)+CHR$(*scan_code*)

The KEY statement is used to enable, disable, list, and change the assignments of the function keys. It is also used to define some special keys for trapping with the KEY() ON and ON KEY() GOSUB statements. The function keys F1 to F10 insert up to 15 characters at the prompt when they are pressed. When GW-BASIC is started, they are given their default definitions, and the first six characters of their definitions are printed along the bottom of the screen. The default definitions are

F1	LIST	F6	,"LPT1:"←
F2	RUN←	F7	TRON←
F3	LOAD"	F8	TROFF←
F4	SAVE"	F9	KEY
F5	CONT←	F10	SCREEN 0,0,0î

The ← signifies that a carriage return has been inserted at the indicated point.

To change the definition of a key, use the first syntax shown above. Insert the key number in *key_num* and a string containing the new definition in *key_string$*. Here, *key_num* must be in the range of one to ten. The string can contain any characters, including control characters that are part of the CHR$() function. For example, the default definition of key number two is set with KEY 2,"RUN"+CHR$(13) (CHR$(13) is the carriage return).

The KEY ON statement turns on display of the first six characters of the key definitions along the bottom of the GW-BASIC screen. This is the default condition. The KEY OFF statement does not disable the keys; it turns off the printing of the definitions. The KEY LIST statement lists the key definitions on the screen. To disable a key and make it available for key trapping, define it as the null string. For example, to disable key number one, use KEY 1,"".

The third syntax shown for the KEY statement is used to define special keys for trapping with the KEY() ON and ON KEY() GOSUB statements. The special user keys, *user_key_num*, are numbered 15 through 20 and don't refer to any real keys on the keyboard. Using the third syntax, define a key on the keyboard as a special user key. Once defined, you can use it in a KEY() ON statement to trap that key. The syntax for the keyboard key consists of a modifier code and a scan code: CHR$(*modifier_code*)+CHR$(*scan_code*). The number *scan_code* identifies the key. Note that the scan codes are not ASCII codes but identifiers for the physical keys on the keyboard. The number *modifier_code* identifies the modifier keys that must be pressed at the same time as the special key. The modifier codes can be added together to cover situations where more than one modifier key is pressed. The scan codes and modifier codes are listed here. See the INKEY$ function for a list of the extended key codes. For example, to make Shift-A special user code 15, use KEY 15, CHR$(3)+CHR$(30).

Modifier Codes

Code	Modifier key	Code	Modifier key
0	No modification	8	Alt
1	Left Shift	32	Num Lock
2	Right Shift	64	Caps Lock
3	Either Shift	128	Extended
4	Ctrl		

Key Scan Codes

Code	Key	Code	Key
1	Esc	41	' ~
2	1 !	42	Left Shift
3	2 @	43	\ |
4	3 #	44	Z
5	4 $	45	X
6	5 %	46	C
7	6 ^	47	V
8	7 &	48	B
9	8 *	49	N
10	9 (	50	M
11	0)	51	, <
12	- _	52	. >
13	= +	53	/ ?
14	Backspace	54	Right Shift
15	Tab	55	* PrtSc
16	Q	56	Alt
17	W	57	Spacebar
18	E	58	Caps Lock
19	R	59	F1
20	T	60	F2
21	Y	61	F3
22	U	62	F4
23	I	63	F5
24	O	64	F6
25	P	65	F7
26	[{	66	F8

Code	Key	Code	Key
27	] }	67	F9
28	Enter	68	F10
29	Ctrl	69	Num Lock
30	A	70	Scroll Lock
31	S	71	7 Home
32	D	72	8 Up arrow
33	F	73	9 Page Up
34	G	74	-
35	H	75	4 Left arrow
36	J	76	5
37	K	77	6 Right arrow
38	L	78	+
39	; :	79	1 End
40	' "	80	2 Down arrow
		81	3 Page Down
		82	0 Ins
		83	. Del

See also INKEY$, KEY() ON|OFF|STOP, ON KEY() GOSUB.

KEY( ) ON|OFF|STOP
Enables/disables trapping of keystrokes

KEY(*key_num*) ON|OFF|STOP

The KEY() ON statement turns on the trapping of keys. To use key trapping, you must first execute an ON KEY() GOSUB statement to set the subroutine to branch to whenever specific key presses occur. Set the key to watch for with the integer key code *key_num*, which can have a value in the range 1 through 20. The key codes refer to the following keys:

Key code	Key
1 to 10	Function keys F1 through F10
11	Up Arrow
12	Left Arrow
13	Right Arrow
14	Down Arrow
15 to 20	User-defined special keys, defined with the KEY*user_key_num*,CHR$(*modifier_code*)+ CHR$(*scan_code*) statement (see KEY)

When key trapping is turned on, GW-BASIC starts checking the keyboard between the execution of each program statement. If the indicated key has been pressed, the program branches to the subroutine set with the ON KEY() GOSUB statement.

The KEY() OFF statement disables key trapping, and GW-BASIC stops checking for key presses. Any key presses that take place with event trapping off are lost. The KEY() STOP statement disables key trapping but does not lose any key presses. Any key presses that arrive with this statement in force are saved until a KEY() ON statement is executed. Note that a KEY() STOP is automatically executed whenever a key trap takes place, and unless a KEY() OFF is executed in the trap subroutine, a KEY() ON is automatically executed when you return from it.

See also KEY, ON KEY() GOSUB.

KILL
Deletes a file

    KILL *file_name$*

The KILL statement is used to delete the disk file named in the string. If the file is not in the working directory, include a path along with the file name.

See also CHDIR, FILES, MKDIR, NAME AS, RESET, RMDIR.

LEFT$( )
Extracts the left side of a string

LEFT$(*source_string$,num_char*)

The LEFT$() function extracts and returns *num_char* characters from the left side of *source_string$*.
See also Chapter 5, RIGHT$(), MID$(), INSTR(), LEN().

LEN( )
Gets the length of a string

LEN(*string$*)

The LEN() function returns the length of the string *string$*.
See also Chapter 5, LEFT$(), RIGHT$(), MID$(), INSTR().

LET
Assigns values to variables

[LET] *variable = formula*

The LET statement is used to assign values or the results of calcula-tions to variables. This statement is primarily for compatibility with older versions of BASIC, since variable assignment in GW-BASIC is done without LET. A GW-BASIC assignment statement and the LET statement differ in that the LET statement requires all the values and vari-ables in *formula* to be of the same type as *variable*. If you do not use the LET keyword, GW-BASIC automatically converts any values that are not of the same type.
See also LSET, RSET.

LINE
Draws lines or boxes

LINE [(*x1,y1*)]-(*x2,y2*)[,[*line_color*][,B[F]][,*line_style%*]]

The LINE statement is used for drawing lines and open and filled boxes on the screen. The two pairs of *x,y* coordinates (*x1,y1*) and (*x2,y2*) define two points on the screen. If you are drawing a line, it is drawn from one point to the other. If you are drawing a box, it is drawn with these points as the upper-left and lower-right corners of the box. If the first coordinate is omitted, the line or box is drawn from the current position, where the last drawing command ended, to the second coordinate. The coordinates are either screen or user coordinates, depending on the last call to the WINDOW statement. Screen coordinates are referenced in pixels, with the origin in the upper-left corner. The range depends on the monitor and the screen mode set with SCREEN. User coordinates are defined with the WINDOW statement, which maps the user's coordinate system onto the physical screen coordinates.

The optional number *line_color* determines the color to draw the line or box. The allowed values are determined by the screen mode set with the SCREEN statement and the current palette set with the COLOR statement. If *line_color* is omitted, the current foreground color is used. The ,B switch draws a box instead of a line, and the ,BF switch draws a filled box.

The *line_style%* argument is a number that determines the dash pattern used when drawing the line. If it is omitted, a solid line is drawn, and if you try to use it when drawing a filled box, it generates an error. The argument is a 16-bit integer mask used while drawing the line. The line is drawn by turning on pixels on the screen. Before each pixel is turned on, the mask is checked, and if the current bit is a zero, no change is made to the pixel. If the current bit is a one, the pixel is set to the color specified with *line_color* or the foreground color if *line_color* is omitted. The statement then moves on to the next bit for the next pixel. When it reaches the end of the integer, it starts over again at the beginning. For example, the binary form of the hexadecimal number &HF0F0 is 1111000011110000 (four pixels on, four off, etc.). If it is used as the *line_style%* argument, a dashed line is drawn with 4-bit dashes and 4-bit spaces. Since the LINE statement does not change the color in the spaces, draw a solid line first in the color that you want the spaces to be, then draw the dashed line to make a two-color line.

See also CIRCLE, COLOR, DRAW, PAINT, PSET(), SCREEN, VIEW, WINDOW.

LINE INPUT
Inputs a complete line into a string

LINE INPUT[;][*prompt$;*]*string$*

The LINE INPUT statement gets a complete line of text from the keyboard. The variable name *string$* is the variable to which the line of characters is assigned. The prompt string *prompt$* is a quoted string of text that is printed on the screen before the statement begins waiting for input. The prompt string must be a quoted string and not a string variable. If a semicolon follows the word INPUT, the carriage return typed by the user is not printed on the screen, and any other printed output appears to the right of what the user has typed.

The LINE INPUT statement accepts all characters, including leading spaces, commas, and quotation marks, from the keyboard. Input terminates with a single carriage return or when 255 characters have been read. Note that a carriage return immediately preceded by a line feed does not end the input; it becomes part of the string.

See also Chapter 3, INKEY$, INPUT, INPUT#, INPUT$, LINE INPUT#, OPEN.

LINE INPUT#
Inputs a complete line into a string

LINE INPUT#*file_num,string$*

The LINE INPUT# statement gets a complete line of text from a communications path established by the OPEN statement. While this path is normally connected to a disk file, it can be attached to any device, including the keyboard and serial communications ports (COM1: and COM2:). The number *file_num* is the file number assigned to the communications path by the OPEN statement.

Unlike the INPUT and INPUT# statements, this statement accepts all characters from the keyboard or disk file, including commas, quotation marks, and leading blanks. Input terminates only with a single carriage return or when 255 characters have been read. A carriage return immediately preceded by a line feed does not terminate input but becomes part of the string.

See also Chapter 3, INKEY$, INPUT, INPUT#, INPUT$, LINE INPUT, OPEN.

LIST
Lists the program on the screen

LIST [.|*start_line*][-|-.|-*end_line*][,*file_name$*]

The LIST statement prints the current program on the screen or in a disk file. If no arguments are used, the whole program is listed. Using the sequence *start_line-end_line* lists all the lines from *start_line* to *end_line*. The sequence *start_line-* lists all the lines from *start_line* to the end of the program. The sequence *-end_line* lists all the lines from the beginning of the program to *end_line*. If a period is used for either of the line numbers, the current line number is used in its place. The current line number is the last line printed on the screen with the LIST or EDIT statement. If a disk file name is included with the *file_name$* argument, the program lines are listed in that file.

See also Chapter 2, LLIST, SAVE.

LLIST
Lists the program on the printer

LLIST [.|*start_line*][-|-.|-*end_line*]

The LLIST statement sends the current program to the printer. If no arguments are used, the entire program will be listed. The *start_line-end_line* sequence lists all the lines between—and including—the specified lines. Using *start_line-* lists all lines from the specified line to the end of the file; if *-end_line* is used, all program lines up to that point are listed. Using a period instead of a line number causes the current line number, that is, the last line printed with the LIST or EDIT statement, to be used in its place.

See also Chapter 2, LIST.

LOAD
Clears memory and loads a program

LOAD *file_name$*[,R]

The LOAD statement closes all files, clears all programs and variables from memory, and then loads the program specified in the string *file_name$*. If the ,R switch is used, files are not closed and the loaded program is run.

See also Chapter 2, CHAIN, MERGE, RUN, SAVE.

LOC( )
Gets the current file position

LOC(*file_num*)

The LOC() function gets the current position in file number *file_num*. The number *file_num* is the file number assigned to the communications path when it is opened with the OPEN statement. In a sequential file, it returns the number of 128-byte blocks read or written since the file was opened. In a random-access file, it returns the number of the record that was just read or written. In a serial communications path, it returns the number of characters in the communications buffer waiting to be read.

See also LOF(), OPEN.

LOCATE
Moves the cursor to a specific location

LOCATE [*row*][,[*column*][,[*cursor*][,[*start*][,*stop*]]]]

The LOCATE statement moves the cursor to a specific position on the screen. The two numbers *row* and *column* determine the cursor location. The number *row* can range from 1 to 25 (the number of rows on the screen) and *column* can range from 1 to 40 or 80, depending on the current width of the screen (set with the WIDTH statement). Subsequent printing on the screen begins at the location indicated). The LOCATE statement can be used to print text on screen line 25, which is normally not used. You can do this by turning off the key display with the KEY statement; then use LOCATE and PRINT to put text on line 25. Note that line 25 does not scroll as the rest of the display does.

The number *cursor* turns the cursor off if it is zero and on if it is non-zero. The numbers *start* and *stop* determine the vertical size of the cursor in scan lines. Although the values allowed are from 0 to 31, the top of the character is at 0 and the bottom is usually at 7—sometimes at 13—depending on the monitor. Setting *start* greater than *stop* creates a two-part cursor;

the lines scan down and then wrap back up to the top. The arguments *cursor*, *start*, and *stop* have no effect in graphics mode.
See also KEY, WIDTH.

LOCK
Restricts access to a file

LOCK[#]*file_num*[,[*record_num_1*][TO *record_num_2*]]

The LOCK statement is used to restrict access to a networked file. Because in a network environment, more than one computer can have access to a set of files, the LOCK statement reserves access to a particular file while you are using it. The number *file_num* is the number assigned to the file when it was opened with the OPEN statement.

Valid record numbers include 1 through 4,294,967,295. If no record range is given or the file is a sequential-access file, the whole file is locked; a record range on a sequential-access file is ignored. If a record range is given for random-access files, only those records will be locked. If the number *record_num_1* is omitted, it is assumed to be one. If the range TO *record_num_2* is omitted, only the record specified in *record_num_1* is locked.

Be sure to unlock any files with the UNLOCK statement or future access to the file may be jeopardized.
See also OPEN, UNLOCK.

LOF( )
Gets the length of a file

LOF(*file_num*)

The LOF() function returns the length, in bytes, of a file. The number *file_num* is the number assigned when the file was opened with the OPEN statement. Divide the file length by the record length set in the OPEN statement to get the number of records in a random-access file. If the file number refers to a communications path to a serial port (COM1: or COM2:), the function returns the amount of free space in the input buffer.
See also LOC().

LOG( )
Calculates the natural logarithm of a number

LOG(*number*)

The LOG() function calculates and returns the single-precision natural logarithm of the number *number*. The natural logarithm is base **e** (2.718282). To get double-precision results, use the /D switch when invoking GW-BASIC. To get the common logarithm (base 10) of a number, use LOG(*number*)/LOG(10).

See also EXP().

LPOS( )
Gets the position of the printer's print head

LPOS(*dummy*)

The LPOS() function returns the character position of the print head. The argument *dummy* is a dummy numeric argument (for example LPOS(1)). The function works by counting the number of characters printed since the last line feed. If the printer has issued its own line feed, as some narrow-carriage printers do, and has not informed GW-BASIC, the number returned by this function will be wrong.

See also LPRINT.

LPRINT
Prints on the printer

LPRINT [*arg*][{,|;| }[*arg*[{,|;| }[...]]]]

The LPRINT statement prints characters on the printer. The arguments *arg* are numbers, numeric or string variables, quoted strings, or formulas that evaluate to numbers or strings. If the arguments are separated by commas, the print head will move to the next tab stop (one every 14 spaces) to print the next argument. If the arguments are separated by semicolons or spaces, printing of the next argument starts in the character position immediately after the last thing printed. Be careful of space delimiters as they can confuse GW-BASIC.

Normally, when the last argument is printed, GW-BASIC uses a line feed-carriage return sequence to advance to the next line. If the statement ends in a comma, semicolon, or a SPC() or TAB() function, this sequence is suppressed. The statement assumes that you have an 80-column-wide printer unless you've changed the width with a WIDTH statement. If the first item printed on a line is longer than this, it will wrap at the end of the line and start printing on the next line. If printing an item other than the first item on a line would extend beyond the end of a line, a line feed-carriage return is executed before printing the item.

See also Chapter 3, LPOS, LPRINT USING, OPEN, PRINT, PRINT USING.

LPRINT USING
Prints formatted text on the printer

    LPRINT USING *format_string;arg*[{,|;}[*arg*[{,|;}[...]]]]

The LPRINT USING statement prints characters on the printer. The arguments *arg* are numbers, numeric or string variables, quoted strings, or formulas that evaluate to numbers or strings. If the arguments are separated by commas, the print head will move to the next tab stop (one every 14 spaces) to print the next argument. The LPRINT USING statement has an added *format_string* argument that controls where the arguments are printed on a line. See the PRINT USING statement for a list of the formatting codes.

Normally, when the last argument is printed, GW-BASIC uses a line feed-carriage return sequence to advance to the next line. If the statement ends in a comma or semicolon, this sequence is suppressed. The statement assumes that you have an 80-column-wide printer unless you've changed the width with a WIDTH statement. If a line is longer than this, it will wrap at the end of the line and start printing on the next line.

See also Chapter 3, LPOS, LPRINT, OPEN, PRINT, PRINT USING.

LSET
Left-justifies a string in a record buffer

    LSET *field_name$* = *string_expression*

The LSET statement left-justifies a string *string_expression* in a named field *field_name* of the record buffer for a random access file. Records in a random-access file are read to or written from a record buffer. The FIELD statement is used to break that buffer into fields and to name those fields with string variables.

See also Chapter 8, FIELD, CVD(), CVI(), CVS(), LET, MKD$(), MKI$(), MKS$(), RSET.

MERGE
Merges program lines on disk with those in memory

> MERGE *file_name$*

The MERGE statement merges program lines from a disk file with those already in memory. The merge process inserts the lines in exactly the same manner as if they were typed at the keyboard. New lines are inserted in their correct locations according to their line numbers. A new line that has the same line number as an existing line replaces it. The file *file_name$* containing the lines to merge must be an ASCII text file, such as is created using the SAVE statement with the ,A switch. If the file extension for *file_name$* is omitted, .BAS is assumed.

See also CHAIN, LOAD, RUN.

MID$
Replaces a substring

> MID$(*target_string$,start_pos*[,*num_char*]) = *source_string$*

The MID$ statement is used to replace a substring in a string. Starting at character number *start_pos* in *target_string$*, *num_char* characters are replaced with characters from *source_string$*. If *num_char* is omitted, all of *source_string$* is used. No matter what values are used for *num_char*, however, the resulting string is the same length as *target_string$*, and any additional characters are ignored. To replace a substring with one of a different length, use LEFT$(*target_string$,start_pos*–1)+*source_string$* +MID$(*target_string$,start_pos*+*num_char*).

See also Chapter 5, INSTR(), LEFT$(), LEN(), MID$(), RIGHT$().

MID$( )
Extracts a substring

MID$(*source_string$,start_pos*[,*num_char*])

The function MID$() is used to extract a substring from a string. It returns *num_char* characters from *source_string$*, starting at character *start_pos*. The number *num_char* must be in the range 0 to 255, and *start_pos* must be in the range 1 to 255. If *num_char* is omitted, the whole right side of the string is extracted, starting at *start_pos*. If *start_pos* is greater than the length of the string, the null string ("") is returned.

See also Chapter 5, INSTR(), LEFT$(), LEN(), MID$, RIGHT$().

MKD$( )
Converts double-precision numbers into 8-byte strings

MKD$(*double#*)

The function MKD$() converts a double-precision value into a string that can be stored in a random-access file. Because only strings can be stored in random-access files, double-precision values are made to appear to be strings. The binary values of the numbers are not changed, and they still occupy the same number of bytes (double-precision numbers take eight bytes). Although the strings created by these functions can be printed, the results would be meaningless. The CVD() function reverses the action of MKD$() and converts the strings back into double-precision values.

See also Chapter 8, CVD(), CVI(), CVS(), FIELD, LSET, MKI$(), MKS$(), OPEN, RSET.

MKI$( )
Converts integers into 2-byte strings

MKI$(*integer%*)

The function MKI$() converts an integer value into a string that can be stored in a random-access file. Because only strings can be stored in random-access files, integers are made to appear to be strings. The binary values of the numbers are not changed, and they still occupy the same number of bytes (integers take two bytes). Although the strings created by these functions can be printed, the results would be meaningless. The CVI() function reverses the action of MKI$() and converts the strings back into integers.

See also Chapter 8, CVD(), CVI(), CVS(), FIELD, LSET, MKD$(), MKS$(), OPEN, RSET.

MKS$( )
Converts single-precision numbers into four-byte strings

MKS$(*single!*)

The function MKS$() converts a single-precision value into a string that can be stored in a random-access file. Because only strings can be stored in random-access files, single-precision values are made to appear to be strings. The binary values of the numbers are not changed, and they still occupy the same number of bytes (single-precision numbers take four bytes). Although the strings created by these functions can be printed, the results would be meaningless. The CVS() function reverses the action of MKS$() and converts the strings back into single-precision values.

See also Chapter 8, CVD(), CVI(), CVS(), FIELD, LSET, MKD$(), MKI$(), OPEN, RSET.

MKDIR
Creates a subdirectory

MKDIR *directory_path$*

The MKDIR statement creates a new subdirectory. The string *directory_path$* must be a standard DOS directory path that does not exceed 63 characters.

See also CHDIR, FILES, KILL, NAME AS, RESET, RMDIR.

NAME AS
Changes a file's name

NAME *old_file_name$* AS *new_file_name$*

The NAME AS statement changes the name of a disk file. The file *old_file_name$* has its name changed to *new_file_name$*. If *old_file_name$* doesn't exist, or *new_file_name$* is being used by another file, an error results.

See also CHDIR, FILES, KILL, MKDIR, RESET, RMDIR.

NEW
Clears all memory

NEW

The NEW statement closes all files and clears all memory, including the program and variables.

See also CLEAR, DELETE.

OCT$( )
Converts a number into an octal string

OCT$(*number*)

The OCT$() function converts the numeric value *number* into an octal (base 8) string. The number must be in the range −32,768 to 65,535. The numbers 0 through 65,535 are changed into the octal values &O0 through &O177777. The numbers −1 through −32768 are changed into the two's complement octal values &O177777 through &O100000. The &O prefix used to denote octal values in GW-BASIC is not returned in the string by the function.

See also HEX$(), STR$(), VAL().

ON COM( ) GOSUB
Specifies a communications event trap

ON COM(*com_port*) GOSUB *line_num*

The ON COM() GOSUB statement specifies the subroutine to execute when activity is detected at a serial port. When communications event trapping is turned on with the COM() ON statement, GW-BASIC starts checking the serial port between the execution of all program statements.

Set the serial port that this subroutine applies to with the number *com_port*, which can have a value of one or two for serial ports COM1: or COM2:. If communications activity is detected, the executing program is interrupted and immediately branches to the subroutine starting at line *line_num*. That subroutine then processes the communications event until a RETURN statement is reached, at which time the program returns to the point of interruption.

See also COM() ON|OFF|STOP.

ON ERROR GOTO
Enables trapping of GW-BASIC errors

        ON ERROR GOTO *line_num*

The ON ERROR GOTO statement enables trapping of GW-BASIC errors and specifies the routine to handle the error events. The number *line_num* is the starting line of the error-handling routine. Normally, GW-BASIC stops executing and prints an error message when an error occurs. When error trapping is enabled, error messages are not printed, and the program branches to the error-handling routine instead.

Use the functions ERR and ERL to get the error code and the line number in which the error occurred. After handling the error, return to the executing code with a RESUME statement. Error trapping is disabled while the error-handling routine is executing. It is enabled when the RESUME statement is executed, unless it has been explicitly disabled in the error-handling routine. You can disable error trapping with the ON ERROR GOTO 0 statement.

See also ERDEV, ERDEV$, ERR, ERL, ERROR, EXTERR(), RESUME.

ON GOSUB
Makes computed branch to subroutines

        ON *index* GOSUB *line_num*[,*line_num*[,...]]

The ON GOSUB statement causes a computed branch to one of several subroutines. The number *index* is rounded to an integer and then used to determine which subroutine to branch to. The numbers *line_num* are the starting line numbers of subroutines. If *index* equals one, execution branches to the subroutine starting at the first line number. If it is two, execution branches to the second line number, and so forth. When the subroutines execute a RETURN statement, execution continues with the next statement after the ON GOSUB statement. If *index* is zero or greater than the number of line numbers (but less than 255), execution continues with the next statement after ON GOSUB. If *index* is negative or greater than 255, an error results.

See also GOSUB, GOTO, ON GOTO, RETURN.

ON GOTO
Makes a computed branch

ON *index* GOTO *line_num*[,*line_num*[,...]]

The ON GOTO statement causes a computed branch to one of several line numbers. The number *index* is rounded to an integer and then used to determine which of the lines *line_num* to branch to. If *index* equals one, execution branches to the first line number; if it is two, execution branches to the second line number, and so forth. If *index* is zero or greater than the number of line numbers (but less than 255), execution continues with the next statement after the ON GOTO statement. If *index* is negative or greater than 255, an error results.

See also GOSUB, GOTO, ON GOSUB, RETURN.

ON KEY( ) GOSUB
Specifies a keystroke event trap

ON KEY(*user_key_num*) GOSUB *line_num*

The ON KEY() GOSUB statement specifies the subroutine to branch to when a specific key is pressed, and the number *line_num* is the starting line number of the subroutine to execute. Key trapping is enabled with the KEY() ON statement and disabled with the KEY() OFF and KEY() STOP statements. The number *user_key_num* is the number of the key to be trapped; it must be in the range 1 to 20. Key numbers one through ten are predefined to the function keys F1 through F10. Number 11 is the up arrow key, 12 is left arrow, 13 is right arrow, and 14 is the down arrow key. Key numbers 15 through 20 can be defined to be any key on the keyboard with the KEY statement, including combinations of keys and modifier keys (Shift, Alt, Ctrl). The KEY and KEY() ON|OFF|STOP statements provide more information on the key definitions.

See also INKEY$, KEY, KEY() ON|OFF|STOP.

ON PEN GOSUB
Specifies a light pen event trap

        ON PEN GOSUB *line_num*

The ON PEN GOSUB statement specifies the subroutine to branch to when a light pen is used. Actual event trapping is enabled with the PEN ON statement and disabled with the PEN OFF and PEN STOP statements. The number *line_num* is the starting line number of the subroutine to execute when the light pen event occurs.

See also PEN, PEN ON|OFF|STOP.

ON PLAY( ) GOSUB
Specifies a music event trap

        ON PLAY(*notes*) GOSUB *line_num*

The ON PLAY() GOSUB statement specifies the subroutine to branch to when a background music event occurs, and the number *line_num* is the starting line number of the subroutine to execute. Background music is started with the PLAY statement, using the MB command. The number *notes* specifies the number of notes left in the music queue that generates a music event trap; it must be in the range 1 through 32. When note *notes – 1* starts to play, a music event occurs. The music event subroutine is normally used to refill the music queue with more notes to play. Use small numbers for *note* or your program will constantly be moving to the music event subroutine.

See also PLAY, SOUND.

ON STRIG( ) GOSUB
Specifies joystick trigger event trap

        ON STRIG(*trigger*) GOSUB *line_num*

The ON STRIG() GOSUB statement specifies the subroutine to branch to when a joystick trigger is pressed. The number *line_num* is the starting line number of the subroutine to execute when the specific trigger is pressed. Actual event trapping is enabled with the STRIG() ON statement and disabled with the STRIG() OFF and STRIG() STOP statements. Trigger events that cause trapping are not seen by the STRIG() function. The number *trigger* is a code for the specific trigger to trap.

Joystick A		Joystick B	
Code	Trigger	Code	Trigger
0	1	2	1
4	2	6	2

See also STRIG(), STRIG ON|OFF, STRIG() ON|OFF|STOP.

ON TIMER( ) GOSUB
Specifies a timer event trap

ON TIMER(*seconds*) GOSUB *line_num*

The ON TIMER() GOSUB statement specifies the subroutine to branch to when the timer goes off. The number *line_num* is the starting line number of the subroutine to execute when the amount of time specified in *seconds* has elapsed since the TIMER ON statement. The number *seconds* must be in the range 1 to 86,400. Actual event trapping is enabled with the TIMER ON statement and disabled with the TIMER OFF and TIMER STOP statements.
See also TIMER ON|OFF|STOP.

OPEN
Opens a communications path to a disk file

OPEN *mode$*,[#]*file_num,file_name$*[,*rec_len*]
OPEN *file_name$* [FOR *mode*][ACCESS *access*][*lock*] AS [#]*file_num*
[LEN=*rec_len*]

The OPEN statement is used to open communications paths to an output device. Normally, it is used to open disk files, but it can also be used for access to the keyboard, printer, screen, or serial ports (see OPEN COM). The two versions of the syntax allow compatibility with older versions of BASIC.

The *mode* controls how and where a file is opened and what type of access is allowed. In the first syntax, the argument *mode$* is a string variable or quoted string containing a single character. The second syntax spells out the variable *mode* rather than using a quoted string or string variable. If the *mode* is omitted, RANDOM is assumed.

Mode

Syntax 1	Syntax 2	Result
I	INPUT	Inputs from a sequential file
O	OUTPUT	Outputs to a sequential file
A	APPEND	Outputs to a sequential file starting at the end
R	RANDOM	Inputs or outputs to a random-access file

The second syntax also has an argument *access*, which controls the type of file access. The allowed values are READ, WRITE, and READ WRITE. This argument is redundant for sequential-access files that have their access fixed by the file mode and will cause a syntax error if used. The access variable is only useful with random-access files, to make them READ ONLY (cannot be written to) or WRITE ONLY (cannot be read). Random-access files default to READ WRITE.

The second syntax has a variable *lock* for use with networked files. The allowed values are shown below; the default is essentially LOCK READ WRITE if *lock* is omitted. See the LOCK and UNLOCK statements for more information, including how to lock only parts of a file.

Lock	Result
SHARED	The file can be accessed by anyone else but cannot be locked.

Lock	Result
LOCK READ	The file cannot be read by another process.
LOCK WRITE	The file cannot be written to by another process.
LOCK READ WRITE	The file cannot be read or written by another process.

The number *file_num* is the file number to assign to this file. All other input and output to this file are done by using this number. The file number can range from 1 to the number of files allowed open at any one time. Set the number of files with the /F switch when invoking GW-BASIC. Because the default number of open files is three, the numbers 1, 2, and 3 are possible file numbers. The number *rec_len* sets the size of the record buffer for random-access files. The range is 1 to 32,767; 128 is the default. To use buffer sizes larger than 128 bytes, use the /S switch when invoking GW-BASIC. The most efficient use of memory is achieved if the record length is evenly divisible into 512 (the internal disk buffer size).

The string *file_name$* is the name of the file to open, which can include a directory path. It can also be one of the following keywords, which open other devices.

Keyword	Device	Options
KYBD:	Keyboard	Input
SCRN:	Screen	Output
LPT1:	Parallel printer 1	Output
LPT2:	Parallel printer 2	Output
LPT3:	Parallel printer 3	Output
COM1:	Serial port 1	Input/Output
COM2:	Serial port 2	Input/Output

See also Chapters 3 and 8, CLOSE, INPUT#, LINE INPUT#, LOCK, OPEN COM, PRINT#, UNLOCK, WRITE#.

OPEN COM
Opens a serial communications channel

OPEN "COM*port*:[*baud_rate*][,*parity*][,*data_bits*][,*stop_bits*]
[,RS][,CS[n]] [,DS[*n*]][,CD[*n*]][.LF][,PE]" AS [#]*file_num*
[LEN=*rec_len*]

The OPEN COM statement opens a communications channel to a serial port and sets the port parameters. All the port parameters and the port name are contained in a string.

- The number *port* is 1 or 2, to select one of the two serial ports (COM1:, COM2:).

- The number *baud_rate* is the speed at which data moves through the port, with allowed values of 75, 110, 150, 300, 600, 1200, 1800, 2400, 4800, and 9600. The default speed is 300.

- The character *parity* sets the parity of the port. Allowed values are S (space), M (mark), O (odd), E (even), and N (none). The default parity is even.

- The integer *data_bits* is the character length in bits. The allowed values are 4, 5, 6, 7, and 8. The default setting is 7 data bits.

- The integer *stop_bits* is the number of stop bits. The allowed values are 1 or 2, with 1 as the default for all speeds but 75 and 110 (the default here is 2).

The rest of the port options cause the following results. The timeout numbers (*n*) are the number of milliseconds to wait before a timeout occurs. A timeout is the amount of time for the program to wait before it decides that something is wrong and to stop and generate an error. If *n* is omitted, a zero timeout is set.

Option	Default	Result
RS	Follow	Suppresses RTS
CS[*n*]	CS1000	Sets CTS timeout
DS[*n*]	DS1000	Sets DSR timeout
CD[*n*]	CD0	Sets CD timeout

Option	Default	Result
LF	CR only	Sends an LF with each CR
PE	Disabled	Enables parity checking

RTS stands for request to send, CTS for clear to send, DST for data set ready, CD for carrier detect, LF for line feed, and CR for carriage return. If RS is set, CS changes its default to CS0.

The number *file_num* is the file number to assign to this communications path. All other input and output to this port are performed by using the file number, which can range from 1 to the number of files allowed open at any one time. Set the number of files with the /F switch when invoking GW-BASIC. The default number of open files is three, so 1, 2, and 3 are possible file numbers. The number *rec_len* sets the maximum number of characters transferred to or from the communications buffer with the GET or PUT statements. The default is 128 bytes.

See also COM() ON|OFF|STOP, ON COM() GOSUB, CLOSE.

OPTION BASE
Sets the lower limit for array subscripts

OPTION BASE *number*

The OPTION BASE statement sets the lower limit for array subscripts. Normally, array subscripts start at zero and count up to the size set in a DIM statement. The OPTION BASE statement is used to change that to one. The argument *number* can have a value of zero or one, with zero being the default. The OPTION BASE statement must be executed before any arrays are dimensioned or used.

See also DIM.

OUT
Sends a byte to a machine port

OUT *port_num,data*

The OUT statement sends a byte to machine port number *port_num*. The number *port_num* must be in the range 0 to 65,535and must be a valid machine port. See the technical reference manual for your computer for a list of valid machine ports. The number *data* is the numeric value of the byte to send to the machine port and must be in the range 0 to 255. The OUT statement serves the same function as the assembly language command OUT.

See also INP(), WAIT.

PAINT
Fills a graphic region

PAINT (*x,y*)[,*fill*[,*border_color*][,*background$*]]

The PAINT statement is used to fill bounded regions with a color or pattern. The region must be completely surrounded by a colored border. Filling starts at the coordinates *x,y* (which must be within the region to be filled and not on a border line) and continues in all directions until it encounters a border. The coordinates can be screen coordinates or user coordinates set with the WINDOW statement.

The argument *fill* is a number or string that determines the fill color or pattern. If it is omitted, the current foreground color is used (see the COLOR statement for more information about colors). If *fill* is a number, it specifies the color attribute to use to fill the region. If *fill* is a string, it specifies the painting of a pattern rather than a solid color. A pattern is created with an 8-bit-wide by up to 64-bit-tall mask. The eight bits from each character in the string form one row in the mask. This pattern mask is then replicated all over the area to be filled. The pattern is aligned with the coordinate system, so patterns on different parts of the screen will line up.

The bits in the mask are used to set the color of each pixel on the screen. The number of bits assigned to each pixel is determined by the current screen mode set with the SCREEN statement. Screen mode 2 uses one bit per pixel, so each bit in the mask corresponds to a bit on the screen. Screen mode 1 uses two bits per pixel to get four colors, so every pair of bits in the mask corresponds to a single pixel on the screen. For example, in screen mode 1, the string CHR$(&HA5) makes vertical magenta and cyan lines, and CHR$(&HA5)+CHR$(&H5A) makes a magenta and cyan checkerboard.

The argument *border_color* specifies the color at which to stop filling, defaulting to the fill color. A border of the correct color must surround the region being filled, or the fill statement may color the whole screen. For example, if you have a blue circle on the screen and want to fill its center, the *border_color* argument must be set to blue otherwise the fill will not stop at the blue circle.

The string *background$* is a one-byte string that specifies the background color to *ignore* while filling a region. The PAINT statement stops filling if it encounters two successive bytes with the same color as the fill color. If you are painting a horizontal line pattern over a region that has already been colored one of the colors in the pattern, you must use the *background$* argument to prevent the existing background from stopping the fill.

See also CIRCLE, COLOR, LINE, PSET, SCREEN, VIEW, WINDOW.

PALETTE
Defines the colors on the palette

   PALETTE *attribute,color*

The PALETTE statement is used to remap screen colors; it requires an EGA monitor. Colors are selected by attribute numbers that are normally fixed to specific colors. With the PALETTE statement you can change the color associated with an attribute. (See the COLOR statement for a list of colors and default attributes.) Changes in the palette affect everything already drawn on the screen as well as what you then draw. The PALETTE statement changes a single color attribute. The number *attribute* is the attribute number to change and the number *color* is the screen color to which it should be changed. For example, in screen mode 1, color attribute 2 defaults to light magenta. The statement PALETTE 2,4 changes 2 to red (4).

See also COLOR, PALETTE USING, SCREEN.

PALETTE USING
Defines the colors on the palette

   PALETTE USING *color_array%(start_index)*

The PALETTE USING statement is used to remap screen colors; it requires an EGA monitor. Colors are selected by attribute numbers that are normally fixed to specific colors. (See the COLOR statement for a list of colors and default attributes.) Changes in the palette affect everything already drawn on the screen as well as what you then draw.

The PALETTE USING statement changes all the colors in a palette at one time. The integer array *color_array%* contains a color number in each element starting with element number *start_index*. Each attribute is then assigned its counterpart in the array element (starting from *start_index*.) That is, attribute 0 is assigned the color number stored in array element *start_index*, and attribute 1 is assigned the color number stored in array element *start_index*+1. The array must have enough elements to set all the attributes allowed in the screen mode in use.

See also COLOR, PALETTE, SCREEN.

PCOPY
Copies one screen page to another

> PCOPY *source_page,destination_page*

The PCOPY statement is used to copy one screen page to another. The number *source_page* is the page to copy, and the number *destination_page* is the page to which it is to be copied. The arguments range from zero to the number of pages of screen memory (see SCREEN).

See also GET, PUT.

PEEK( )
Gets the contents of a memory location

> PEEK(*location*)

The PEEK() function returns the contents (one byte) of a memory location. The number *location* is an offset (in bytes) into the current segment set with the DEF SEG statement. The offset must be in the range 0 to 65,535. See the DEF SEG statement for more information on memory addressing.

See also DEF SEG, POKE.

PEN ON|OFF|STOP
Enables/disables trapping light pen events

PEN ON|OFF|STOP

The PEN ON statement turns on trapping of light pen events. You must first execute an ON PEN GOSUB statement to set the subroutine to branch to whenever a light pen is used. When the trapping is turned on, GW-BASIC starts checking the light pen between the execution of the program statements. If an event occurs, the program branches to the subroutine set with the ON PEN GOSUB statement.

The PEN OFF statement disables pen event trapping, and GW-BASIC stops checking for pen events and any that then take place are lost. The PEN STOP statement disables the trapping, but does not lose any pen events; they will be saved until a PEN ON statement is executed. A PEN STOP is automatically executed whenever a pen event trap takes place, and a PEN ON is automatically executed when you return from the trap subroutine unless a PEN OFF is executed in that subroutine.

See also ON PEN GOSUB, PEN().

PEN( )
Reads the light pen

PEN(*code*)

The PEN() function is used to read the coordinates of the light pen. A PEN ON statement must be executed before this function is active. The number *code* determines the value to be returned by the function. Locations are in screen coordinates, which have their origin in the upper-left corner; positive values read down and right from there in pixels. See the SCREEN statement for the number of pixels in each direction for different screen modes.

Code	Results
0	Returns −1 if the pen was down; otherwise it returns 0.
1	Returns the *x* coordinate of the last pen down.
2	Returns the *y* coordinate of the last pen down.

Code	Results
3	Returns the current pen state; −1 if down, 0 if up.
4	Returns the last known *x* coordinate.
5	Returns the last known *y* coordinate.
6	Returns the character row of the last pen down. The range is 1 to 24.
7	Returns the character column of the last pen down. The range is 1 to 40 or 1 to 80 depending on the width set with the WIDTH statement.
8	Returns the last known character row.
9	Returns the last known character column.

See also ON PEN GOSUB, PEN ON|OFF|STOP.

PLAY
Plays a music macro language string

PLAY *mml_string$*

The PLAY statement is used to play music coded as a music macro string. The string *mml_string$* contains music macro language codes for the music to be played. If the music is to be played in the background, a maximum of 32 notes can be stored at any one time in the music queue. Use the PLAY ON and ON PLAY GOSUB statements to set a subroutine to be branched to when most of the background music has been played. The subroutine then adds more notes to the music queue.

The music macro language consists of single character codes for the notes and rests and some longer codes to set music parameters. Numbers can be literal numbers or program variables using the format =variable; (the semicolon is required to separate the variable names from other macro commands). The music macro language is similar to the Graphics Macro Language used with the DRAW statement.

Code	Result
A to G	Plays notes A to G.
#	Makes the note preceding it sharp.
+	Makes the note preceding it sharp.
-	Makes the note preceding it flat.
L*n*	Sets the length of the following notes. The number *n* can have values from 1 to 64, where L1 is a whole note, L4 is a quarter note and so forth. The number *n* may also follow the note. For example B2 is a half note B.
MF	Plays following notes in the foreground. This is the default. The program will wait at this statement until all of the notes are played.
MB	Plays following notes in the background. Up to 32 notes are saved in the music queue and will begin to play. The statement does not wait for the notes to play but continues with the rest of the program.
MN	Music normal. Notes play for seven-eighths of the time set with L, with a one-eighth pause between notes.
ML	Music legato. Notes play continuously (full length) with no pause between notes.
MS	Music staccato. Notes play three-quarters of the time set with L and pause for one-quarter of the time.
N*n*	Plays note number *n*, where *n* ranges from 0 to 84 over 7 octaves. A value of 0 is a rest.
O*n*	Sets the current octave to n, where *n* ranges from 0 to 6. Octave 3 contains middle C. The default is 4.
P*n*	Pauses n, where *n* ranges from 1 to 64.

Code	Result
T*n*	Sets the tempo for a quarter note, with n quarter notes per minute. The number *n* ranges from 32 to 255 with 120 as the default.
	Increases the length of the note it follows by three halves. Multiple periods are allowed; each one increases the previous total length by three halves.
X*mml_string$*;	Plays another music macro string named *mml_string$* and returns. This is much like calling a subroutine.
>	Moves all notes after it up one octave.
<	Moves all notes after it down one octave.

See also BEEP, ON PLAY GOSUB, PLAY ON|OFF|STOP, SOUND.

PLAY( )
Gets the number of notes left in the music queue

PLAY(*dummy*)

The PLAY() function returns the number of notes left to play in the music queue. Use the PLAY statement to insert notes into the music queue, which can store a maximum of 32 notes (and pauses) for music playing in the background. You can use an ON PLAY() GOSUB statement to cause an event trap when the contents of the queue reaches a certain level. If music is playing in the foreground, the PLAY function returns 0.

See also ON PLAY() GOSUB, PLAY.

PMAP( )
Maps screen and user coordinates

PMAP(*coordinate,map_type*)

The PMAP() function is used to map user coordinates to screen coordinates or screen coordinates to user coordinates. Screen coordinates are by pixels, with their origin (0,0) in the upper-left corner. The range depends on the monitor as well as screen mode set with SCREEN. User coordinates are defined with the WINDOW statement, which maps a user's coordinate system onto the physical screen coordinates, and VIEW, which determines the part of the screen on which to draw. The number *coordinate* is the coordinate to translate and *map_type* is the type of mapping to do. The allowed values of *map_type* follow.

Value	Result
0	Maps user *x* coordinate to screen *x* coordinate.
1	Maps user *y* coordinate to screen *y* coordinate.
2	Maps screen *x* coordinate to user *x* coordinate.
3	Maps screen *y* coordinate to user *y* coordinate.

See also SCREEN, VIEW, WINDOW.

POINT( )
Gets the attributes of a screen pixel

```
POINT(x,y)
POINT(code)
```

The POINT function returns the color attribute of a screen pixel or the color and location of the current graphics location. The first syntax returns the color attribute of the pixel located at the point (*x,y*) in screen coordinates. If the point is not in range, it returns −1. See the SCREEN statement for the ranges for the different screen modes and the COLOR statement for valid color attributes.

The second syntax returns the current graphics location, the last point moved or drawn to with a graphics statement. The number *code* determines which part of the coordinate is returned.

Code	Result
0	Returns *x* in screen coordinates.
1	Returns *y* in screen coordinates.
2	Returns *x* in user coordinates if they have been set with WINDOW; otherwise, it returns *x* in screen coordinates.

Code   Result

3   Returns *y* in user coordinates if they have been set with
         WINDOW; otherwise, it returns *y* in screen coordinates.

See also COLOR, PMAP(), SCREEN, VIEW, WINDOW.

POKE
Sets the contents of a memory location

POKE *location,data*

The POKE statement changes the contents (one byte) of a memory location. The number *location* is an offset (in bytes) into the current segment set
with the DEF SEG statement. The offset must be in the range 0 to 65,535.
(See the DEF SEG statement for more information on memory addressing.)
The number *data* is the data byte to insert in the memory location; it must
be in the range 0 to 255.

See also DEF SEG, PEEK.

POS( )
Get the current cursor position in a line

POS(*dummy*)

The POS() function returns the cursor's current position in a line. The
position is counted from the left, by characters, with the first character
as number 1. The argument is a dummy numeric argument (for example,
POS(1)). To find the row containing the cursor use the CSRLIN function.

See also CSRLIN, LOCATE, POINT(), SCREEN().

PRESET( )
Displays a point on the screen

PRESET[STEP](*x,y*)[,*color*]

The PRESET() function displays a point on the screen. The STEP option
causes the points to be drawn relative to the current graphic position. If this

option is omitted, the point is drawn at the absolute coordinate (*x,y*), which can be screen or user coordinates.

Screen coordinates are in pixels, with the origin in the upper-left corner. The range depends on the monitor and on the screen mode set with SCREEN. User coordinates are defined with the WINDOW statement, which maps a user's coordinate system onto the physical screen coordinates, and VIEW, which defines the part of the screen on which to draw.

The number *color* is the color attribute to use in making the point. (See the COLOR statement for a list of valid color attributes.) If the *color* option is omitted, the PRESET statement draws in the background color.

See also COLOR, POINT(), PSET, VIEW, WINDOW.

PSET
Displays a point on the screen

PSET[STEP](*x,y*)[,*color*]

The PSET function displays a point on the screen. The STEP option causes the points to be drawn relative to the current graphic position. If this option is omitted, the point is drawn at the absolute coordinate (*x,y*), which can be screen or user coordinates.

Screen coordinates are in pixels, with the origin in the upper-left corner. The range depends on the monitor and on the screen mode set with SCREEN. User coordinates are defined with the WINDOW statement, which maps a user's coordinate system onto the physical screen coordinates, and VIEW, which defines the part of the screen on which to draw.

The number *color* is the color attribute to use in making the point. (See the COLOR statement for a list of valid color attributes.) If the *color* option is omitted the PSET statement draws in the foreground color.

See also COLOR, POINT(), PRESET, VIEW, WINDOW.

PRINT
Prints text

PRINT[*arg*][{,|;| }[*arg*[{,|;| }[...]]]]

The PRINT statement prints characters on the screen. The arguments *arg* are numbers, numeric or string variables, quoted strings, or expressions that evaluate to numbers or strings. If the arguments are separated by commas, the next argument is printed at the next tab stop (one every 14 spaces). If the arguments are separated by semicolons or spaces, printing of the next argument starts at the next character position after the last thing printed. Be careful of space delimiters, as they can confuse GW-BASIC.

Normally, when the last argument is printed, GW-BASIC prints a carriage return to advance to the next line. If the statement ends in a comma, semicolon, SPC(), or TAB() function, the carriage return is suppressed. If the first item printed on a line extends longer than the width of the screen, it wraps at the end of the line and starts printing on the next line down. If printing an item other than the first item on a line would extend beyond the end of a line, a carriage return is executed before printing the item.

PRINT USING
Prints formatted text

PRINT USING *format string*;*arg*[{,|;}[*arg*[{,|;}[...]]]]

The PRINT USING statement prints formatted text on the screen. The arguments *arg* are numbers, numeric or string variables, quoted strings, or expressions that evaluate to numbers or strings, separated by commas or semicolons. If the statement ends in a comma or semicolon, the carriage return is suppressed.

See also Chapter 3, CSRLIN, LOCATE, LPRINT, LPRINT USING, POINT(), POS(), PRINT USING, PRINT#, PRINT# USING, OPEN, WRITE, WRITE#.

The PRINT USING statement has an added formatting argument. The format string *format_string* controls where the arguments are printed on a line. A format string consists of characters and fields. The characters are printed exactly where they are located in the string. Fields define places to put the arguments that follow the format string. The arguments and fields must be consistent, since the first argument is inserted into the first field, and the second argument is inserted in the second field and so forth. If a format string runs out of fields before the statement runs out of arguments, the format string starts over. The following codes in the format string define the fields and format for printed output:

Code	Result
!	Defines a one-character text field. The first character of a string argument is printed at this location.
\ \	Defines a multiple-character field. The length of the field consists of the two backslash characters plus the spaces between them. Characters from a string expression are inserted into the field until it is filled, and any additional characters in the string are ignored. If there are not enough characters to fill the field, the remainder is filled with blanks.
&	Defines a variable-length string field. The entire contents of a string argument are inserted here, and the line width is increased to hold it.
#	Defines a numeric field. To create a numeric field, type a pound sign for each digit, inserting commas and the decimal point where they belong. If a number does not use the complete width of the field, unused positions are filled with blanks. If a number has too many digits to the right of the decimal point, the number is rounded to fit in the field. If the number has too many characters to the left of the decimal, they are printed with a percent sign on the left to indicate field overflow. For example ##,###.## defines a numeric field with five digits to the left of the decimal, a comma after every third digit on the left (reading from the decimal point), a decimal point, and two digits on the right.
+	Prints the sign of the number. If it is placed at the beginning or end of a numeric field, the sign of the number (+ or −) is printed there. Normally, only negative numbers have their signs printed.
−	Prints minus signs for negative numbers. If it is placed after a numeric field, negative numbers will have a minus sign there and positive numbers will have a blank.

Code	Result
**	Fills leading spaces. If you place these at the beginning of a numeric field, leading spaces will be filled with asterisks instead of spaces. The two asterisks also define two more digit positions of the numeric field.
$	Prints a dollar sign. Place it on the left side of a numeric field and a dollar sign is printed there. There can be spaces between the dollar sign and the leftmost number.
$$	Prints a dollar sign. When placed on the left side of a number, a dollar sign is printed up against the printed number, with no spaces between the number and the dollar sign. The two dollar signs count as an additional digit position plus the position for the dollar sign in the numeric field.
**$	Prints a dollar sign and fills leading spaces. Place the code on the left side of a numeric field, and a dollar sign is printed up against the number and any leading spaces are filled with asterisks. This symbol defines three more digit positions, including the dollar sign.
^^^^	Inserts an exponent. Place on the right side of a numeric field to specify exponential notation (for example, 1.234E+23). These symbols define the four positions needed for the letter *E*, a sign, and a two-digit exponent.
_	Inserts a literal character. To insert any of the formatting characters as literal characters, preface them with an underscore. For example, _** prints two asterisks instead of filling the leading blanks with asterisks. To print an underscore, insert two underscores in the format string.

See also Chapter 3, CSRLIN, LOCATE, LPRINT, LPRINT USING, POINT(), POS(), PRINT, PRINT#, PRINT# USING, OPEN, WRITE, WRITE#.

PRINT#
Prints text in a disk file

PRINT[#*file_num*,][*arg*][{,|;| }[*arg*[{,|;| }[...]]]]

The PRINT# statement prints characters in a disk file. The number *file_num* is the file number assigned to a file when it was opened with the OPEN statement. (If the file number is omitted, the printing is done on the screen.) The arguments *arg* are numbers, numeric or string variables, quoted strings, or expressions that evaluate to numbers or strings. If the arguments are separated by commas, the next argument is printed at the next tab stop (one every 14 spaces). If the arguments are separated by semicolons or spaces, printing of the next argument starts at the next character position after the last thing printed. Be careful of space delimiters, as they can confuse GW-BASIC. To print delimited text and numbers that can be more easily read with the INPUT# statement, use the WRITE# statement.

Normally, when the last argument is printed, GW-BASIC prints a carriage return to advance to the next line. If the statement ends in a comma, semicolon, SPC(), or TAB() function, the carriage return is suppressed. If the first item printed on a line extends longer than the width of the screen, it wraps at the end of the line and starts printing on the next line down. If printing an item other than the first item on a line would extend beyond the end of a line, a carriage return is executed before printing the item.

See also Chapter 3, CSRLIN, LOCATE, LPRINT, LPRINT USING, POINT(), POS(), PRINT, PRINT USING, PRINT# USING, OPEN, WRITE, WRITE#.

PRINT# USING
Prints formatted text in a disk file

PRINT[#*file_num,*]USING *format_string;arg*[{,|;}[*arg*[{,|;}[...]]]]

The PRINT# USING statement prints formatted text in a disk file. The number *file_num* is the file number assigned to a file when it was opened with the OPEN statement. (If the file number is omitted, the printing is done on the screen.) The arguments *arg* are numbers, numeric or string variables, quoted strings, or expressions that evaluate to numbers or strings. Normally, when the last argument is printed, GW-BASIC prints a carriage return to advance to the next line. If the statement ends in a comma or semicolon, function, the carriage return is suppressed.

The PRINT# USING statement has an added formatting argument. The format string *format_string* controls where the arguments are printed on a line (see the PRINT USING statement for details).

See also Chapter 3, CSRLIN, LOCATE, LPRINT, LPRINT USING, POINT(), POS(), PRINT, PRINT USING, PRINT#, OPEN, WRITE, WRITE#.

PUT
Copies an image to the screen

PUT (*x,y*),*graphics_array*[,*comb_opt*]

The graphics version of the PUT statement transfers a screen image stored in an array variable to the screen. (The GET statement is used to copy a screen image and store it in an array variable.) The image is inserted with its upper-left corner at (*x,y*). The coordinates can be either screen units or user units set with the WINDOW statement.

The options *comb_opt* determine how the image is combined with what is already on the screen.

Option	Result
PSET	Replaces what is on the screen with the image.
PRESET	Replaces what is on the screen with the inverse of the image. That is, black changes to white and white to black, and so forth.
AND	Combines the screen contents with the image contents using a Boolean AND. The image replaces only those regions on the screen that already have an image.
OR	Combines the screen contents with the image contents using a Boolean OR. The screen contents and the image contents are added together.
XOR	Combines the screen contents with the image contents using a boolean XOR. The screen contents are inverted wherever the image appears; this is the default mode.

See also GET, LINE, SCREEN, WINDOW.

PUT
Copies a record buffer to a disk record

PUT[#]*file_num*[,*record_num*]

The file version of the PUT statement writes the contents of the record buffer to a record in a random-access disk file. (Use the GET statement to read the contents of a record into the record buffer.) The number *file_num* is the one assigned to the file when it was opened with the OPEN statement. The number *record_num* is the number of the record on disk where the buffer contents are stored. Records in the file are numbered sequentially starting with the first record as number 1. The record number ranges from 1 to 4,294,967,295. If the record number is omitted, the default is the next record in the file after the last one written with the PUT statement.

Access to the record buffer is with the FIELD statement, which equates string variables to fields in the buffer. If the file is to a communications port instead of a disk file, the record number is the number of characters to be read from the communications buffer.

See also Chapter 8, CVD(), CVI(), CVS(), FIELD, GET, LSET, MKD$(), MKI$(), MKS$(), OPEN, RSET.

RANDOMIZE
Reset the random number generator

RANDOMIZE [*seed*|TIMER]

The RANDOMIZE statement is used to reset the seed of the random number generator. The seed can also be reset with the RND() function by using a negative argument. The numbers are generated with the RND() function using a formula that produces pseudorandom values between zero and one. Since the function uses a formula, the random numbers are the same every time a program is run unless you seed the random number generator each time with a different starting value. The number *seed* is the new seed for the generator. You can also use the result of the TIMER function, which returns the number of seconds since midnight, as the seed value. If you omit the seed, GW-BASIC will stop and ask you for one.

See also RND().

READ
Reads data from an internal data statement

READ *variable*[,*variable*[,...]]

The READ statement is used to read values from an internal DATA statement and store them in some variables. Any number of DATA statements can be in a program, and they do not have to be contiguous. The first value read is from the lowest-numbered DATA statement, and reading continues to the highest-numbered one. To read a specific DATA statement or to reread a DATA statement, execute a RESTORE statement.

See also DATA, RESTORE.

REM
Remark statement, does nothing

REM [*comments*]
'[*comments*]

The REM statement is used to insert comments into a program. The text *comments* can be any text and does not have to be surrounded with double quotation marks. Everything from REM or a single quotation mark to the end of a line is ignored when a program executes. Remark statements can be the target statements of GOTO or GOSUB statements.

RENUM
Renumbers the program

RENUM [*new_num*][,[*start_num*][,*increment*]]

The RENUM statement renumbers the lines in a program, including line numbers contained within statements, such as the line number following GOTO. The number *new_num* is the first new line number. If *new_num* is omitted, the default is line 10. The number *start_num* is the number of the first statement to renumber, and line numbers lower than this are not changed. Renumbering continues through all the higher numbered statements. The default for *start_num* is 0, which will renumber the entire program. The number *increment* is the step between each of the new line numbers. The default is 10. Renumbering cannot reorder a program, so *new_num* must be at least one greater than the number of the statement before *start_num*.

See also AUTO.

RESET
Prepares a disk for removal

   RESET

The RESET statement is used to prepare floppy disks for removal. This statement closes all files, empties all file buffers, and writes all directory information to a disk. If the contents of a disk have been changed, the directory pointing to those changes may still be in memory, and the directory on the disk would still refer to the old data. Removing the disk at this point could make the data on it inconsistent. Use RESET statement whenever you have made changes in direct mode and want to remove a floppy disk to avoid the problem. Executing a CLOSE statement for every open file on a disk, or executing an END statement at the end of a program has the same effect.

See also CLOSE, END.

RESTORE
Resets internal data statements

   RESTORE [*line_num*]

The RESTORE statement sets the number of an internal DATA statement where reading with a READ statement is to begin. Any number of DATA statements can be in a program, and they do not have to be contiguous. Reading normally starts at the lowest-numbered statement. Use the RESTORE statement to select the DATA statement starting at *line_num* as the first one to read. Reading continues from there to the highest-numbered DATA statement. If the argument *line_num* is omitted, the lowest-numbered DATA statement in the program is selected. This also allows rereading of the data in DATA statements.

See also DATA, READ.

RESUME
Continues program execution after an error

RESUME [0|NEXT|*line_num*]

Use the RESUME statement to continue program execution after an error-recovery procedure specified with an ON ERROR GOTO statement. When a GW-BASIC program error occurs, the error-recovery procedure is executed to correct it. When that procedure has completed, the RESUME statement is used to continue execution of the program. Using RESUME with no arguments or with 0 as the argument starts execution with the statement that originally caused the error. Using the NEXT argument starts execution at the next statement after the one that caused the error. If the number *line_num* is used, execution resumes at that line number. Be careful of this last option, because all loops, loop counters, and GOSUB returns are still in force.

See also ON ERROR GOTO.

RETURN
Returns from a subroutine

RETURN[*line_num*]

The RETURN statement is used to return from a subroutine to the statement following the GOSUB statement that called it. While you can use the number *line_num* to return to some other location, use it with care, since all loops and GOSUB returns are still active. The line number option is used primarily for event trapping routines.

See also GOSUB, ON COM GOSUB, ON KEY() GOSUB, ON PEN GOSUB, ON PLAY() GOSUB, ON STRIG() GOSUB, ON TIMER() GOSUB.

RIGHT$( )
Extracts the right side of a string

RIGHT$(*source_string$,num_char*)

The RIGHT$() function extracts and returns *num_char* characters from the right side of *source_string$*.

See also Chapter 5, INSTR(), LEFT$(), LEN(), MID$().

RMDIR
Deletes a subdirectory

RMDIR *directory_path$*

The RMDIR statement deletes a subdirectory. The string *directory_path$* must be a standard DOS directory path that does not exceed 63 characters. The last subdirectory in the path is the one to be deleted and must be empty of all files or an error results.

See also CHDIR, FILES, KILL, MKDIR, NAME AS, RESET.

RND( )
Gets a random number

RND[(*seed*)]

The RND() function returns a pseudorandom number between zero and one. The numbers are generated using a formula, and unless the seed number is changed, will be the same every time a program is run. To prevent this from happening, seed the random number generator with a new starting value using either the RANDOMIZE statement or a negative value for the number *seed*. If the number *seed* is equal to 0, the previous value of the random number is returned. If seed is greater than 0 or omitted, the next random number in the sequence is returned.

See also RANDOMIZE.

RSET
Right-justifies a string in a record buffer

RSET *field_name$* = *string_expression*

The RSET statement right-justifies the string *string_expression* in the field *field_name$* of a record buffer for a random-access file. The FIELD statement is used to break the record buffer into fields and to name those fields with string variables. (Use LSET to left-justify strings into the field names.)

See also Chapter 8, CVD(), CVI(), CVS(), FIELD, LSET, LET, MKD$(), MKI$(), MKS$().

RUN
Runs a program

RUN [*line_num*|*file_name$*][,R]

The RUN statement runs a GW-BASIC program. If no options are used, the program currently in memory is run, starting at the lowest line number. If the number *line_num* is used, the program currently in memory is run, starting at that line number. If the string *file_name$* is used, GW-BASIC closes all files, erases memory, loads the indicated file and runs it. If the ,R switch is used, files are not closed before running a program.

See also CHAIN, CONT, END, LOAD, MERGE, RESUME, STOP.

SAVE
Saves a program in a disk file

SAVE *file_name$*[,A|,P]

The SAVE statement saves a copy of the program in memory in a disk file. The string *file_name$* names the file on disk and may include a directory path if the file is to be saved in a directory other than the default directory. If the file name does not include an extension, .BAS is assumed. If a file with the same name already exists on the disk, it is replaced by the new file.

GW-BASIC program files are normally stored in a compressed binary format. Using the ,A switch causes them to be saved as ASCII text that can be opened and edited with any word processor. The ,P switch causes the file to be saved in a protected (encrypted) binary format that allows it to be run, but neither listed nor edited. Be sure to save an unencrypted copy if you ever plan to make any changes to the program.

See also Chapter 2, BLOAD, BSAVE, CHAIN, LIST, LOAD, MERGE.

SCREEN
Sets the display screen attributes

SCREEN [*mode*][,[*color_switch*]][,[*active_pg*][,*visual_pg*]]]

The SCREEN statement is used to set the screen mode. Screen modes include both character and several graphics modes. The modes available on a particular system depend on the monitor and monitor card in that system. The number *mode* takes on the values 0, 1, 2, 7, 8, 9, and 10. The table below details the capabilities of each mode and the systems that they are available on. Note that mode 0 is text, and the rest are all graphics modes. (See the COLOR statement for a list of the colors available in each mode.)

For composite video monitors and TVs, the number *color_switch* sets only black and white for the modes that allow color. In the graphics modes, a value of 0 disables color and a value of 1 turns color on again. For text mode (0), a value of 0 turns color on and a value of 1 disables it.

The two numbers *active_pg* and *visual_pg* specify which graphics page is the active page and which is the visual page. The active page is the one that the drawing statements affect; the visual page is the one that is being displayed. (This is allowed only in graphics cards that have sufficient memory to support more than one page of graphics memory.) Switching active and visual pages is one method of achieving animation: you draw on one page while you view the other.

The following table lists the graphic attributes for the different screen modes. An MDPA (monochrome display and printer adapter) card can display only mode 0 on a monochrome monitor. A CGA (color graphics adapter) card can display modes 0, 1, and 2, and an EGA (enhanced graphics adapter) card can display all these modes (except 10) on a color monitor; mode 10 is for a monochrome monitor attached to an EGA card. Modes 7 and 8 are enhanced versions of modes 1 and 2 and make use of the EGA card's greater capabilities. Mode 9 makes full use of the EGA card's capabilities.

Mode	Resolution	Memory Pages	Attributes	Colors	Bits per pixel
0	Text only	1		16	
1	320 x 200	1	4	16	2
2	640 x 200	1	2	16	1
7^1	320 x 200	$2,4,8^2$	16	16	4
8^1	640 x 200	$1,2,4^2$	16	16	4

Mode	Resolution	Memory Pages	Attributes	Colors	Bits per pixel
9^1	640 x 350	2^4	$4,16^3$	64	$2,4^3$
10^5	640 x 350	2^4	4	9^6	2

[1] EGA only.

[2] With 64K, 128K, or 256K of EGA memory.

[3] With 64K of EGA memory, 4 attributes, and 2 bits per pixel.
   With 128K and 256K of EGA memory, 16 attributes, and 4
   bits per pixel.

[4] With 256K of EGA memory.

[5] EGA with a monochrome monitor.

[6] Pseudocolors, blinking black and white patterns.

See also COLOR, PALETTE WIDTH.

SCREEN( )

Gets the character at a location

SCREEN(*row,column*[,*color*])

The SCREEN() function returns the ASCII code of the character at a location on the screen. (See Figure 5.1 for a list of ASCII codes and characters.) The location is specified with the numbers *row* and *column*. The number of rows ranges from 1 to 25 and counts down from the top of the display. The number of columns ranges from 1 to 40 or 80, depending on the width of the display set with the WIDTH statement. The argument *color* is allowed only in text mode (0); if the argument is non-zero the color attribute of the character is returned instead of its code. If it is zero, the ASCII code is returned.

See also CSRLIN, LOCATE, POINT(), POS(), SCREEN().

SGN( )

Returns the sign of a number

SGN(*number*)

The SGN() function returns the sign of a number. The function returns the value 1 with the sign (plus or minus) of *number*. If *number* is 0, the function returns 0.

See also ABS(), CINT(), FIX(), INT().

SHELL
Executes DOS commands without exiting GW-BASIC

    SHELL [*dos_command_string$*]

The SHELL statement executes DOS commands and runs other programs without removing GW-BASIC from memory. The memory containing GW-BASIC is partitioned off and the remaining memory is used for DOS commands or other programs. If SHELL is executed without any arguments, it runs COMMAND.COM, the DOS command processor, in the remaining memory. You can then execute the necessary commands. To return from DOS to GW-BASIC, type EXIT. To execute a single DOS command and immediately return to GW-BASIC, put the command, including arguments, in the string *dos_command_string$*.

See also CHDIR, ENVIRON, ENVIRON$, FILES, KILL, MKDIR, NAME AS, RMDIR.

SIN( )
Calculates the sine of a number

    SIN(*angle*)

The SIN() function calculates the single-precision sine of *angle*. The number *angle* must be in radians. To convert from degrees to radians, multiply the degrees by &p/180. To get double-precision values of the sine, use the /D switch when invoking GW-BASIC.

See also ATN(), COS(), TAN().

SOUND
Emits variable frequency and duration tones

    SOUND *frequency,duration*

The SOUND statement emits variable frequency and variable duration tones. The number *frequency* is the frequency of the sound in Hertz (cycles per second). The allowed values are 37 to 32,767, although most people can't hear tones above about 13,000 Hz. The number *duration* is the length of the tone in clock ticks. The allowed values are 0 to 65,535, and there are 18.2 clock ticks per second. The value 0 turns off a tone, as does a PLAY statement. Values of *duration* greater than 0 but less than 0.022 produce a continuous tone.

The tone plays in the foreground unless background sound has been set with the PLAY statement. Foreground sound must play to completion before any other statements can run. Background sounds are put in a queue, and play while the program continues running.

See also BEEP, ON PLAY() GOSUB, PLAY, PLAY().

SPACE$( )
Returns a string of spaces

SPACE$(*num_spaces*)

The SPACE$() function returns a string of *num_spaces* spaces. The number *num_spaces* must be in the range 0 to 255.

See also SPC(), STRING$().

SPC( )
Skips spaces in PRINT statements

SPC(*num_spaces*)

The SPC() function skips *num_spaces* spaces in a PRINT, PRINT#, or LPRINT statement. The number *num_spaces* must be in the range 0 to 255.

See also SPACE$(), STRING$(), TAB().

SQR( )
Calculates the square root of a number

SQR(*number*)

The SQR() function calculates the single-precision square root of *number*, which must be greater than zero. To get double-precision values of the square root, use the /D switch when invoking GW-BASIC.

See also ABS(), EXP(), LOG().

STICK( )
Gets the coordinates of a joystick

STICK(*code*)

The STICK() function returns the *x* and *y* coordinates of the joystick. The number *code* determines which coordinate is returned. Execute the function with a code of 0 first to store all the coordinates at one point in time, then read them with the other codes.

Code	Results
0	Stores the *x* and *y* coordinates of both joysticks and returns the *x* coordinate of joystick A.
1	Returns the *y* coordinate of joystick A.
2	Returns the *x* coordinate of joystick B.
3	Returns the *y* coordinate of joystick B.

See also ON STRIG(), GOSUB, STRIG(), STRING ON|OFF|STOP.

STOP
Breaks the execution of a code without closing files

STOP

The STOP statement breaks the execution of a program, and leaves it in a state that can be restarted with the CONT statement. A STOP statement is equivalent to pressing Ctrl-Break. After a program is stopped, the variables can be examined using PRINT statements, or their values changed in direct mode. As long as none of the program lines have been changed, the program can be restarted by executing CONT. A program that has been stopped using the END statement cannot be restarted and must be rerun with RUN. Use a GOTO statement instead of CONT to make execution restart at a different place.

See also Chapter 9, CONT, END, RUN.

STR$( )
Converts a number to a string

STR$(*number*)

The STR$() function returns a string representation of the value of *number*. The string has a leading space or minus sign and no trailing space. The VAL() function converts a string representation of a number into a value.

See also VAL().

STRIG ON|OFF
Enables/disables tracking joystick triggers

STRIG ON|OFF

The STRIG ON|OFF statement enables or disables tracking the joystick trigger state. The STRIG ON statement enables tracking the joystick triggers so that their state can be read with the STRIG() function. The STRIG OFF statement disables checking the triggers. Note that this is different from the STRIG() ON|OFF|STOP statement.

See also ON STRIG() GOSUB, STRIG(), STRIG() ON|OFF|STOP.

STRIG( ) ON|OFF|STOP
Enables/disables trapping joystick triggers

STRIG(*code*) ON|OFF|STOP

The STRIG() ON statement turns on trapping of joystick trigger events (presses). To use trigger-event trapping, you must first execute an ON STRIG() GOSUB statement to set the subroutine to branch to whenever a trigger is used. When trapping is turned on, GW-BASIC starts checking the joystick triggers between execution of the program statements. If a trigger event occurs, the program branches to the subroutine set with the

ON STRIG() GOSUB statement. The number code determines for which trigger the event trapping takes place.

Joystick A		Joystick B	
Code	Trigger	Code	Trigger
0	1	2	1
4	2	6	2

The STRIG() OFF statement disables trigger event trapping, GW-BASIC stops checking for trigger events, and any ensuing events are lost. The STRIG() STOP statement disables trigger event trapping but does not lose any events, saving them until a STRIG() ON statement is executed. A STRIG() STOP is automatically executed whenever a trigger event trap takes place, and a STRIG() ON is automatically executed when you return from the trap subroutine, unless a STRIG() OFF is executed in the trap subroutine.

See also ON STRIG() GOSUB, STRIG().

STRIG( )
Gets the state of the joystick triggers

STRIG(*code*)

The STRIG() function returns the state of the joystick triggers. The STRIG ON statement must have been executed before this function is called. The number code determines what is returned by the function.

Code	Result
0	Trigger A1; returns −1 if the trigger has been pressed since the last STRIG(0) statement, or 0 if it has not.
1	Trigger A1; returns −1 if the trigger is currently pressed, or 0 if it is not.

Code	Result
2	Trigger B1; returns −1 if the trigger has been pressed since the last STRIG(2) statement or 0 if it has not.
3	Trigger B1; returns −1 if the trigger is currently pressed, or 0 if it is not.
4	Trigger A2; returns −1 if the trigger has been pressed since the last STRIG(4) statement or 0 if it has not.
5	Trigger A2; returns −1 if the trigger is currently pressed, or 0 if it is not.
6	Trigger B2; returns −1 if the trigger has been pressed since the last STRIG(6) statement or 0 if it has not.
7	Trigger B2; returns −1 if the trigger is currently pressed, or 0 if it is not.

See also ON STRIG() GOSUB, STRIG ON|OFF|STOP.

STRING$( )
Returns a string of characters

STRING$(*num_char*,{*code*|*char$*})

The STRING$() function returns a string of *num_char* characters. The number *num_char* must be in the range 0 to 255. The character returned is selected with the second argument, which can be either the ASCII code of the character (*code*) or a string containing the character (*char$*). If there is more than one character in *char$*, only the first character is reproduced.

See also SPC(), SPACE$().

SWAP
Exchanges the values of two variables

SWAP *variable_1*,*variable_2*

The SWAP statement exchanges the values of two variables. Both *variable_1* and *variable_2* must be of the same type.

SYSTEM
Ends GW-BASIC and returns to DOS

    SYSTEM

The SYSTEM statement closes all files, quits GW-BASIC, and returns to DOS.
See also SHELL.

TAB( )
Spaces to a specific position in a line

    TAB(*position*)

The TAB() function in a print statement moves the cursor to a specific character position in a PRINT, PRINT#, or LPRINT statement. The number *position* must be in the range 1 to 255. If the current character position of the cursor is beyond *position*, the cursor is moved to that character position on the next line down. If the function is the last item in a PRINT statement the cursor is not advanced to the next line.
See also LOCATE, SPACE$(), SPC(), STRING$().

TAN( )
Calculates the tangent of a number in radians

    TAN(*angle*)

The TAN() function calculates the single-precision tangent of *angle*. The number *angle* must be in radians. To convert from degrees to radians, multiply the degrees by $\pi/180$. To get double-precision values of the tangent, use the /D switch when invoking GW-BASIC.
See also ATN(), COS(), SIN().

TIME$
Sets the current time

TIME$ = *new_time_string$*

The TIME$ statement is used to set the system clock to the time specified in the string *new_time_string$*. The format of the string must be: hh[:mm[:ss]], where hh equals hours, mm equals minutes, and ss equals seconds. Any omitted values default to 00.

See also DATE$, ON TIME() GOSUB, TIME$, TIMER.

TIME$
Gets the current time

TIME$

The TIME$ function returns an eight-character string containing the time in the following form hh:mm:ss where hh equals hours, mm equals minutes, and ss equals seconds. For hours, minutes or seconds less than ten, a leading zero is inserted to keep the string eight characters long.

See also DATE$, ON TIME() GOSUB, TIME$, TIMER.

TIMER
Gets the number of seconds since reset

TIMER

The TIMER function returns a single-precision number containing the number of seconds since system reset or midnight, whichever is smaller.

See also DATE$, ON TIME() GOSUB, TIME$.

TIMER ON|OFF|STOP
Enables/disables timer-event trapping

TIMER ON|OFF|STOP

The TIMER ON statement turns on trapping of timer events. To use timer event trapping, you must first execute an ON TIMER() GOSUB statement to set the subroutine to branch to whenever timer events occur, and to set the number of seconds between the events. When timer-event trapping is turned on, GW-BASIC starts checking the time between the execution of the program statements. If the number of seconds set in the ON TIMER() GOSUB have elapsed, the program branches to the subroutine set in that statement.

The TIMER OFF statement disables timer-event trapping, GW-BASIC stops checking, and any subsequent timer events are lost. The TIMER STOP statement disables timer event trapping but does not lose a timer event that arrives with this statement in force. The event is saved until a TIMER ON statement is executed. A TIMER STOP is automatically executed whenever a timer event trap takes place, and a TIMER ON is automatically executed when you return from the trap subroutine, unless a TIMER OFF is executed in the trap subroutine.

See also ON TIMER GOSUB, TIME$, TIMER.

TROFF
Turns program tracing off

    TROFF

The TROFF statement turns tracing off.
See also Chapter 9, CONT, STOP, TRON.

TRON
Turn program tracing on

    TRON

The TRON statement turns tracing on. When tracing is on, the line number of the statement being executed is printed on the screen in square brackets, allowing you to trace the execution of a code by watching the line numbers. This is used for debugging operations.
See also Chapter 9, CONT, STOP, TROFF.

UNLOCK
Releases access restrictions to a file

    UNLOCK[#]*file_num*[,[*record_num_1*][TO *record_num_2*]]

The UNLOCK statement is used to release restrictions placed on a networked file by LOCK, so that other processes can get access to it. In a network environment, more than one computer can have access to a set of files, and the LOCK statement is to reserve access to a particular file while you are using it. The number *file_num* is the file number assigned to the file when it was opened with the OPEN statement.

If no record range is given or the file is a sequential-access file, the whole file is unlocked. Valid record numbers range from 1 to 4,294,967,295. If a record range is given for random-access files, only those records will be unlocked (record ranges on sequential-access files are ignored). If *record_num_1* is omitted, the number is assumed to be 1. If the range TO *record_num_2* is omitted, only one record is unlocked. Be sure to unlock any locked file before closing it or future access to the file may be jeopardized.

See also LOCK, OPEN.

USR( )
Calls a machine language subroutine

USR[*num*](*argument*)

The USR function is used to call machine language functions. There are ten USR functions—USR0 through USR9—called with the number *num*. The function's offset must be set with a DEF USR statement before it can be used. If the function is stored in other than GW-BASIC's data segment, the DEF SEG statement must be executed to set the current data segment to the one containing the function. The function has one argument and must understand the type of variable being sent. If it does not need an argument, a dummy variable must be used. This statement is used primarily for compatibility with older versions of BASIC.

See also DEF SEG, DEF USR(), CALL.

VAL( )
Converts a string to a number

VAL(*numeric_string$*)

The VAL() function is used to convert a string representation of a number to a numeric value. Leading spaces, tabs, and linefeeds in *numeric_string$* are ignored when extracting the number. If the first nonblank character is not numeric, VAL() returns 0.

See also STR$().

VARPTR( )
Gets the memory address of variables or file control blocks

    VARPTR(*variable_name*|#*file_num*)

The VARPTR() function is used to get the memory address of a variable or file control block. This function is primarily used to get the locations of variables to pass to machine language subroutines (see CALL and USR()). If a variable name is used for the argument of VARPTR(), the function returns the address of the first byte of that variable in memory. The VARPTR() function should be called just before its value is to be used because variables, especially arrays, are moved around in memory as new variables are defined. The number returned by the function ranges from −32,768 to 32,767. Adding 65,536 to any negative values received gives the correct memory address. Variables must be defined by assigning something to them before using them in a VARPTR() statement.

If a pound sign and a file number are used as the argument, VARPTR() returns the address of the start of the file control block for the file with that number. The file control block contains file type information, the file buffer, the record buffer (see FIELD), and other information pertaining to the open file.

VARPTR$( )
Gets a variable's address as a string

    VARPTR$(*variable_name*)

The VARPTR$() function is mainly used to get variable locations to be passed to machine language subroutines (see CALL and USR()). It returns the location of a variable in memory as a three-byte string. The first byte contains the type of variable, with values of 2 for integer, 3 for string, 4 for single-precision, and 8 for double-precision. The second byte contains the least-significant byte and the third contains the most-significant byte of the memory address.

See also PEEK, POKE.

VIEW

Sets the viewport for drawing

VIEW[SCREEN][(*x1,y1*)-(*x2,y2*)[,[*back_color*][,[*border_color*]]]]

The VIEW statement is used to define the viewport, that is, the limits of the drawing area on the screen. Normally, drawing with the drawing statements (CIRCLE, LINE, DRAW, PAINT, PSET(), and so forth) can take place anywhere on the screen. The VIEW statement limits drawing to the rectangle defined with the coordinates (*x1,y1*), and (*x2,y2*) as opposing corners. All drawing now takes place only in that rectangle. Any attempt to draw to a point outside of that rectangle is clipped when it reaches the rectangle, and any drawing outside of the rectangle is ignored. The coordinate system has the origin in the upper-left corner, with increasing values of the *x* and *y* coordinates going down and to the right. (See the SCREEN statement for the range of the *x* and *y* coordinates for different screen modes.) A RUN statement or a VIEW statement with no arguments resets the viewport to the whole screen.

If the SCREEN option is omitted, the origin of the coordinate system (0,0) is moved to the upper-left corner of the rectangle. If it is included, the origin stays in the upper-left corner of the screen. The coordinate system is not scaled when the viewport is created (to scale the viewport, see the WINDOW statement).

The optional number *back_color* is the attribute of a color to paint the viewport rectangle. The number *border_color* is the attribute of a color to draw a rectangular border around the viewport. (See the COLOR statement for a list of valid color attributes.)

When a viewport is set, CLS clears only the viewport. To clear the whole screen, reset the viewport to the whole screen, then execute CLS.

See also COLOR, SCREEN, VIEW PRINT, WINDOW.

VIEW PRINT
Set the viewport for printing

> VIEW PRINT [*upper_line* TO *lower_line*]

The VIEW PRINT statement sets the viewport for text display on the screen. Normally, text can be displayed on all 25 lines of the screen. Lines 1 through 24 are scrolled while line 25 is fixed. The VIEW PRINT statement redefines the scrollable portion of the screen. A VIEW PRINT statement with no arguments resets the text area to the default values. The default values of *upper_line* and *lower_line* are 1 and 24. Use the LOCATE statement to print on line 25.

See also VIEW.

WAIT
Pauses for input from a machine port

> WAIT *port_num,and_mask*[,*xor_mask*]

The WAIT statement halts execution of the program and waits for a byte with a specific bit pattern to appear. The number *port_num* is the machine port number to watch for the byte to appear. It must be in the range 0 to 65,535 and must be a valid machine port. (You will need a technical reference manual for your computer for a list of valid machine ports.) When a byte appears at a machine port, it is first XORed (exclusive OR, see the *GW-BASIC Logical Operators* at the beginning of this Appendix) with *xor_mask* and then ANDed with *and_mask*. If the result is zero, the statement waits for another byte. If the result is nonzero, execution of the program continues with the next statement after the WAIT statement. The numbers *and_mask* and *xor_mask* must be in the range 0 to 255.

See also INP(), OUT.

WHILE/WEND
Defines a logically terminated loop

> WHILE *logical_expression*
>
> . other statements

WEND

The WHILE and WEND statements specify a logically terminated loop. When the WHILE statement is encountered the argument *logical_expression* is evaluated. If the expression is true (nonzero) all the statements between the WHILE and WEND statements are executed. Execution then loops back to the WHILE statement and evaluates *logical_expression* again. This continues until *logical_expression* is false (zero), at which point execution continues with the statement after the WEND statement. WHILE and WEND statements can be nested to any level, with each WEND statement looping back to the most recently executed WHILE statement.

See also FOR/NEXT.

WIDTH
Sets the width for printed output

WIDTH [*file_num|device_name$*],*line_length*

The WIDTH statement sets the length of a line for printed output. The number *line_length* is the length of a line in characters. A carriage return is automatically inserted in the output whenever *line_length* characters are output to a device. The value of *line_length* can range from 0 to 255; for the screen it is restricted to 40 or 80. If it is set to 255 for the line printer, it has the effect of setting an infinite line width. The printer then has to perform the line wrapping.

The argument *file_num* is the file number assigned to a file when it is opened with the OPEN statement. The string *device_name$* must contain a valid output device name. Allowed device name strings are COM1:, COM2:, LPT1:, LPT2:, LPT3:, SCRN: (see the OPEN statement).

See also OPEN, PRINT, PRINT#, SCREEN.

WINDOW
Defines user coordinates for the viewport

WINDOW[[SCREEN](*x1,y1*)-(*x2,y2*)]

The WINDOW statement defines the user coordinate system for graphics output on the screen. When GW-BASIC is initialized, drawing on the screen must be done in screen coordinates. Screen coordinates have the origin (0,0) in the upper-left corner of the screen, and positive values of *x* and *y* are to the right and down. The range of screen coordinates is determined by the active screen mode set with the SCREEN statement and the viewport set with the VIEW statement. The VIEW statement restricts graphics to a specific rectangle on the screen; the WINDOW statement defines the coordinate system used in that rectangle.

The WINDOW statement defines a user coordinate system for the whole screen or for the current viewport if one was set with VIEW. A user coordinate system is just that, a coordinate system defined by the user. The range of *x* and *y* values in the current viewport are set to any range of valid GW-BASIC numbers that you want. Graphics statements (except DRAW) then use the user coordinate system to draw on the screen, and GW-BASIC automatically converts the user coordinates to screen coordinates. The *x, y* coordinate pairs *(x1,y2)* and *(x2,y2)* define the coordinates of the lower-left and upper-right corner of the graphics viewport. The values of the coordinates now increase up and to the right, unless the SCREEN option is used, in which case they read down and to the right. A RUN, SCREEN, or WINDOW statement with no options resets the screen to the screen coordinate system.

See also CIRCLE, LINE, PAINT, POINT(), PSET(), SCREEN, VIEW.

WRITE
Prints with delimiters

WRITE[*arg*][,|;[*arg*[,|;[...]]]]

The WRITE statement is used to print delimited data on the screen.

This statement is similar to the PRINT statement, except that each printed argument is separated from the next with a comma, and printed strings are enclosed in double quotation marks. The WRITE statement does not tab to the next tab stop when arguments are separated by commas, and no leading spaces are inserted in printed numbers.

See also Chapter 3, INPUT, INPUT#, OPEN, PRINT, PRINT#, WRITE#.

WRITE#
Prints with delimiters

WRITE#*file_num*,[*arg*][,|;[*arg*[,|;[...]]]]

The WRITE# statement is used to print delimited data to a disk file. The number *file_num* is the file number assigned to a file when it was opened with the OPEN statement.

This statement is similar to the PRINT# statement, except that each printed argument is separated from the next with a comma, and printed strings are enclosed by double quotation marks. The WRITE# statement does not tab to the next tab stop when arguments are separated by commas, and no leading spaces are inserted in printed numbers.

Numeric and string data written to a disk file using the WRITE# statement are accurately recoverable with the INPUT# statement in exactly the same form as written. A mixture of numeric and string data written with a PRINT# statement can be input as a single string with the INPUT# statement. See the INPUT# statement for a description of the characters that terminate input.

See also Chapter 3, INPUT, INPUT#, OPEN, PRINT, PRINT#, WRITE.

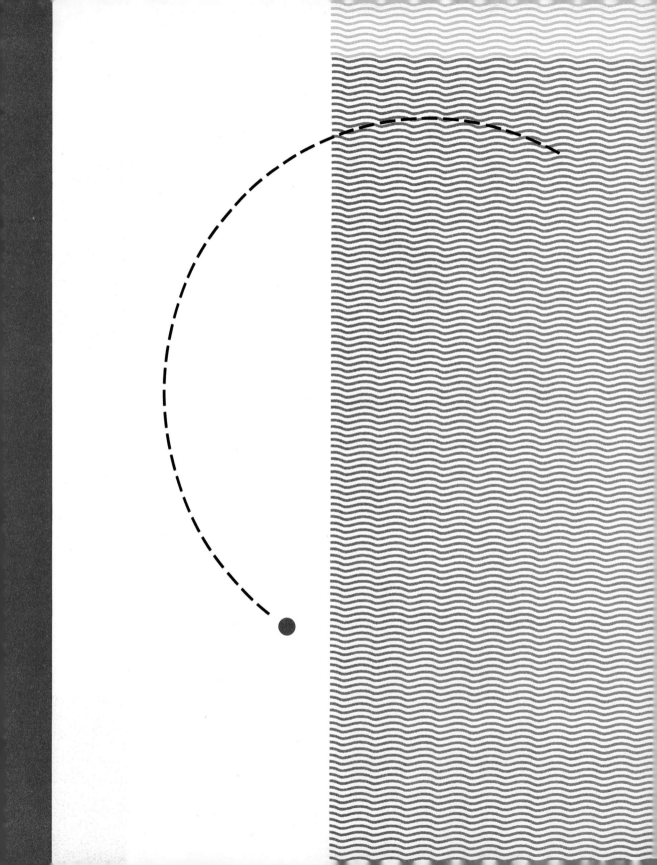

GW-BASIC
Error Codes

Code	Error
1	NEXT without FOR
2	Syntax error
3	RETURN without GOSUB
4	Out of DATA
5	Illegal function call
6	Overflow
7	Out of memory
8	Undefined line number

Code	Error	Code	Error
9	Subscript out of range	52	Bad file number
10	Duplicate Definition	53	File not found
11	Division by zero	54	Bad file mode
12	Illegal direct	55	File already open
13	Type mismatch	56	Unprintable error
14	Out of string space	57	Device I/O Error
15	String too long	58	File already exists
16	String formula too complex	59, 60	Unprintable error
		61	Disk full
17	Can't continue	62	Input past end
18	Undefined user function	63	Bad record number
19	No RESUME	64	Bad file name
20	RESUME without error	65	Unprintable error
21	Unprintable error	66	Direct statement in file
22	Missing operand	67	Too many files
23	Line buffer overflow	68	Device Unavailable
24	Device Timeout	69	Communication buffer overflow
25	Device Fault		
26	FOR Without NEXT	70	Permission Denied
27	Out of Paper	71	Disk not Ready
28	Unprintable error	72	Disk media error
29	WHILE without WEND	73	Advanced Feature
30	WEND without WHILE	74	Rename across disks
31–49	Unprintable error	75	Path/File Access Error
50	FIELD overflow	76	Path not found
51	Internal error		

INDEX

! (exclamation mark)
   in PRINT USING statement, 32
   for single-precision numbers, 55, 58
(pound sign), 55
   for double-precision variable
      names, 58
   and file input and output, 37
   in INPUT$() function, 240
   in PRINT USING statement, 33
$ (dollar sign), in string variable
   name, 56, 76
% (percentage sign)
   for integer variable names, 58
   in printed output, 34
      (ampersand), in PRINT USING
      statement, 32
* (multiplication) operator, 199
+ (addition) operator, 200
- (unary negation) operator, 199
/ (floating point division), 199
< (less than) operator, 89, 201
≤ (less than or equal to) operator, 201
<> (inequality operator), 201
= (equality) operator, 201
> (greater than) operator, 89, 201
≥ (greater than or equal to) operator, 202
? (question mark), from INPUT statement, 35–36
\ (integer division), 199–200
\\ (backslashes) in PRINT USING
   statement, 32
^ (exponential) operator, 199

A

A> prompt, 3
ABS() function, 61, 204
addition operator (+), 200
address
   physical, 221

segment, 221–222
   starting for USR function, 222
ALL option, in CHAIN statement,
   208
Alt key, for ASCII code, 79
American Standard Code for Information Exchange. See ASCII code
AMORT.BAS programs, 130–141
amortization table, program for,
   130–141
ampersand (@INDEX LV 2 =), in
   PRINT USING statement, 32
AND logical operator, 108, 202–203
angle, for drawing, 226
animation, 288
appending data to file, 38, 198
arc, drawing, 210
arccosine, 205
arcsine, 205
arctangents, 61, 205
arguments, 12
   in functions, 60
   of INPUT statement, 35
   multiple, for INPUT statement, 36
   in PRINT statement, 29
   in PRINT USING statement,
      277–278
   separation of, 30–31
   in user-defined functions, 220
arithmetic
   Boolean, 202
   operators for, 199–200
array subscripts, setting lower limit
   for, 266
array variables, 224
   erasing, 228
arrays, 64–69, 116
   for copying screen image, 234
   defining, 66–67
   deleting, 67
   dimensions for, 113
   indices for, 68

of loan payments, 67–69
   multidimensional, 65–66
   random access to elements of, 145
ASC() function, 78, 204–205
ASCII code, 75
   converting characters to, 204–205
   converting to character, 77–78,
      208–209
ASCII text files, 39
   saving, 287
assignment statements, 52, 58–59, 63
ATN() function, 61, 205
attributes, 212
AUTO command, 205
AUTOEXEC.BAT file, 45

B

background color, 212–213, 268
background music, 261, 271–272
background sound, 291
backslashes (\\), in PRINT USING
   statement, 32
backspace, control character for, 35,
   77, 204
Backspace key, 19
.BAS file name extension, 21
BASIC, features of, 2–3. See also
   GW-BASIC
BASICA, xx
batch files, 45–46
baud rate, 265
BEEP statement, 186, 206
bell (beep), 20
   control character for, 35, 77, 204
binary format, 21, 52
binary memory image file, 206
bits, 52
bits per pixel, 234
blank line, 29
blank records, inserting, 148
blinking text, 213

S

/S: flag, 198
SAVE command, 21, 41–42, 198, 287
save process
  for memory image to disk file,
    206–207
  for program, 6–7, 21–22
  for record buffer contents, 175–176
  for variables in chained pro-
    grams, 217
scale factor, 225–226
scan codes for keys, 237–238,
  244–245
scientific notation, 54
scientific symbols, 78
screen
  clearing, 22, 211–212
  communication with, 29
  copying image to, 281
  displaying point on, 275–276
  drawing area on, 301
  echoing contents of, 34, 182–183
  messages on, 140
  opening, 113, 264
  printing messages to, in debugging,
    185–186
  printing to, 29–34, 133
screen buffers, 221–222
screen colors, 212
  remapping, 268
screen coordinates, 210, 248, 276, 304
  mapping, 273–274
screen format, 139
screen image, copying to variable,
  234
screen mode, 212, 214, 288
screen page, copying, 269
screen pixels, attributes of, 274–275
SCREEN statement, 210, 225, 234,
  267, 270, 274, 287–289, 304
SCREEN() function, 289
SCRN: keyword, 91, 182
scrolling, 251
searching, subroutine for, 173–174
second-level subroutines, 130
seed, of random number generator, 282

segment address, 221–222
semicolons, separating arguments
  with, 30–31
sequential disk files, 37–40
serial communications, buffer size
  for, 198
serial communications port
  checking, 258
  input from, 240, 249
  opening, 264–266
  trapping, 216–217
SGN() function, 61, 289–290
shared files, 263
SHELL command, 23, 227, 290
sign, of numbers, 289–290
SIN() function, 61, 290
single-precision numbers, 54–55
  converting to, 61, 218
  converting strings to, 219
  converting to 4-byte strings, 257
  declaring variables as, 223
  stored as strings, 150
  variable names for, 58
sound signals, 186–188, 192
SOUND statement, 187, 192, 290–
  291
source-code debugger, 181
SPACE$() function, 77, 79, 85, 291
spaces
  as delimiters, 253
  in formulas, 59
  in strings, 81
  separating arguments with, 30–31
  skipping in PRINT statement, 291
SPC() function, 30, 254, 291
SQR() function, 61, 291–292
square brackets [], 197
square root, 61, 291–292
starting GW-BASIC, 3–4, 11–12,
  197–198
statements, 12, 204
statistics, collecting on computer
  use, 40
STEP function, 189–191
STEP option, in PRESET() function, 275
step size, 101

STICK() function, 292
stop bits, 265
STOP statement, 189, 217, 227,
  292–293
stopping program, 16
storage. *See* data storage
STR$() function, 78, 150, 293
straight-line depreciation, 5
STRIG ON|OFF|STOP statement,
  262, 293–294
STRIG() function, 294–295
string variables, 56
  declaring, 223
  names for, 58
  reading text from file into, 40
STRING$() function, 75–76, 295
strings, 74–95
  comparison of, 200
  concatenating, 85
  conversion to double-precision num-
    ber, 218
  conversion to numeric values, 151
  conversion of single-precision num-
    bers to 4-byte strings, 257
  converting double-precision num-
    bers to, 256
  converting integers to 2-byte
    strings, 256–257
  converting numbers to, 293
  converting to integer, 219
  converting to numeric values, 78,
    299–300
  converting to single-precision num-
    ber, 219
  in DATA statement, 219
  empty, 75
  extracting left side of, 247
  extracting right side of, 285
  from GW-BASIC environment
    string table, 228
  getting information about, 85–86
  in INPUT statement, 36
  inputting, 240, 249
  left-justifying in record buffer,
    254–255
  length of, 85, 247
  locating substring in, 241

ABCs of GW-BASIC Examples Disk

If you would like to use the examples in this book but don't want to enter them yourself, you can obtain them on disk. In addition, the disk contains many other examples of GW-BASIC statements and functions. Complete the following order form and return it along with a check or money order for $20.00 in U.S. funds. For orders from countries other than the U.S. or Canada, please add $1.00 for shipping. For California orders, please add your local sales tax. The BASIC Examples Disk will be sent to you by first class mail. The disk is a 5 1/4" 360K disk.

William J. Orvis
226 Joyce St.
Livermore, CA 94550

Name _____

Address _____

_____

City/State/ZIP _____

Cost $20.00

Overseas shipping (not U.S. or Canada) $ 1.00

Local sales tax (California only)   _____

Total   _____

Enclosed is my check or money order for $_____ in U.S. funds
(Make checks payable to William J. Orvis).
Please send me the BASIC Examples Disk.

SYBEX is not affiliated with William J. Orvis and assumes no responsibility for any defect in the disk programs.

TO JOIN THE SYBEX MAILING LIST OR ORDER BOOKS
PLEASE COMPLETE THIS FORM

NAME _____ COMPANY _____

STREET _____ CITY _____

STATE _____ ZIP _____

☐ PLEASE MAIL ME MORE INFORMATION ABOUT **SYBEX** TITLES

ORDER FORM (There is no obligation to order)

PLEASE SEND ME THE FOLLOWING:

TITLE	QTY	PRICE
_____	___	___
_____	___	___
_____	___	___
_____	___	___

TOTAL BOOK ORDER   ___ $___

CUSTOMER SIGNATURE _____

SHIPPING AND HANDLING PLEASE ADD $2.00 PER BOOK VIA UPS   ___

FOR OVERSEAS SURFACE ADD $5.25 PER BOOK PLUS $4.40 REGISTRATION FEE   ___

FOR OVERSEAS AIRMAIL ADD $18.25 PER BOOK PLUS $4.40 REGISTRATION FEE   ___

CALIFORNIA RESIDENTS PLEASE ADD APPLICABLE SALES TAX   ___

TOTAL AMOUNT PAYABLE   ___

☐ CHECK ENCLOSED   ☐ VISA
☐ MASTERCARD   ☐ AMERICAN EXPRESS

ACCOUNT NUMBER _____

EXPIR. DATE _____ DAYTIME PHONE _____

CHECK AREA OF COMPUTER INTEREST:

☐ BUSINESS SOFTWARE

☐ TECHNICAL PROGRAMMING

☐ OTHER: _____

THE FACTOR THAT WAS MOST IMPORTANT IN YOUR SELECTION:

☐ THE SYBEX NAME

☐ QUALITY

☐ PRICE

☐ EXTRA FEATURES

☐ COMPREHENSIVENESS

☐ CLEAR WRITING

☐ OTHER _____

OTHER COMPUTER TITLES YOU WOULD LIKE TO SEE IN PRINT:

_____

_____

OCCUPATION

☐ PROGRAMMER   ☐ TEACHER

☐ SENIOR EXECUTIVE   ☐ HOMEMAKER

☐ COMPUTER CONSULTANT   ☐ RETIRED

☐ SUPERVISOR   ☐ STUDENT

☐ MIDDLE MANAGEMENT   ☐ OTHER:

☐ ENGINEER/TECHNICAL   _____

☐ CLERICAL/SERVICE

☐ BUSINESS OWNER/SELF EMPLOYED

CHECK YOUR LEVEL OF COMPUTER USE

☐ NEW TO COMPUTERS

☐ INFREQUENT COMPUTER USER

☐ FREQUENT USER OF ONE SOFTWARE

   PACKAGE:

   NAME _____

☐ FREQUENT USER OF MANY SOFTWARE

   PACKAGES

☐ PROFESSIONAL PROGRAMMER

OTHER COMMENTS:

_____

_____

_____

_____

_____

_____

_____

PLEASE FOLD, SEAL, AND MAIL TO SYBEX

SYBEX, INC.
2021 CHALLENGER DR. #100
ALAMEDA, CALIFORNIA USA
                              94501

SEAL

SYBEX Computer Books are different.

Here is why . . .

At SYBEX, each book is designed with you in mind. Every manuscript is carefully selected and supervised by our editors, who are themselves computer experts. We publish the best authors, whose technical expertise is matched by an ability to write clearly and to communicate effectively. Programs are thoroughly tested for accuracy by our technical staff. Our computerized production department goes to great lengths to make sure that each book is well-designed.

In the pursuit of timeliness, SYBEX has achieved many publishing firsts. SYBEX was among the first to integrate personal computers used by authors and staff into the publishing process. SYBEX was the first to publish books on the CP/M operating system, microprocessor interfacing techniques, word processing, and many more topics.

Expertise in computers and dedication to the highest quality product have made SYBEX a world leader in computer book publishing. Translated into fourteen languages, SYBEX books have helped millions of people around the world to get the most from their computers. We hope we have helped you, too.

For a complete catalog of our publications:

SYBEX, Inc. 2021 Challenger Drive, #100, Alameda, CA 94501
Tel: (415) 523-8233/(800) 227-2346   Telex: 336311
Fax: (415) 523-2373

Character Output: Screen

CLS	Clears the screen.
CSRLIN	Gets the number of the row containing the cursor.
LOCATE	Moves the cursor to a specific location.
POS()	Gets the current cursor position in a line.
PRINT	Prints text.
PRINT USING	Prints formatted text.
SCREEN()	Gets the ASCII code of the character at a location.
SPC()	Skips spaces in a PRINT statement.
TAB()	Spaces to a specific line position.
VIEW PRINT	Sets the boundaries of the screen text window for printing.
WIDTH	Sets the width for printed output.
WRITE	Prints with delimiters.

Character Output: Printer

LPOS()	Gets the position of the print head.
LPRINT	Prints to the printer.
LPRINT USING	Prints formatted text to the printer.
SPC()	Skips spaces in an LPRINT statement.
TAB()	Spaces to a specific position in a line.
WIDTH	Sets the width for printed output.

Character Input: Keyboard

INKEY$	Gets one character.
INPUT	Gets delimited input.
INPUT$	Gets a specified number of characters.
LINE INPUT	Inputs a complete line into a string.

Disk I/O: General

CLOSE	Closes any open disk files.
LOC()	Gets the current file position.
LOCK	Restricts access to a file.
LOF()	Gets the file length in bytes.
OPEN	Opens a path to a disk file.
UNLOCK	Releases access restrictions to a file.

Disk I/O: Sequential Files

EOF()	Checks for the end of file.
INPUT#	Gets delimited input.
INPUT$()	Gets a specific number of characters.
LINE INPUT#	Inputs a complete line into a string.
PRINT#	Prints characters.
PRINT# USING	Prints formatted characters.
WRITE#	Prints with delimiters.

Disk I/O: Random-Access Files

CVD()	Converts an eight-byte string into a double-precision number.
CVI()	Converts a two-byte string into an integer.
CVS()	Converts a four-byte string into a single-precision number.
FIELD	Defines a record buffer.
GET	Reads a record into a record buffer.
LSET	Left justifies a string into a field.
MKD$()	Converts a double-precision number into an eight-byte string.
MKI$()	Converts an integer into a two-byte string.
MKS$()	Converts a single-precision number into a four-byte string.
PUT	Writes the record buffer into a disk record.
RSET	Right justifies a string into a field.

Internal Data Statements

DATA	An internal data statement.
READ	Reads data from an internal data statement.
RESTORE	Resets internal data statement for rereading.

Other I/O

ERDEV	Gets a device error number.
ERDEV$	Gets the name of the device with an error.
INP()	Returns a byte from a machine port.
IOCTL	Sends a control string to a device driver.
IOCTL$()	Receives a control string from a device driver.